Texts in Computer Science

Series Editors

David Gries, Department of Computer Science, Cornell University, Ithaca, NY, USA

Orit Hazzan⬢, Faculty of Education in Technology and Science, Technion—Israel Institute of Technology, Haifa, Israel

Chellammal Surianarayanan •
Pethuru Raj Chelliah

Essentials of Cloud Computing

A Holistic Perspective

 Springer

Chellammal Surianarayanan
Department of Computer Science
Bharathidasan University Constituent
Arts and Science College
Navalurkuttapattu, Tiruchirappalli
Tamil Nadu, India

Pethuru Raj Chelliah
Site Reliability Engineering (SRE) Division
Reliance Jio Infocomm. Ltd. (RJIL)
Bengaluru, Karnataka, India

ISSN 1868-0941   ISSN 1868-095X   (electronic)
Texts in Computer Science
ISBN 978-3-030-13136-4   ISBN 978-3-030-13134-0   (eBook)
https://doi.org/10.1007/978-3-030-13134-0

Library of Congress Control Number: 2019932608

This Springer imprint is published by the registered company Springer Nature Switzerland AG
The registered company address is: Gewerbestrasse 11, 6330 Cham, Switzerland

Foreword

Business organizations across the globe are keenly focused on various digital transformation initiatives and implementations such that they are right and relevant for their customers, consumers, partners, employees, etc. The primary business objective today is to wisely leverage proven and potential digital technologies (IoT, AI, data analytics, blockchain, enterprise mobility, containerization, microservices architecture, software-defined cloud environments, etc.) to be extremely competitive and competent in their core activities. With cloudification processes becoming integrated and insightful, IT infrastructures are bound to be highly optimized and organized to efficiently host and run a dazzling array of business workloads; that is, applications are becoming cloud infrastructure aware and cloud resources, on the other hand, are all set to become application aware. The praiseworthy innovations and changes made in the cloud space will without an iota of doubt bring forth a bevy of delectable business transformations; that is, advances in the IT landscape will result in delivering pioneering and premium business solutions and services.

The book relates the story of the humble beginning and the continued journey of enigmatic cloud philosophy. The book makes a heady start by describing the fundamental and foundational aspects of cloud computing, and then proceeds with the various cloud service and deployment models. Popular cloud realization technologies are well expressed and exposed in this book. Cloud networking, storage, and security details are etched beautifully. Other important traits and tenets, such as cloud migration, monitoring, measurement, management, orchestration, and brokerage, are explained in detail and should empower readers. The final chapter describes how the cloud concept is invaluable in fulfilling business continuity as a result of its disaster recovery (DR) capability.

The book is a must for every cloud architect and software developer. Research scholars and academic professors will benefit greatly from this carefully crafted book on the cloud paradigm.

Tiruchirappalli, Tamil Nadu, India

Dr. Gopinath Ganapathy, Ph.D.
Registrar
Bharathidasan University

Preface

The cloud paradigm has generated a tectonic shift in IT space. The extreme agility, adaptability, and affordability of cloud-enabled IT systems have substantially and strategically impacted business operations, offerings, and outputs. The goals of business automation and acceleration are being easily and quickly met through various noteworthy advances in the cloud space. This book relates the story of the cloud computing journey and much more.

Chapter 1 is dedicated to introducing the concept of cloud computing. It presents a quick refresher on traditional computing models—namely, monolithic computing, client–server computing, distributed computing, cluster computing, and grid computing, etc. Furthermore, it compares and contrasts cloud computing with other computing models. By the end of the chapter readers should understand the primary purpose for which cloud computing has been developed.

Chapter 2 introduces the fundamentals of cloud computing. It covers many features of cloud computing such as cloud computing architecture, different service classes, and deployment models. In addition, it gives a brief overview of different public cloud service providers.

Chapter 3 illustrates the enabling technologies and tools of cloud computing including service-oriented architecture (SOA), microservices architecture (MSA), compartmentalization (virtualization and containerization), and computing models such as cluster, grid, on-demand, utility, and DevOps. The greater maturity and stability of a number of technological paradigms has led to the rapid proliferation of cloud environments. The way in which this has happened raises a number of questions: How does cloud computing permit elastic resource sharing using the same physical hardware infrastructure for different users engaged in different kinds of computing tasks? What is it that enables an infrastructure, platform, or software system to be available to many users in a multi-tenancy environment? What technologies are key to the cloud taking its solid shape? This chapter aims to present answers to these question. By the end of this chapter readers should have an understanding of the key technological foundations of cloud computing.

Chapter 4 explains the nuances and nitty-gritty of cloud networking. The cloud computing environment is a huge computing environment that consists of many computational resources dispersed over different geographical locations. It goes without saying that resources are tied together with the help of networks. However, this chapter aims to describe how these networks evolved from the simple design of the flat network model to the software-defined networking model for the cloud. By the end of this chapter readers should have gained an overall idea of enterprise networking, cloud networking, and how they work together to achieve business goals.

Chapter 5 digs deeper and describes what is involved in cloud storage. Data are a major if not core asset of every organization. Every organization of course has a need for its data to be stored. There are different types of storage devices with different characteristics such as capacity, scalability, reliability, performance, and cost. Navigating and selecting the appropriate storage device for a specific purpose requires an understanding of these different types of storage. The objective of this chapter is to progressively describe various types of storage, from conventional storage to cloud storage, and at the same time describe the evolution of data and the need for digitization.

Chapter 6 is all about security, the challenges it poses, and approaches taken to solve them. Cloud solutions are third-party solutions for any enterprise or user. Since cloud users avail themselves of the many different services that are deployed on the cloud provider's infrastructure, security naturally becomes a major concern. The objective of this chapter is to detail security-related concepts in the cloud. Readers will be shown how security is provided in different service models such as IaaS, PaaS, and SaaS. By the end of this chapter readers should understand that implementing security is a shared responsibility and the cloud user is responsible for data security, compliance, and regulatory and privacy requirements.

Chapter 7 details the intricacies of cloud migration. As a result of the cloud being deemed a game-changer, individuals, innovators, and institutions are migrating and modernizing their personal, social, and business workflows to cloud environments (private, public, and hybrid). Hence there are a number of cloud migration techniques, tools, and tips. The objective of this chapter is to introduce readers to the fundamentals of cloud migration. By the end of this chapter readers should understand the migration processes, migration strategies, and taxonomies of cloud-enabled, cloud-optimized, and cloud-native applications.

Chapter 8 explains the relevance of cloud monitoring. Cloud environments comprise physical and virtual infrastructures, IT platforms, and business applications. The number of participative, interactive, and collaborative cloud components is constantly growing. Therefore, meticulous and minute monitoring of each participant and constituent is essential to bringing about the originally envisaged benefits of cloud computing. The objective of this chapter is to highlight the basic concepts behind cloud monitoring. By the end of the chapter readers should understand how monitoring plays a crucial role in achieving the fundamental characteristics of cloud computing and optimizing the cloud.

Chapter 9 addresses the hot topic of cloud management. Monitoring and measuring the various cloud systems in a systematic manner requires cloud management. Having learned the technological, migration, and monitoring aspects readers will be interested in knowing about how the cloud computing environment is managed. The objective of this chapter is to introduce the basics of cloud management. By the end of the chapter readers should understand the different cloud management functionalities and how they are managed by cloud management platforms and tools.

Chapter 10 explains the importance of cloud brokerage. As a result of the surge in popularity of the cloud the number of cloud and communication service providers (CSPs) is growing steadily. There are state-of-the-art cloud infrastructures and integrated platforms for design, development, debugging, deployment, delivery, decommissioning, etc. Hence the solutions and services provided by cloud brokerage could not have come at a better time. This chapter introduces the basics of cloud service brokerage (CSB). By the end of this chapter readers should understand what CSB is, why enterprises need CSB, and what its typical capabilities and architecture are.

Chapter 11 throws light on the growing importance of cloud orchestration. The objective of this chapter is to introduce the basics of cloud orchestration in multi-cloud environments. By the end of the chapter readers should understand why we need multi-cloud environments and hybrid IT, the challenges involved in bringing them about, and how cloud orchestration helps to resolve some of these challenges. Readers will also learn about the currently available tools for cloud orchestration.

Chapter 12 is all about cloud-based application and data recovery. Like security, disaster recovery (DR) is a major concern in the IT industry. Enterprises want to maintain business continuity (BC) in the event of disasters. The objective of this chapter is to present the basics of DR and highlight how DR plans can be prepared and implemented using the cloud.

Tiruchirappalli, India   Chellammal Surianarayanan
Bengaluru, India   Pethuru Raj Chelliah

Acknowledgements

First, I thank the Almighty with whom I always realize a lot of blessings, confidence, bliss and peace. He has given me passion and made my dream of writing a book true. I feel writing this book as a gift of God. He has given me strength and mental will to work continuously without any interruption.

I feel my deepest gratitude to my co-author Dr. Pethuru Raj, The Chief Architect and Vice President, Site Reliability Engineering (SRE) Division, Reliance Jio Infocomm. Ltd. (RJIL), Bangalore, India who travelled along with me in making the technical and technological stuff of cloud computing as a book. In fact, one of his presentations in cloud set fire in me. He is the sole inspiration for writing this book. Like cloud, he is very elastic enough to deliver his unlimited support at any time from anywhere. His readiness and helping tendency create several sparks in me. Through this note, I convey my sincere gratitude to him from my heart, brain and soul.

I express my sincere thanks to Dr. P. Manisankar, Honourable Vice-Chancellor, Bharathidasan University, Tiruchirappalli, India for his support and encouragement.

I refresh all my memories and convey my heartfelt thanks to Dr. G. Gopinath, Professor and Respected Registrar of Bharathidasan University, Tiruchirappalli, India for being an exemplary mentor of my academic and professional life. I would not be where I am today without his mentorship.

I convey my sincere thanks to Dr. N. Rajaraman, Principal(i/c) of Bharathidasan University Constituent Arts and Science, Navalurkuttapattu, Trichirapalli, India for his support.

I thank my best friend, Mr. N. Ramesh, Scientific Officer, Indira Gandhi Centre for Atomic Research, Department of Atomic Energy, Kalpakkam, TamilNadu for all his moral support.

I have great pleasure in expressing my deep sense of thanks to my awesome husband, R. Ganesan and my lovely son G. Srimurugan for their kindness, support and care.

I sincerely convey my thanks to everyone on the Editing, Proof Reading and Publishing team of Springer.

Chellammal Surianarayanan

I extend my sincere gratitude to Wayne Wheeler, Senior Editor and Simon Rees, Associate Editor, Computer Science, Springer, UK for their contributions in bringing forth this book. I thank Prof. Chellammal Surianarayanan, Ph.D. for her unwavering zeal in putting together her vast and varied technical competency in producing this prestigious book. I appreciate her unflinching determination and discipline in completing this book with all the right and relevant details in time. Her expertise and experience in crafting this textbook on cloud computing in a precise and concise manner for a larger audience is really laudable. Let God appropriately reward for all her hard work.

I solemnly submit here my profound gratitude to my Managers Mr. Anish Shah and Mr. Kiran Thomas, the President at Reliance Industries Limited, Bombay for their moral support. I also appreciate my former Manager Mr. Sreekrishnan Venkateswaran, Distinguished Engineer (DE), IBM Cloud, for all the enchanting technical discussions. I appreciate my colleagues Senthil Arunachalam and Vidya Hungud for their cooperation.

At this moment, I reflect the selfless sacrifices of my parents during my formative days. I thank my wife (Sweetlin Reena) and my sons (Darren Samuel and Darresh Bernie) for their extreme patience. Above all, I give all the glory and honour to my Lord and Saviour Jesus Christ for granting the physical strength and the knowledge required towards contributing a bit for this book.

Pethuru Raj Chelliah

Contents

About the Authors

Chellammal Surianarayanan is an Assistant Professor of Computer Science at Bharathidasan University Constituent Arts and Science College, Tiruchirappalli, Tamil Nadu, India. She earned a Doctorate in Computer Science by developing novel optimization techniques for discovery and selection of semantic services. She has published research papers in *Springer Service-Oriented Computing and Applications, IEEE Transactions on Services Computing, International Journal of Computational Science, Inderscience*, and the *SCIT Journal of the Symbiosis Centre for Information Technology*, etc. She has produced book chapters with IGI Global and CRC Press. She has been a life member of several professional bodies such as the Computer Society of India, IAENG, etc. Before coming to academic service, Chellammal Surianarayanan served as Scientific Officer in the Indira Gandhi Centre for Atomic Research, Department of Atomic Energy, Government of India, Kalpakkam, TamilNadu, India. She was involved in the research and development of various embedded systems and software applications. Her remarkable contributions include the development of an embedded system for lead shield integrity assessment, portable automatic air sampling equipment, embedded system for detection of lymphatic filariasis in its early stage and development of data logging software applications for atmospheric dispersion studies. In all she has more than 20 years of academic and industrial experience.

Pethuru Raj Chelliah is the Chief Architect and Vice President of the Site Reliability Engineering (SRE) division, Reliance Jio Infocomm Ltd. (RJIL), Bangalore. His previous stints include cloud architect in the IBM Cloud CoE, enterprise architect in Wipro consulting services (WCS), and lead architect in Robert Bosch Corporate Research (CR) division. In total, he has gained more than 18 years of IT industry experience and 8 years of research experience. He completed a CSIR-sponsored PhD degree at Anna University, Chennai, and continued with UGC-sponsored postdoctoral research in the Department of Computer Science and Automation, Indian Institute of Science, Bangalore. Thereafter, he was granted a couple of international research fellowships (JSPS and JST) to work as a research scientist for 3.5 years in two leading Japanese universities. He has published more than 30 research papers in peer-reviewed journals such as *IEEE, ACM, Springer-Verlag, Inderscience*, etc. He has authored sixteen books thus far on some of the emerging technologies such as The Internet of Things (IoT), Artificial intelligence (AI), Blockchain technology, Digital twin, Docker Platform, Data science, microservices architecture, fog/edge computing, etc. He has contributed 30 book chapters thus far for various technology books edited by highly acclaimed and accomplished professors and professionals.

Introduction to Cloud Computing

1

Learning Objectives

The objective of this chapter is to introduce the concept of cloud computing by presenting a quick refresher of traditional computing models—such as monolithic computing, client–server computing, distributed computing, cluster computing, and grid computing—as well as comparing and contrasting it with other computing models. By the end of the chapter the reader should understand the primary purposes for which cloud computing came into existence.

Motivational Questions
1. Why do we need yet another means of computing called cloud computing?
2. Are we reinventing the wheel?
3. How does cloud computing differ from other computing models?
4. Is cloud computing an entirely new computing paradigm? Or can we perceive it as an evolution and extension of existing models?
5. What are the motivational ideas behind cloud computing?

Preface
In this chapter the reader is, first, introduced to computing models that are the predecessors of cloud computing. Monolithic computing, client–server computing, three-tier client–server computing, cluster computing, and grid computing are discussed. This enables the reader to understand the limitations of previous computing models. At the same time the reader is exposed to the current needs of enterprises. On the one hand, there are small and medium-sized enterprises that suffer huge capital and

© Springer Nature Switzerland AG 2019

S. Chellammal and C. Pethuru Raj, *Essentials of Cloud Computing*,
Texts in Computer Science, https://doi.org/10.1007/978-3-030-13134-0_1

time costs in establishing the startup infrastructure necessary to run their businesses. On the other hand, there are large enterprises such as Amazon Web Services (AWS) and Microsoft Azure that want to rent out their infrastructure to others on a pay-per-use basis. Meeting these two needs led to the invention of cloud computing.

Insight is provided to readers by discussing: (i) how cloud computing differs from previous computing models; (ii) the primary purpose of cloud computing; (iii) some applications where cloud computing is used; and (iv) limitations of cloud computing. Since an enterprise is moving its services to an infrastructure provided by a third party it should have strong technical and business motivations for cloud migration. Guidelines outlining when and where cloud migration should be considered are highlighted.

1.1   Introduction

An overview of traditional computing models starting from monolithic centralized computing to distributed computing will help the reader perceive cloud computing in the correct way. There are different computing models that fit different orientations or

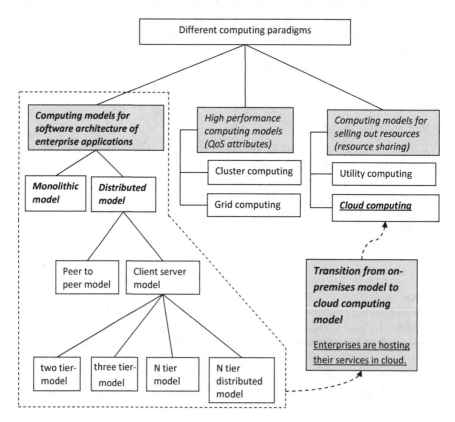

Fig. 1.1 Categories of computing paradigms

aspects. Different computing models have been developed for different purposes. Different computing models can be categorized according to the ***purposes***, ***orientations***, or ***aspects*** for which they were developed (as given in Fig. 1.1):

(i)   computing models that represent applications architectures of enterprise applications;
(ii)   computing models for high performance; and
(iii) computing models for selling IT resources.

1.2 Computing Models for Software Architecture of Enterprise Applications

The applications architecture of enterprise applications is primarily based on the concept of modular programming. Modular programming is a software design technique that promotes the decomposition of a large software application into its constituent but independent and replaceable modules such that each module contains everything necessary to accomplish only one aspect of a particular functionality. Modular programming helps in

(i)   reducing complexity;
(ii)   achieving separation of concerns;
(iii) achieving flexibility;
(iv)   obtaining better maintainability; and
(v)   reducing rework and effort while performing changes in the modules and hence reducing cost.

In any software development (whether project or product), as a rule of thumb, a software application is logically divided into three modules—namely, *presentation logic, business logic, and database access logic. Now, based on how these modules are deployed in physical machines different computing architectures have evolved*.

1.2.1 Monolithic Centralized Computing

In monolithic centralized computing a software application is developed using a single-tier architecture in which presentation logic, business logic, and database access code are combined into a single program and deployed in a single physical machine (as shown in Fig. 1.2).

This kind of computing is suitable for simple and small applications. However, this kind of architecture is not suitable for organizations where more than one user needs to access the data stored in a system simultaneously.

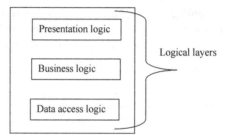

Physically deployed in single machine

Fig. 1.2 Monolithic centralized computing

1.2.2   Peer-to-Peer Model

A peer-to-peer (P2P)) network is created when two or more PCs/nodes are connected and share resources without using a separate server. Each node is a peer and each peer can serve both as client and server. Each peer is connected to every other peer (as in Fig. 1.3).

Peer-to-peer networks are suitable only for very small businesses. This model can support around 10 peers. If more peers are connected, it suffers from serious performance and management problems. A peer-to-peer network is primarily used for sharing files and printers within a small network of computers so as to achieve low cost. Since there is no centralized control in this network it is very difficult to administer. In addition, nodes are allowed to control access to resources on their own; security becomes very risky in a peer-to-peer environment. There's no central security or any way to control who shares what. Data recovery or backup is very difficult. Each computer should have its own backup system. Thus this network model is suitable to connect a small number of computers where high security is not required.

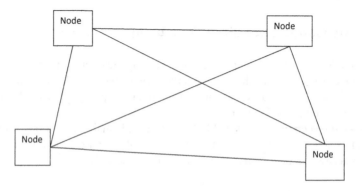

Fig. 1.3 Peer-to-peer network

1.2.3 Client–Server Model

In contrast to peer-to-peer computing the client–server model follows a master–slave configuration. In this model there is a separate dedicated server that serves as a master to which clients (i.e., slaves) are connected. Moreover, this model is primarily adopted for enterprise applications. Depending on the requirements of scalability, availability, performance, etc., there are client–server models with different numbers of tiers. As mentioned earlier the logical separations are presentation logic, business logic, and database access logic. When these tiers are deployed in different physical machines they give the real deliverables for which they are meant. According to the physical deployment there are different client–server models in use—namely, (i) two-tier client–server model; (ii) three-tier client–server model; (iii) *N*-tier client–server model; and (iv) *N*-tier distributed client–server model.

1.2.3.1 Two-Tier Client–Server Computing

Typically, client–server computing is an extension of modular programming where the presentation logic is deployed in a separate physical machine called the client that accesses the application deployed in another physical machine called the server. Client–server computing establishes a fundamental request–response communication model where the client requests services from the server and the server provides services to clients over a network. Of the abovementioned logical separations of an application, presentation logic is deployed in the client machine. Data access logic is deployed in the server. Application logic is deployed either in the client (*thick client–thin server model*, Fig. 1.4) or in the server (*thin client–thick server model*, Fig. 1.5) depending on the particular application. Obviously, client–server computing enables multiple users to access the server at a remote location. Hence it provides scalability by allowing up to 100 users. Typically, a two-tier architecture is implemented over a local area network (LAN). This kind of architecture is suitable for small businesses.

Initially there were two kinds of computers: the *mainframe computer* that had sufficient input and output peripheral supports, processing power, storage, and communication support and *computer terminals* that had input and output

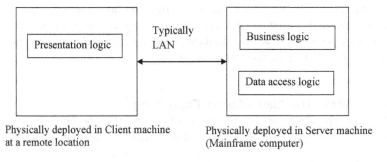

Physically deployed in Client machine at a remote location

Physically deployed in Server machine (Mainframe computer)

Fig. 1.4 Two-tier client–server (thin client–thick server) computing

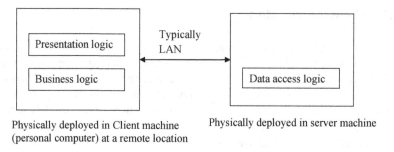

Fig. 1.5 Two-tier client–server (thin server–thick client) computing

capability. Mainframe computers were configured as server machines and terminals were configured as client machines. This kind of deployment led to the *thin client–thick server* architecture.

Advances in hardware technology and invention of the personal computer were responsible for the *thin server–thick client* architecture in which business logic is deployed in the client machine (as shown in Fig. 1.5).

Common applications of a two-tier client–server architecture include (i) desktop to database server communication, (ii) browser to web server communication, and (iii) FTP client to FTP server communication.

Advantages of two-tier architecture

- Implementation of a two-tier architecture is simple.
- A two-tier model gives fast performance as it provides direct communication between the client and server.
- The cost of hardware, network, maintenance, and deployment is low.

Disadvantages of two-tier architecture

- The client application has to be installed for each client and in the event of any change each client has to be updated.
- The performance of a two-tier model decreases as the number of users increases.
- Two-tier models have low scalability, security, and fault tolerance, etc.
- Heterogeneous/Business environments with rapidly changing rules and regulations are not suitable since the database server has to handle the business logic, which slows down database performance.

1.2.3.2 Three-Tier Client–Server Computing

Enterprises typically have different teams of people who specialize in the development of front-end, server back-end, and data back-end interfaces. Modularizing

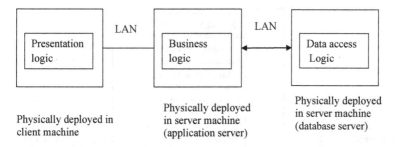

Fig. 1.6 Three-tier client–server computing

an application into different tiers enables different development teams, such as a
GUI development team, a core business logic team, and a database team, to develop
their work faster by allowing the different teams to focus only on their core com-
petencies. In addition, large-enterprise applications need to be horizontally scalable
to meet various quality of service (QoS) factors such as availability, performance,
and scalability. This business need led to three-tier client–server architecture, which
involved the deployment of application modules in three different physical
machines (as shown in Fig. 1.6).

Advantages of three-tier architecture

- Scalability is the great advantage of a three-tier architecture. Each tier can scale
  independently. For example, if an application receives many web requests, then
  web servers alone will be scaled out without disturbing the application server or
  database. Similarly, if an application deals with more database requests (but not
  more web requests), then the database server will be scaled out without disturbing
  the web server. So the concept of three tiers helps in achieving higher performance with minimum resources.
- The concept of three tiers increases reliability and availability by hosting different
  parts of an application on *different servers and utilizing cached results*. When all
  three tiers are deployed in a single physical tier this will lead to a huge performance issue during server failure. Three-tier deployment in different physical
  machines minimizes performance issues when a server goes down.

Disadvantages of three-tier architecture

- A three-tier model is complex to implement.
- The implementation of a three-tier model is time consuming.
- A three-tier model requires enhanced expertise in object-oriented programming.
- As the number of tiers increases the complexity of communications between tiers
  also increases.

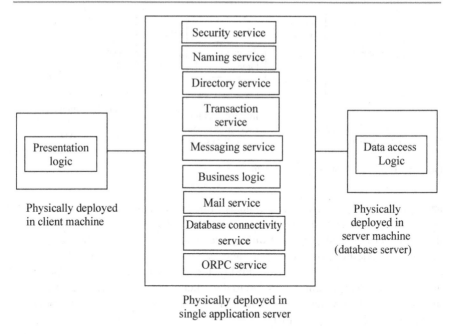

Fig. 1.7 Three-tier *N*-layer client–server architecture

1.2.3.3   Three-Tier–*N*-Layer Client–Server Model

To meet the various vertical needs of enterprise applications, such as transaction service support, naming and directory services, asynchronous messaging services, and email services, different logical layers were introduced into the business tier. This led to the *N-layer three-tier client–server* computing model (as shown in Fig. 1.7).

As shown in Fig. 1.7 there are different functional layers even though they are deployed in the same physical machine (middle tier).

1.2.3.4   *N*-Tier Distributed Client–Server Computing

How the *N*-tier client–server architecture has evolved as a distributed client–server computing model as shown in Fig. 1.8.

As shown in Fig. 1.8 different layers of both business logic components and common services are distributed over different physical machines and accessed over a network, which may be an enterprise-level LAN to the global Internet. The expected QoS attributes and the number of user/loads of the application will help in determining the number of servers necessary for the deployment of different components.

It is understood here that different function-specific business logic modules and common functions/services of applications can be physically distributed in the middle tier. The concept of distribution introduces **heterogeneity at various levels**. There may be heterogeneity regarding machines, networks, software platforms, and

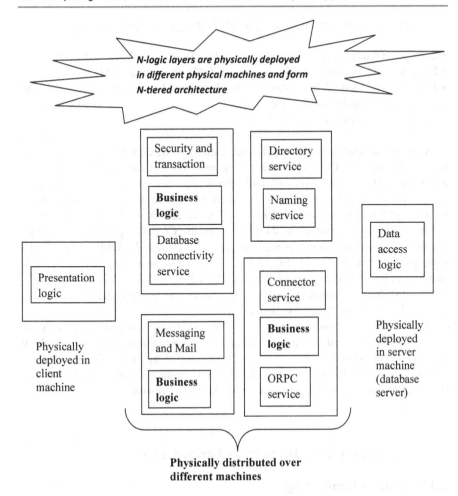

Fig. 1.8 Distributed *N*-tier client–server computing

communication protocols. *But there is always a necessity to invoke and reuse business components.*

Another aspect of enterprise computing is that the development of complex components (e.g., stock exchange component) is very tedious and time consuming. Frequently changing customer demands and business agility necessitates the sharing of functional components not only between the business to consumer (BtoC) model, but also the business to business (BtoB) model.

Different industries and business associations, such as Object Management Group (OMG), Sun Microsystems, and Microsoft, have developed various industry standard specifications and frameworks that facilitate the communication, sharing, and reusability of various distributed modules (or components) despite heterogeneity.

A short illustrative group of *distributed computing standards* includes

- Common Object Request Broker Architecture (CORBA) developed by OMG;
- Distributed Component Object Model (DCOM) developed by Microsoft;
- Java Remote Method Invocation (RMI) developed by Sun Microsystems (now procured by Oracle Corporation); and
- Web of Services developed by W3C.

Although different standards and specifications arise, each has its own focus or target. For example, CORBA facilitates the invocation of distributed components using the ORB protocol over different operating systems (*heterogeneity of operating systems*). This has a limitation when an application needs to be deployed on the Internet (ORB is not firewall friendly). That is, as long as the client and server has the ORB layer deployed in their machines the CORBA specification enables sharing of functional components. Similarly, Microsoft DCOM facilitates the sharing and reusability of functional components over different languages (*heterogeneity of languages*) on Windows-based machines. Similarly, RMI provides a distributed computing model using Java as the development language (and hence achieves platform independence).

Web of Services introduces *interoperability* to software components irrespective of the heterogeneity of operating systems and programming languages. Web of Services is an XML-based protocol stack developed by W3C. These protocols include XML, SOAP, WSDL, and UDDI. These protocols work over the existing HTTP and hence are firewall friendly over the global Internet.

1.3 Computing Models for High Performance

1.3.1 Cluster Computing

High performance is a critical need in *both general business applications and computation-intensive scientific calculations*. Consider the following examples:

- *Online railway applications* or *online flight-booking applications*: At any given instant a few thousand users will be accessing the application. Hence applications should be readily available.
- *Data recovery during disaster*: High-performance recovery is essential for scientific applications such as apps designed for the *study of genetic analysis and fluid dynamics* (which involves huge scientific calculations), for *weather forecasting* (which has to complete the processing of a huge amount of data within a stipulated time), for *scientific or engineering simulation modeling*, for *banks and stock exchanges*, for *astrophysics-related analysis*, and for *problems solved using neural networks*.

Conventionally, *supercomputers* were used to satisfy High-performance requirements. There are supercomputers that give high performance on the order of a hundred quadrillion floating point operations per second. Supercomputers were developed with special hardware, massive parallel design and special energy usage and heat management. *The big issue in using a single supercomputer is its cost*. As an alternative cluster computing was developed in which *two or more computers were connected together via a high-speed network called a cluster and the connected computers work together as a single system*.

The primary purpose of cluster is to provide applications with greater **performance, availability, load balancing, and fault tolerance** than was available on a single machine.

1.3.1.1 Generic Architecture of Cluster

The generic architecture of high-performance cluster computing is shown in Fig. 1.9. The core part of the architecture is the cluster. Each computer in the cluster is called a node. Within a cluster the nodes are connected using a high-speed LAN. There are two types of nodes: (i) a head node or master node and (ii) compute nodes. The head node or master node of the cluster is a node that can access the cluster and is responsible for providing users with the environment to work and to distribute tasks to other nodes (compute nodes). *An important feature of cluster computing is that the nodes in the cluster are homogeneous. That is, the nodes use the same hardware and software. The cluster is physically located at a single site and owned by a single organization.*

The essential components of a cluster computer include

1. Multiple single computers
2. High-speed network
3. Cluster middleware to support a **single-system image** and the required infrastructure
4. Communications protocols
5. Parallel programming environment
6. Applications and user interfaces.

As shown in the block diagram the applications that require high availability or fault tolerance or load balancing may be sequential or parallel processing based. In either case the distribution of tasks to compute nodes or the allocation of parallel tasks or mapping of jobs and scheduling are carried out at a *single centralized control*.

1.3.1.2 Types of Clusters

According to the requirement for which clusters are designed there are different types of clusters [1] (as shown in Fig. 1.10).

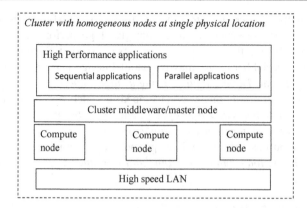

Fig. 1.9 Generic architecture of cluster computing

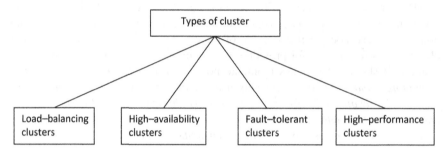

Fig. 1.10 Different types of clusters

Load-Balancing Clusters

Load balancing is often required when applications deal with large numbers of client requests. The main purpose of a load-balancing cluster is to distribute client requests to different active compute nodes. This is shown in Fig. 1.11. All the compute nodes in a load-balancing cluster are *actively executing the same kind of service simultaneously.*

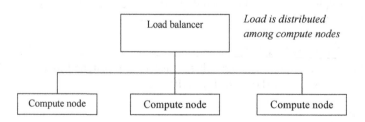

Fig. 1.11 A load balancer distributes requests to compute nodes (active–active cluster)

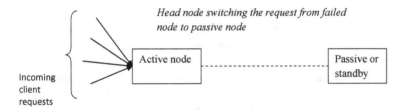

Fig. 1.12 High-availability cluster configuration

Load balancing can be implemented either by algorithms (software-based load balancing) or by specialized hardware (hardware-based load balancing). Load balancing is also called horizontal scaling or scale-out. Horizontal scaling is implemented by adding new nodes with identical functionality to existing ones, redistributing the load among all of them. Typically, web servers scale out by adding more servers to a load-balanced network so that incoming requests can be distributed among all of them.

High-Availability Clusters

Availability is a function of scaling systems up or out and implementing system, network, and storage redundancy. High-availability clusters are also called failover clusters. A group of nodes are combined as a cluster. When a node in a group fails the standby node will restart the application. It involves a minimum amount of downtime. For example, in a two-node availability cluster there are two nodes, but they are *not simultaneously active*. This is shown in Fig. 1.12.

The active node serves requests submitted by the client. In case it fails to serve the requests the passive node will immediately restart the application that had been earlier served by the failed node. The passive device detects the failure of active node by means of two common techniques: (i) the interface link method and (ii) the heartbeat method. In the interface link method the standby node detects whether the interface link to the active node is going *down*. As soon as it detects the link to active node is going down it restarts the application concerned. In the heartbeat method the active node is configured to send a heartbeat signal to the standby node at regular intervals. If standby node does not receive the heartbeat signal, it restarts the application concerned.

Fault-Tolerant Clusters

Basically, fault-tolerant clusters are high-availability clusters with zero downtime. This is generally achieved by combining many nodes to form a cluster. The nodes in the cluster deliver the same service and do so simultaneously. For example, in a two-node fault-tolerant cluster there are a pair of tightly coupled systems that provide redundancy. The two systems are in lockstep, so when any instruction is executed on one system it is also executed on the secondary system. *The two nodes are mirrored* (as shown in Fig. 1.13).

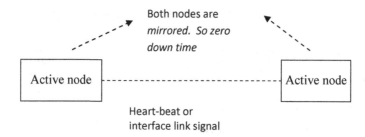

Fig. 1.13 Fault-tolerant clusters

In the event the main system suffers a hardware failure the secondary system takes over and there is zero downtime.

High-Performance Clusters

High-performance clusters are used when time to respond to a request (i.e., response time) is critical. High-performance clusters are used to increase computing throughput. The easiest way to do this is to allow the cluster to act as a *compute farm*. Instead of running a job on a single machine it is submitted to the cluster for execution. The cluster will manage the resources needed for the job and assign the job to a work queue. Depending on the resources all the jobs may run at the same time or some may wait in the queue while other jobs finish. The cluster middleware finds the availability of resources and assigns jobs. *It maintains the workflow.* Once the jobs are over the results are combined and returned to users. Users can submit hundreds of jobs and allow the cluster to manage the workflow. High-performance can be achieved by means of both vertical scaling and horizontal scaling.

1.3.2 Grid Computing

Grid computing was first developed in the 1990s to meet very large–scale computational needs. This happens when a single cluster alone is not sufficient to satisfy computational requirements. Grid computing involves multiple organizations that are geographically dispersed sharing their resources to achieve a common goal. By their very nature the computational nodes in grid computing are heterogeneous. Grid computing can be visualized as shown in Fig. 1.14. A grid is an environment that allows a heterogeneous network of resources set up for compute-intensive tasks to be shared.

As shown in Fig. 1.14, grid resources are resources of partners or collaborators involved in the grid that can be shared among themselves. Generally, the resources of each partner would be a cluster. Grid computing enables combining the resources of different autonomous, heterogeneous, and geographically dispersed organizations into a single virtual entity and provides the required resources to remote users

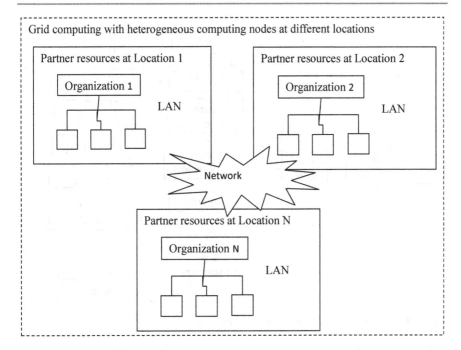

Fig. 1.14 Concept of grid infrastructure

over the network among the partners. The users of grid computing are the partners of the network. The focus of grid computing is to share resources among collaborators.

Another important aspect of the grid environment is that the resources belong to different collaborators with different administrative and security policies. But the grid coordinates all heterogeneous and decentralized resources.

Once the grid infrastructure is ready in grid computing a user can access a virtual computer, which consists of a heterogeneous network of computing resources. Much as in an electric grid, where the consumer does not know the source of electric power, in the grid infrastructure (called a computational grid) the users do not know which individual resources are available. Initially business organizations built their own private grids called *intragrids* and later many intragrids were interconnected according to the Open Grid Services Architecture (OGSA)—the grid standard—and tools provided by the Globus Toolkit framework.

1.3.2.1 Essential Components of a Grid

The essential components of a grid are (as shown in Fig. 1.15):

- *User interface*: Generally the user interface is a web portal that provides an interface for a user to access the variety of resources in the grid.

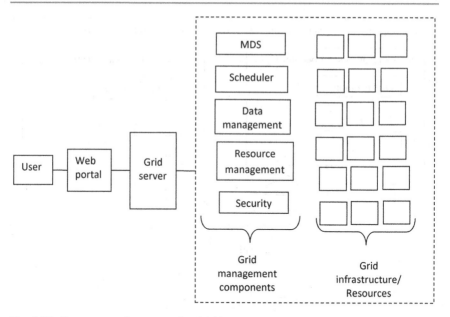

Fig. 1.15 Components of a computational grid environment

- *Grid server*: The grid server coordinates and manages different networks of heterogeneous resources.
- *Grid infrastructure*: A huge collection of heterogeneous networks of resources is held by the grid infrastructure.
- *Grid server component*: A grid portal that allows authenticated users to access grid resources. The broker component discovers and identifies the resources requested in the grid using a grid information service, also called a monitoring and discovery service (MDS).
- *Scheduler*: After the resources are identified the scheduler component will schedule the user job to run in the grid. The task will be moved to the grid at the scheduled time.
- *Data and resource management*: During execution of a task in the grid, data management and resource management are achieved using grid access to secondary storage (GASS) and grid resource allocation manager (GRAM) components.

In a nutshell, grid computing can be perceived as a computing model that allows geographically distributed and preinstalled resources over enterprise-level networks to be shared. Multiple organizations collaborate as a single virtual organization in the grid to achieve a unified goal according to the resource-sharing rules defined by collaborators. Scientific and engineering domains, high-energy physics, bioinformatics, and other academic domains utilize a computational grid for complex research work involving computation-intensive and data-intensive tasks. For example, enabling grid for e-science (EGEE), a European grid infrastructure, is available to scientists for their experiments. This overview shows the primary purpose of a grid is to solve a massive or complex problem by splitting the problem into several small units and distribute them over grid nodes.

1.4 Computing Models to Sell Information Technology Resources

1.4.1 Utility Computing

Utility computing can be visualized as a kind of computing that shows how computing resources can be provided to users in much the same way as domestic utility services such as electricity, gas, and water. Consumers in turn pay service providers according to their usage. Hence, utility computing is based on a service-provisioning model, where users pay providers only for the computing power they use. Utility computing focuses on a business model in which customers receive computing resources from a paid service provider. Cloud computing is a broader form of computing that has evolved with different purposes in mind (as discussed in the subsequent sections).

1.4.2 What's the Point of Cloud Computing?

The reason grid computing was developed was to solve the massive problem that entailed supporting the demands for resources by collaborators of the grid and achieving a unified goal or research goal. Grid computing does not allow a business model to be defined to provide existing resources to common/public users, *whereas cloud computing sets its primary objective as providing hardware and software (which involves high cost when building and deploying from scratch) over the Internet according to the dynamic demands of users on a pay-as-you-go basis.*

Let us now turn to the key motivational ideas that underlie cloud computing's existence.

1.4.2.1 Motivational Ideas Behind Cloud Computing

Cloud computing can be regarded as a kind of Internet-based computing model where computing resources are rented out, in much the same way as a utility like electricity, over the Internet. The first breakthrough in cloud computing was the advent of Salesforce.com, which delivered applications as a utility to users over the Internet. Salesforce.com has completely eliminated the need for millions of dollars of capital costs that would be needed to implement an application from scratch (which could take years to develop), let alone ongoing maintenance and upgrades. Amazon.com began as an online bookstore in 1995. In addition to books it started selling music, movies, houseware, electronics, toys, and many other goods, either directly or as a mediator between other retailers and its customers.

In course of time Amazon became the first company to realize that only 10% of its capacity or infrastructure was being effectively utilized by the company and that the remaining 90% of its capacity was not being used. *The company decided to utilize all its capacity by selling it to its* customers. At the same time Amazon realized that small or medium-sized IT companies had little choice but to incur capital costs. That is, an IT company has to invest a huge amount of money before it can start trading. The capital cost includes a building cost, electricity cost, purchase of computers, UPS, storage devices, and networking hardware and software. In addition to the capital cost the company has to spend a significant amount of time, typically on the order of months, before it can start trading. *Most small and medium-sized companies are unable to invest the upfront capital cost.* Amazon exploited the critical needs of small IT companies and developed its Simple Storage Service (S3) cloud to sell data storage over the Internet as a utility in March 2006. Amazon is responsible for the pay-per-use pricing model that now stands as the de facto standard for cloud pricing. In addition, in August 2006 Amazon expanded its Elastic Compute Cloud (EC2) to rent out computer-processing power in small or large increments. S3 and EC2 quickly succeeded and helped popularize the idea that companies and individuals do not need to own their own computing resources. These two computing platforms shifted Amazon from a simple online retailer to a pioneer cloud service provider. In 2008 Google launched Google App Engine as a developer tool, which allows users to run their web application on the Google App Engine platform. In 2009 Microsoft launched its cloud—Azure—with the objective of building, testing, deploying, and managing applications and services through the internet.

The motivation behind cloud computing is to efficiently utilize the computing resources of cloud providers by renting out computing resources as a utility (like electricity or LPG) to organizations or individuals over the internet. Figure 1.16 shows the motivation behind cloud computing.

From one perspective cloud computing may be viewed as a combination of grid computing and utility computing. However, cloud computing is strongly motivated by the desire to remove the need to purchase infrastructure/software, which is a major cost when establishing IT support for an enterprise. The primary objective of

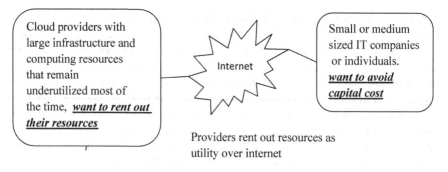

Fig. 1.16 Motivation behind cloud computing

grid computing is to provide a well-scheduled resource-sharing facility for its partners. Typically, grid computing only supports its users as collaborators of the grid and not the public. Therefore the demands of users are more or less prede-termined and there is little need to scale up resources. In grid computing resources are provisioned as per the service level agreement between providers and con-sumers. Nevertheless, grid computing suffers from the fact that resources are underutilized. In the following we will elaborate on a number of factors: *(i) pro-viding resources according to the elastic and dynamic demands of users, (ii) uti-lizing the available resources in the best way possible, and (iii) monitoring and metering the usage of resources, which differentiates cloud computing from grid computing.*

Another objective of cloud computing is to establish IT infrastructure support for its users/enterprises in a very short time—from minutes to a couple of hours. But, if an enterprise elects to establish its own IT from scratch, then it will take months. Worse still, in most cases the enterprise may not be able to fully utilize the capa-bility of the IT infrastructure.

In addition, the cloud computing infrastructure is typically established in line with the commodity hardware, whereas the grid computing infrastructure is established for High-performance computing. So, mission-critical, safely-critical, High-performance, or real-time analytics-based applications should not be deployed in the cloud. Further, in cloud computing resources are centrally managed, whereas in grid computing resources are distributed to sites that have has their own administrative control.

1.4.2.2 Why the Name Cloud Computing?

Cloud computing is based on the internet, which consists of several networks connected together. Although the networks are connected with one another, one network may not know all the details of another that is outside the domain of the first network. Traditionally, network engineers used a cloud symbol to represent the fact that the global internet had several domains that were unknown to one another. Cloud computing is internet-based computing. Network engineers considered the same cloud symbol to more appropriately indicate cloud computing since con-sumers do not precisely know what is inside the cloud.

1.4.2.3 Defining Cloud Computing

Cloud computing is a type of internet-based computing where cloud service pro-viders rent out their computing resources, such as servers, storage devices, network devices, platforms, and software applications, as a utility to consumers over the internet using a pay-per-use pricing model according to the dynamic demands of consumers.

1.4.2.4 Stakeholders in Cloud Computing

Stakeholders who participate in cloud computing can be perceived as using an architecture [2, 3] that has a higher level of abstraction (as shown in Fig. 1.17). The cloud is provided by *cloud service providers*. The cloud service provider owns,

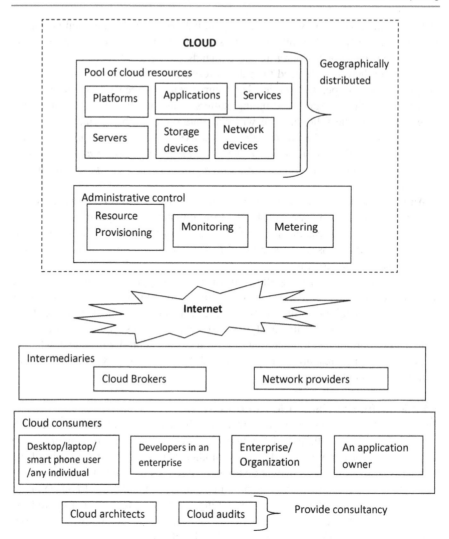

Fig. 1.17 Stakeholders in cloud computing

controls, and manages the cloud platform. Figure 1.17 shows that the cloud consists of resources and administrative control. *Cloud consumers* may range from a variety of users, from an individual to a company developer to an application owner. Further, a cloud consumer can use a desktop, laptop, smartphone, or any pervasive or wearable device that has internet connectivity.

In addition, cloud consumers can use *cloud brokers* who serve as intermediaries between cloud service providers and cloud consumers. Brokers help in

(i)   identifying the right cloud service provider;
(ii) obtaining consistent billing and support; and
(iii) integrating different service providers, if needed.

Cloud architects are third-party consultants who help cloud consumers to design a cloud solution and choose appropriate architecture for a given problem. *Cloud auditors* are third-party consultants who assess the cloud solution for its security, vulnerability, and performance-related issues. Typically, when a cloud consumer submits his/her request for cloud resources the administrative control part of the cloud receives the request and provides the required resources from the pool of resources that are geographically distributed. The usage of provisioned resources is monitored, metered, and billed according to a pay-as-you-go model.

1.4.2.5 Cloud Computing Versus Grid Computing
Cloud computing evolved from grid computing by taking onboard the need to address dynamic scalability, reliability, and other QoS (quality of service) issues. Cloud computing and grid computing share the same visions such as resource sharing, reducing computing cost, and increasing flexibility and reliability:

- *Resource sharing*: Grid computing enhances resource sharing across organizations, whereas cloud computing provides resources based on demand from the user—there is no actual sharing due to isolation provided through virtualization.
- *Coordination*: Grid computing needs to coordinate service workflow and location, whereas in cloud computing it is not necessary.
- *Scalability*: In grid computing scalability is mainly enabled by increasing the number of working nodes, whereas in cloud computing the virtualized hardware is resized automatically.
- *Pricing model*: Grid computing has not defined an explicit pricing model for offering resources to the organization involved, whereas cloud computing can be basically perceived as a combination of grid computing and utility computing.
- *Network grid resources* are generally accessed over private or enterprise networks, whereas cloud computing uses the internet as its backbone.
- *Administration and control of resources*: In the grid environment resources are distributed at different physical locations and they have decentralized local administrative control (along with a grid server), whereas in the cloud environment resources are centrally managed.

1.4.2.6 Applications of Cloud Computing
Let us now discuss some applications to illustrate the role cloud computing plays in various domains.

Cloud Computing in Business Applications
Cloud computing has now evolved into being almost a standard way of implementing IT infrastructure for small companies to large enterprises. Cloud

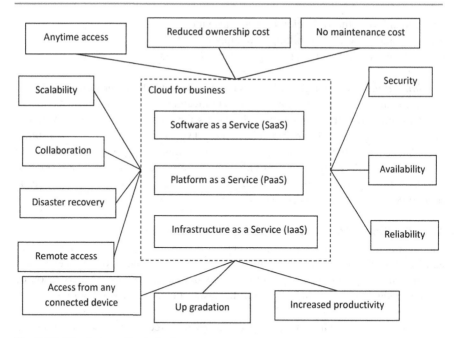

Fig. 1.18 Cloud computing in business

computing basically provides three types of services to any business: infrastructure (such as processors, hardware, storage, and network infrastructure), platforms (such as operating systems, development tools, and environments), and software applications (such as customer relationship management and supply chain management). The benefits of cloud computing in business are shown in Fig. 1.18.

The primary benefits of cloud computing in business include

- dynamic scale-up and scale-out;
- flexibility;
- reliability;
- increased productivity;
- lower cost of ownership;
- easy upgradation;
- off-site data storage;
- reduced cost of ownership;
- no maintenance cost;
- anytime and anywhere access;
- access from mobile (smartphone) or any connected device.

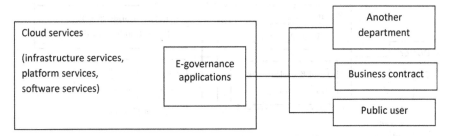

Fig. 1.19 Cloud-based e-governance

Cloud Computing in E-governance

E-governance is a process that has reformed the way governments work, share information, and deliver services to its users. Government applications need to support different types of interactions: between any two governments (e.g., communication among different departments), government and business (e.g., contract management), and government and public consumer (e.g., electronic billing). As E-governance needs to use distributed services it requires a huge infrastructure. Cloud computing provides such an infrastructure with reduced cost, sufficient security, increased scalability, high availability, and quick implementation of various E-governance applications. The generic architecture of cloud-based E-governance is as shown in Fig. 1.19. E-governance applications can be deployed in cloud computing.

Cloud Computing in Healthcare

Being able to access cloud services using any device with internet connectivity at anytime from anywhere has made cloud technology highly attractive to the healthcare industry. Figure 1.20 shows a number of healthcare situations where cloud computing is the natural choice for storage and monitoring:

(i)   Once a patient is registered with a hospital his/her information will be entered into a *Hospital Management Information System* (HMIS), thus enabling his/her data to be accessed by doctors at their convenience, at anytime, and from anywhere. Hence, HMIS is a good candidate for deployment in the cloud.

(ii) Data are generated in huge volumes by various medical devices such as *computed tomography (CT) scanners, magnetic resonance imaging (MRI) scanners,* and remote monitoring devices. These data need to be stored and readily available for diagnosis. Hence such data are good candidates to be stored in the cloud.

(iii) Very frequently it is essential to monitor patients at risk continuously. Since monitoring applications are easily deployed in the cloud, which enables serving remote patients, the corresponding data are also suitable for archiving in the cloud.

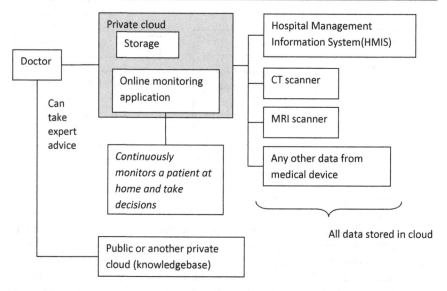

Fig. 1.20 Some of the roles cloud computing plays in healthcare

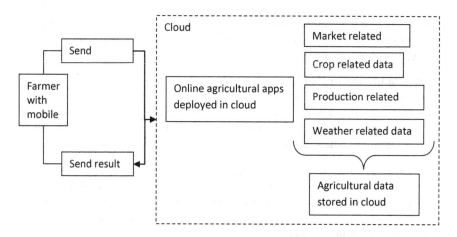

Fig. 1.21 Cloud computing in agriculture

Cloud Computing in Agriculture

All agriculture-related information, such as crop-related data, market-related data, weather-related data, and production-related data, can be stored in the cloud (as shown in Fig. 1.21).

Farmers need to be kept up to date with such information as market rate, quality of soil, and soil-specific fertilizers. Farmers can query the cloud for their needs at any time using any device such as a mobile phone.

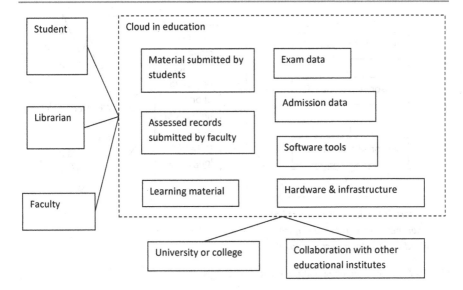

Fig. 1.22 Cloud computing in education

Cloud Computing in Education
A traditional education system suffers from various difficulties such as lack of teachers, lack of lab facilities, lack of hardware and software, and lack of other infrastructure. Cloud computing can offer solutions to these problems (as shown in Fig. 1.22).

Cloud computing allows students and faculty to access information and a wide range of tools at anytime from anywhere using any connected device. It also enables educational institutions to use new technologies for different educational needs and research projects. Students, faculty, and educational institutes can collaborate with partners with help from the cloud.

Cloud Computing and Internet of Things
The Internet of Things (IoT) is a collection of interrelated devices or sensors with unique identifiers. It has the ability to transfer acquired data to servers over the internet with human intervention. Like all data, any data acquired by various sensors are preprocessed and analyzed for various purposes. Cloud computing helps in providing a facility to store and process these data (as shown in Fig. 1.23).

Cloud Computing and Big Data
Big data is the term used to represent a large volume of data that cannot be processed by conventional relational database management systems. The important characteristics of big data include

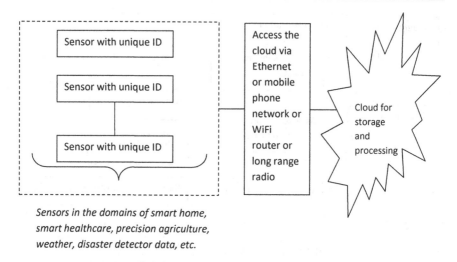

Sensors in the domains of smart home,
smart healthcare, precision agriculture,
weather, disaster detector data, etc.

Fig. 1.23 Cloud computing and the Internet of Things

- large volume or size of data;
- variety of data formats such as images, videos, and text; and
- velocity at which data are generated.

For example, social networks such as Facebook and Twitter generate large amounts of data on the order of terabytes everyday. Sensors and Internet of Things (IoT) not only generate large amounts of data but do so at frequent intervals of time. Global positioning system (GPS) satellites, remote-sensing applications, airplanes, automobiles, and smartphones generate large amounts of dynamic data in various formats. Several sources of big data are shown in Fig. 1.24. The data format can be structured, semi-structured, or unstructured. There are several issues associated with the handling of big data:

- What is the best way to store large volumes of data?
- Which are the best databases to use to store unstructured data?
- What is the best way to process large volumes of data?
- What is the best way to visualize data and information retrieved from data?
- Which are the best file systems to use for big data?
- Which programming models are the most suitable?
- What tools are available to handle big data?

Distributed file systems are predominantly used for storing big data. Therefore, cloud computing is a natural choice for storing data in distributed nodes. Programming models such as MapReduce can be used to process data stored in different nodes simultaneously. Cloud computing inherently supports both batch-processing and real-time analyzing of terabytes of data with open-source tools such as the Hadoop Distributed File System (HDFS) and Apache Spark.

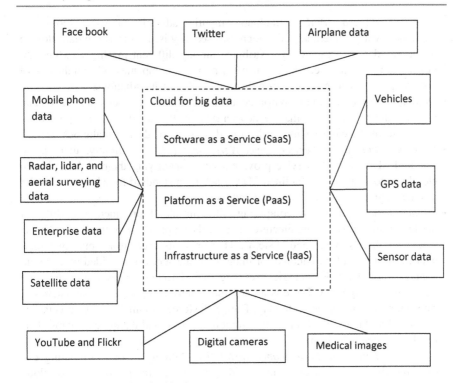

Fig. 1.24 Cloud computing for big data generators

1.4.2.7   Limitations of Cloud Computing

There are a number of limitations with cloud computing:

- *Internet connectivity*: The internet is the backbone of cloud computing. If a consumer does not have access to the internet, then he/she cannot fully utilize the services offered by the cloud.
- *Outage of service*: Outage of service is a serious limitation as all services are accessed via the internet typically with a web browser. For example, problems with the browser itself can lead to failure of service delivery.
- *Data segregation*: Cloud computing possesses a multi-tenancy characteristic, which means that virtual machines of different customers may get co-located in the same server. In this case the isolation of memory between two users becomes difficult and data can leak from one virtual machine to another.
- *Data location*: Knowing the location of data is fundamental to securing data. However, users are unaware of the location of their data in the cloud. As users are unaware of the physical location of their own data they cannot check data integrity. It is very difficult to maintain the ACID (atomicity, consistency, isolation, and durability) properties among geographically distributed servers.

- *Security and privacy of data*: In cloud computing administrative access to data is performed via the internet, which increases security issues [4]. Since data storage in the cloud is geographically distributed among different machines (which are governed by different security and privacy policies) companies will run the risk of not complying with government policies of different jurisdictions.
- *Data deletion*: In the cloud environment if a user finishes his/her storage need and wants to delete the data, it may come as a surprise that the data are not physically deleted from the cloud. This can lead to disclosure of data to malicious users.
- *Lack of standard for Service Level Agreement (SLA)*: Currently, there is no standard SLA to guide service providers when specifying their SLA, and each cloud vendor has his own defined SLA. Lacking a standard for SLAs is a barrier to data migration among different vendors.
- *Vendor lock-in*: In cloud computing different cloud providers use different hardware and software architectures and APIs (application programming interfaces) for their services and systems. This prevents users from migrating their data from one vendor to another or integrating the services provided by different vendors. For example, Google uses Bigtable, Facebook uses Cassandra, and Amazon uses Dynamo. There is no common interface to access these databases. The migration of contact data (say, from Salesforce to Gmail and vice versa) is not possible due to the absence of common interface and database systems. This results in vendor lock-in.
- *Network latency and performance instability*: Although cloud computing can dynamically scale up or down in providing resources, the performance of cloud services becomes unstable during peak loads. The data transfer rate over the internet is slower than the data transfer rate over a fiber-optic network or Ethernet.
- *Lack of standards*: Although clouds have documented interfaces, there are no standards associated with them making it unlikely that most clouds will be interoperable. The Open Grid Forum is developing an open cloud computing interface to resolve this issue and the Open Cloud Consortium is working on cloud computing standards and practices.

1.4.2.8 Ultimately Do We Really Need Cloud Computing?

Cloud computing provides more scalability, reliability, and flexibility than previous computing models. It is becoming increasingly clear that cloud computing is sorely needed as the extension and natural evolution from the grid model that had as its purpose to effectively and efficiently utilize underutilized resources. It is not a new computing model. It is actually a combination of grid computing and utility computing. The major benefit of cloud computing is that its resources are only available on demand from the user and only for the period the resource is requested by the user. Both providers and consumers gain benefits. Cloud computing has the ability to dynamically scale up or down in providing resources to clients. The most important part of cloud computing is that it provides more scalability and flexibility than previous computing models. The second most important part is the pricing model of the cloud. Cost optimization with "pay-as-per-use" relieves enterprises from ownership cost, operational cost, and maintenance cost. Other benefits are increased mobility, ease of use, optimal utilization of resources, and portability of applications. Due to its benefits many organizations are tending toward migrating their IT infrastructure to the cloud.

Should Enterprises Avail Themselves of the Cloud?
Cloud migration refers to the process of moving applications, data, and other business objects from an enterprise's onsite premises to the cloud environment. An enterprise should analyze the benefits and limitations of the cloud [5] before migrating its IT infrastructure to the cloud. Obvious benefits include unlimited scalability, reduced cost, increased storage, flexibility, reliability, automation, and mobility. Major limitations of the cloud environment include security, interoperability, portability, and SLA.

As the limitations of cloud technology clearly show, any enterprise involved *in mission-critical, time-critical, safety-critical work cannot migrate to the cloud as the cloud cannot give 100%* assurance against loss of the above. *Any company that has sensitive data should realize that it is placing the security of its assets into the hands of third parties.*

Therefore it is not wise for a company with sensitive data to migrate to the cloud. Moreover, applications involved in real-time transactions, such as banking, are not advised to migrate to the cloud as network latency will be a serious issue.

Typical reasons enterprises want to migrate

(i)   Many enterprises want to migrate their legacy software assets to the cloud as they have experienced difficulties in adopting new technologies and standards. It takes a long time to establish new services and features.
(ii)   Enterprises that have less important or insensitive information.
(iii) Small to medium-sized businesses that cannot afford operational costs.
(iv)   Enterprises where batch processing of data takes place.

Key Points to Be Considered Before Migration
An enterprise needs to be aware that the cloud is a collection of different providers' (someone else's) infrastructures and services. It is where a company happens to host its data and applications. There are a number of common service offering models of cloud computing: Infrastructure as a Service (IaaS), Platform as a Service (PaaS), and Software as a Service (SaaS). An enterprise needs to decide which of the above three service offering models is most suitable for it. The enterprise has to consider two aspects: (i) the security, performance, scalability, reliability, and other required QoS characteristics of applications, and (ii) capital, operational, and maintenance cost, and return on investment (ROI). With these two aspects in mind an enterprise should choose which service offering model suits it best. An oversimplification of these models is given below.

In an IaaS model an enterprise allows the cloud service provider to host the enterprise's physical infrastructure, equipment, etc. Having hired the infrastructure from the cloud service provider an enterprise can take control of building servers, managing storage, and deploying different applications. But, the enterprise has only limited control over networking devices. Many enterprises use this kind of migration for off-site disaster recovery. An enterprise can deploy continuity of business (COB) or disaster recovery (DR) servers in the cloud.

In a PaaS model the infrastructure and platform are both offered by the cloud service provider and the user will host its applications on the platform offered by the provider. Users will have more limited control than in an IaaS model. This kind of offering is more suitable for web or application developers. Web applications or applications having large numbers of end users can be migrated to this model.

In an SaaS model the cloud service provider offers software applications and the user has no control. In this model the user has access to applications across the Web.

After deciding which service offering model to adopt an enterprise should decide which deployment model it is going to use to migrate its stuff. There are three deployment models: public, private, and hybrid. In public cloud deployment, services are offered to end users across the internet, which is of course shared by the public. In private cloud deployment, services are offered by a cloud owned by a single company at a single location. Private cloud deployment is more secure than public cloud deployment. Typically, an enterprise can construct its own private cloud center to cater for the needs of all its company requirements. However, the problem with this deployment is that the cloud may not be able to provide all customer needs with full dynamic scaling of resources. At times, there may be insufficient resources. For example, an enterprise may suffer from insufficient resources at holiday times due to peak loads. On such occasions an enterprise can opt to combine both private cloud and public cloud deployment. This kind of deployment is hybrid deployment.

An enterprise should weigh the pros and cons of cloud migration and decide whether it is really necessary to migrate to the cloud. It should ask a number of questions of itself:

1. Whether it deals with sensitive data.
2. Whether it deals with mission/safety/time-critical applications.
3. Whether it deals with heavy transactions in daily processing.
4. Whether it deals with real-time analytics.
5. Whether it can afford to meet capital, operational, and maintenance costs.
6. Whether it is fully aware of connectivity issues, performance instability, network latency, and other security-related limitations of the cloud.
7. Whether it is fully aware of the service model it is going to choose and what control it will have over the infrastructure, platform, etc.
8. What kind of deployment model it should go for.
9. How tough the migration process is.
10. Whether it meets ROI.

11. Whether it has disaster recovery mechanisms in case of failures?
12. Whether clear business needs and objectives for cloud migration have been formulated.
13. What to migrate and what not to migrate.
14. Whether the migration and transfer cost have been assessed. Are they reasonable? Because there are times when the migration cost will be more expensive than the capital and operational cost.
15. Whether migration is feasible. How long will migration take?
16. Whether all objectives are defined and specified in the SLA.

Ultimately, an enterprise should understand that it is dealing with all its data and applications. It has to decide, based on cost, connectivity, network capacity, performance, security, and other factors, whether to choose to migrate to the cloud or not.

1.5 Summary

The chapter began by describing the different categories of computing and the different aspects/purposes for which they are intended. It highlighted where cloud computing fits into computing taxonomy. There are different computing models for different aspects/purposes: (i) models for enterprise computing, (ii) models for High-performance computing, and (iii) models for selling IT resources or hiring resources over the internet. With respect to the first aspect, the chapter elaborated how the enterprise computing model gradually evolved from traditional monolithic to two-tier client–server to three-tier models, and then moved on by stating the varying needs of enterprises such as scalability, performance, and availability. It discussed the need for splitting the middle tier into N different layers and tiers, which resulted in the N-tier client–server model.

With respect to the second aspect, the chapter discussed the different High-performance computing models. It introduced the benefit of cluster computing by pointing out the high cost involved in setting up supercomputers to achieve High-performance. It described the cluster as a collection of almost homogeneous nodes deployed at a single physical site capable of delivering the expected High-performance task. The chapter went on to describe different types of clusters such as top-performance clusters, load-balancing clusters, high-availability clusters, and fault-tolerant clusters. It described the inadequacy of clusters when handling scientific, engineering, and other research projects and the need to coordinate work produced at different universities and research centers. In this way the chapter introduced grid computing. In grid computing, resources from more than one organization are coordinated to provide the required infrastructure and other QoS attributes for computation. A grid can be perceived as a huge collection of nodes that are heterogeneous and geographically dispersed. Hence administrative control over different resources is decentralized (but centrally coordinated).

With respect to the third aspect, the chapter discussed utility computing and cloud computing. It introduced the cloud model which has the dual purpose of (i) using the computing resources of service providers (which otherwise remain underutilized) and (ii) meeting the cost burden of small and medium-sized enterprises by offering the computing infrastructure they require on demand according to a pay-as-per-use pricing model.

The chapter highlighted the concepts underlying cloud computing, the need for cloud computing, and the different stakeholders involved in the cloud environment. The chapter described in simple terms how cloud computing could be applied in various domains. It highlighted the drawbacks of cloud computing. Ultimately, it gave guidelines on how an enterprise should decide whether it really needs cloud computing and how to go about it.

1.6 Exercises

1. Compile a list of motivational ideas behind cloud computing.
2. Compile a list of the primary reasons cloud computing came into existence.
3. Are we reinventing the wheel of traditional computing by using the new name of cloud computing? Or does cloud computing really differ from its traditional counterparts? If so, how (write an assignment)?
4. Is cloud computing an entirely new computing paradigm? Or can we perceive cloud computing as an evolution and extension of existing models?
5. Differentiate between scalability and elasticity.
6. Compare and contrast cloud computing with its counterparts.
7. Explain briefly who the beneficiaries of cloud computing are.
8. Do enterprises really need cloud computing? Justify your ideas with different scenarios (write an assignment).

References

1. Kahanwal B, Singh TP (2012) The distributed computing paradigms: P2P, grid, cluster, cloud, and jungle. Int J Latest Res Sci Technol 1(2):183–187. ISSN (Online) 2278–5299. http://www. mnkjournals.com/ijlrst.htm
2. Stifani R, Pappe S, Breiter G, Behrendt M (2012) IBM cloud computing reference architecture. IBM Acad Technol ATN 3(1). http://csrc.nist.gov/publications/drafts/800-145/Draft-SP-800-145_cloud-definition.pdf
3. Chandrasekaran D (2015) Essentials of cloud computing. CRC Press, Taylor & Francis Group
4. Ahmed M, Hossain MA (2014) Cloud computing and security issues in the cloud. Int J Netw Secur Appl (IJNSA) 6(1):25–36
5. Jadeja Y, Modi K (2012) Cloud computing—concepts, architecture and challenges. In: 2012 Proceedings of international conference on computing, electronics and electrical technologies (ICCEET), pp 887–880

Fundamentals of Cloud Computing

2

Learning Objectives

The objective of this chapter is to introduce the fundamentals of cloud computing. This covers the features of cloud computing, the architecture of cloud computing, and different service classes and deployment models of cloud computing. In addition, it gives a brief overview of the different public cloud service providers.

Motivational Questions
1. What are the features or characteristics that are unique to cloud computing?
2. We often come across the terms IaaS, PaaS, and SaaS. What are they?
3. What are the core components of the cloud architecture?
4. How are the clouds deployed?
5. What kinds of services can be rented out from the cloud?
6. Compare cloud and on-premise computing.
7. How can the services be accessed?
8. List a few examples of existing public cloud service providers?

Preface

Chapter 1 made it clear that cloud computing is a computing model that provides convenient and on-demand as well as rapid access to a shared pool of resources provided by cloud service providers over the internet. *This facilitates both service providers, such as Amazon who want their computational resources to be fully and effectively utilized by renting them out to consumers, and small and medium-sized enterprises who want to cut down the capital investment involved in establishing an IT infrastructure.* Moving to the next level a reader may wish to know which needs

© Springer Nature Switzerland AG 2019

S. Chellammal and C. Pethuru Raj, *Essentials of Cloud Computing*,
Texts in Computer Science, https://doi.org/10.1007/978-3-030-13134-0_2

of modern enterprises are essential, how the needs can be fulfilled through the unique features of cloud computing, the architecture of cloud, different kinds of service offerings and deployment models in the cloud. These concepts are addressed in this chapter.

2.1   Essential Needs of Enterprises and How They Are Fulfilled by the Unique Features of Cloud Computing

The essential characteristics that differentiate cloud computing from other computing paradigms are on-demand provisioning, self-service based access, resource pooling and multi-tenancy, rapid elasticity, measured service and pay-as-per-use pricing, and broad network access.

2.1.1   Scalability and On-Demand Provisioning

Very often application load is found to be non-static and varies with respect to time. For example, an online flight-booking application tends to have greater load during holiday times like Christmas. Many users will access the application during such times. Let us consider another example in which a social networking website, such as Facebook, may use a large amount of information during an abnormal situation such as a cyclone or flood. Scalability is the ability of a system to handle growing loads without compromising the existing QoS attributes of service deliverables. Scalability is the ability of the system to accommodate varying loads either by adding additional resources for nodes *(scale-up/vertical scaling)* or by adding additional nodes *(scale-out/horizontal scaling)*. A scalable system is more adaptable to the needs or demands of users. According to the varying loads user demand for computing resources will vary. Further, computing the amount of resources necessary for an application may not be predicted exactly. Because an internet-based application typically consists of three tiers to N tiers, it is essential to discover the computing resources required by different tiers during peak loads. Two major parameters to be taken into account are *how many resources need to be provided* and *when should they be provided*. Hence cloud computing should be capable of meeting such situations and provide the required resources on demand very quickly so that the quality of service (QoS) of the application will be maintained. Variations in loads are often of two types: *long-term variations* (such as variations in load over a period of, say, days to seasons) and *short-term variations* (such as exponential surges in requests for a short time like spikes, also called a flash crowd). Different provisioning schemes, such as predictive provisioning and reactive provisioning, are used in the cloud environment to handle long-term and short-term variations in load, respectively. Scalability is achieved by providing the required resources to handle

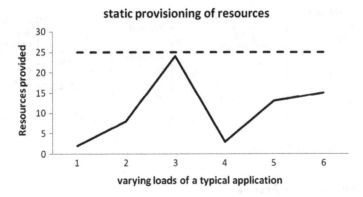

Fig. 2.1 Static provisioning of resources (overprovisioning)

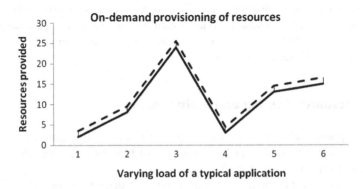

Fig. 2.2 On-demand provisioning

the load. To meet varying loads, resources are generally provided in two ways: static provisioning and dynamic provisioning. In static provisioning resources are over-provisioned to applications, keeping the largest quantity of required resources in mind. As shown in Fig. 2.1 the amount of resources provided is always more than the amount of resources required. With static provisioning of resources the resources will remain underutilized most of the time. An enterprise generally tends to over-provision to meet loads. Since peak load conditions occur only occasionally the resources will remain unused. However, in the cloud environment, scalability is achieved by providing resources as and when needed (i.e., dynamically provisioning resources according to the demands of users), as shown in Fig. 2.2.

The main advantage of dynamic provisioning of resources on demand is the reduced cost for consumers. Consumers only need pay for the actual usage of resources, much like such domestic utilities as liquefied petroleum gas (LPG) or electricity.

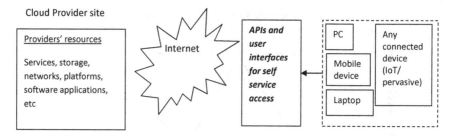

Fig. 2.3 Self–service based access

2.1.2 Self-service Access

In the cloud environment a user can avail himself of the required computational resources through an online interface of his own, without interacting with service providers (called self-access/self-service capability), as in Fig. 2.3. This means that the user interface API allows the user to configure his needs himself (as per his demands) and avail himself of them.

2.1.3 Resource Pooling and Multi-tenancy

Resource pooling allows cloud service providers to accommodate the needs of multiple tenants or consumers by pooling available resources according to the demands of users (as shown in Fig. 2.4).

This means that the number of tenants and their demands vary with respect to time. Computational resources are pooled so that the demands of multiple tenants will be met. This implies that the resources allotted, say, 20 GB in *machine-1* for a particular tenant (*tenant-1*) may get pooled as 20 GB in *machine-2*. This pooling of resources occurs to handle the needs of multiple tenants and their changes in demands. However, consumers are transparent to resource pooling. This means that a user can access his resources with logical mapping without knowing their physical locations in the cloud. Another important aspect is that, although multiple tenants share the same physical resources, their data or application or code or whatever resources they consume will remain logically separated from other tenants.

2.1.4 Rapid Elasticity

Rapid elasticity refers to the capability of providing scalable services rapidly. Cloud computing can be elastic only if the demands of users are rapidly provisioned. Rapidity in provisioning is obtained with automation. Since the demands of any

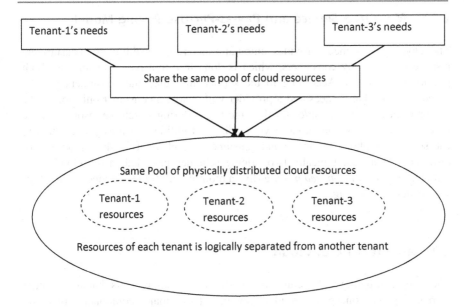

Fig. 2.4 Resource pooling and multi-tenancy

cloud user are dynamic with respect to time, demands may either scale out (increase in demand) or scale in (decrease in demand). Both needs should be automatically met so that there is no or at least a very minimal time gap between *demand* and *capacity*. Capacity should closely follow demand with a very minimal time gap (as shown in Fig. 2.5) so that the cloud becomes rapid elastic in nature. This is in contrast to traditional computing where scalability is achieved by manually adding physical servers, which takes a long time.

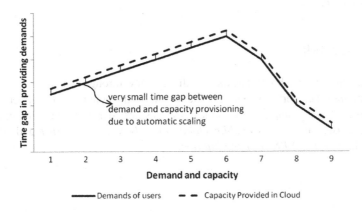

Fig. 2.5 Rapid elasticity of the cloud

2.1.5   Measured Service and Pay-as-Per-Use Pricing Model

The cloud environment provides automatic-metering capability to measure the resources utilized by consumers, which is done in a transparent manner for both providers and users. According to the service measured the consumers will be billed. As for what is measured a provider will charge a consumer only for the IT resources actually used and/or for the time frame during which the resources were used. Similar to how the public pays for different utilities, such as gas, electricity, cab service, or phone service, cloud consumers are charged for their exact use of resources. There are typically two pricing schemes provided in the cloud environment: *subscription-based pricing* (like a monthly bill for the service acquired) or *pay-as-per-use pricing*.

2.2   Architecture of Cloud

The cloud computing architecture comprises the core components that are essential to realizing the concept of cloud computing. Three major components of cloud computing are (i) the front end, (ii) the network, and (iii) the back end or the cloud. This is shown in Fig. 2.6.

2.2.1   Front End

The front-end layer of the cloud refers to the user layer. Typical cloud users are individuals, enterprises, employees of enterprises, employees on the move, mobile users, laptop user, users having any kind of connected device, etc. Cloud service providers provide APIs and interfaces for users themselves to access the required service through a web portal. Users access the APIs over the internet and consume the required service.

2.2.2   Network

Network refers to the broad backbone infrastructure through which cloud service providers offer their services to users. The internet is the core network infrastructure that makes cloud computing feasible. Services are delivered via the internet. Typically, *users can access public clouds directly* via *the internet* and *private clouds* via *a secure VPN over the internet*.

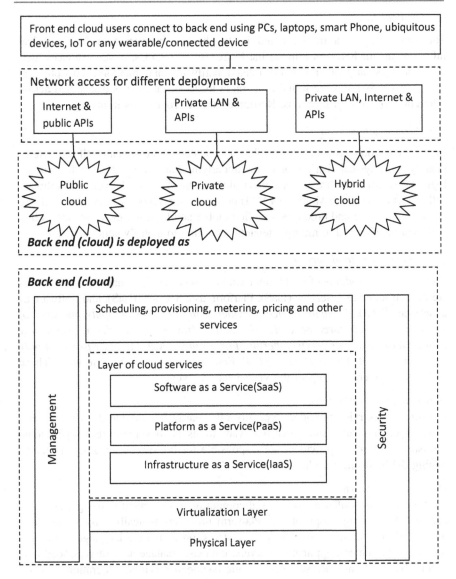

Fig. 2.6 Cloud architecture

2.2.3 Back End

The back-end layer forms the cloud. It consists of six different layers: (i) physical layer, (ii) virtualization layer, (iii) layer of cloud services, (iv) scheduling, provisioning, and pricing layer, (v) security, and (vi) management.

(i) *Physical layer*

The core component of the cloud is its physical infrastructure. The physical infrastructure includes bare metal hardware, servers, CPUs, storage devices, network devices, any other network-related hardware, and memory. The physical infrastructure is not to be found at a single location, rather it is distributed across different geographical locations. Resources are heterogeneous in nature.

(ii) *Virtualization layer*

The virtualization layer is responsible for considering theoretically all the heterogeneity and physical distribution of the underlying hardware and generate a single, logical view for the entire physical layer of the cloud. This is achieved with software called Virtual Machine Monitor (VMM) or hypervisor. Hypervisor combines all the physical hardware and produces a unified global and logical view of resources that will then be allocated to multiple tenants according to their dynamic demands.

(iii) *Layers of cloud services*

Cloud service providers offer different kinds of services. The major service classes are Infrastructure as a Service (IaaS), Platform as a Service (PaaS), and Software as a Service (SaaS). *A cloud service provider generally provides only one kind of services (e.g., Salesforce only provides SaaS). However, a service provider may provide more than one service offering. For example, Azure initially provided only PaaS, but later it started providing both PaaS and even some IaaS services.* These services are offered on top of the virtualization layer.

Infrastructure as a Service

Infrastructure service providers typically offer hardware, storage devices, servers, network components, and other hardware to users to support their operations. Infrastructure service providers are responsible for housing, operating, and maintaining the hardware for clients.

Platform as a Service

Platform providers offer a cloud-based computing environment to design, develop, execute, and manage applications. Platform providers typically provide development platforms, middleware, operating systems, programming languages, libraries, runtime environment, application servers, database management servers, load balancers, business analytics services, mobile back-end services, integration brokers, business process management systems, rules engines, event processors, and other software tools. PaaS providers are responsible for installation, configuration, operation, licensing, upgradation of software tools, and maintenance of tools. *PaaS providers help developers to concentrate only on developing code of concern to them and hence relieve them of the abovementioned common services.*

Software as a Service

Software as a Service provides software applications for consumer use over the internet on demand. Users can subscribe to software applications from SaaS providers with the help of their APIs over the internet.

(iv) *Scheduling, provisioning, and other services*

Various management and orchestration services are needed to be able to manage the cloud environment. Cloud orchestration and management are essential processes that take place within the cloud. A cloud orchestrator automates and orchestrates

- a scheduling component to schedule resources to different tenants;
- a provisioning component that provides scheduled resources;
- monitoring components that monitor the cloud environment;
- metering services that meter the resources provided; and
- a pricing component that bills the consumer according to a subscription-based or use-based model.

(v) *Security*

Security in cloud computing is a responsibility shared among cloud service providers and cloud users. In the case of IaaS, for example, providers take on the responsibility of providing security for their physical infrastructure and consumers take on the responsibility of providing security to a guest operating system (OS), platform, applications, and data that they deploy on the infrastructure consumed.

(vi) *Management*

Since the cloud computing environment is complex cloud service providers use various tools to manage, automate, and orchestrate cloud operations and business services. Cloud Management Platform (CMP) tools, cloud automation tools, cloud orchestration tools, cloud brokerage tools, cloud monitoring tools, cloud security tools, etc. are typically used to manage and optimize the cloud.

2.3 Deployment Models for Cloud Services

Cloud services can be deployed by means of five major models: (i) public cloud deployment, (ii) private cloud deployment, (iii) hybrid cloud deployment, (iv) community cloud deployment, and (v) multi-cloud deployment.

2.3.1 Public Cloud Deployment

In public cloud deployment cloud service providers offer their services and infrastructure off-site over the internet to all public users who have signed up for pay-per-use pricing on demand [1, 2]. This is shown in Fig. 2.7. Service providers provide their services through publicly accessible APIs. Users can self-access their required services using a web interface on their own without any intervention from the provider. When applications are used by large numbers of people, public cloud deployment is suitable. Public cloud vendors include Google, Amazon, Microsoft, and Salesforce.com who offer their services (which may be IaaS, PaaS, or SaaS) to the public over the internet. *The inherent feature of public cloud deployment is multi-tenancy.* Cloud resources are simultaneously accessible to multiple tenants. Internally, resources are virtualized and pooled among multiple customers according to their dynamic demands.

Advantages of public cloud deployment

- The primary benefit of public cloud deployment is cost savings. Organizations do not need to buy, install, operate, or maintain servers or other equipment. Organizations simply develop their own applications and host them in the public cloud.
- Since developers do not need to worry about the runtime environment of applications, public cloud deployment leads to increased productivity.
- Since public clouds support multi-tenancy they are inherently cost-effective for users.

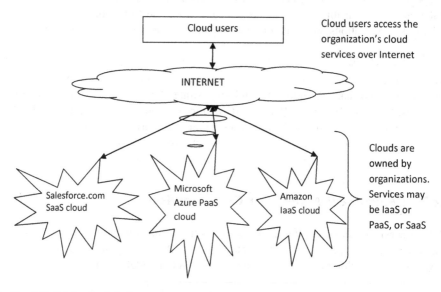

Fig. 2.7 Public cloud deployment

- Public clouds provide infinite elasticity and dynamic scale-out or scale-up.
- Public clouds offer unlimited capacity at lower cost.
- Public clouds use recent technologies and support the modernization of applications.
- Public clouds allow capital expenses to be shifted to operational expenses.
- Public clouds have better utility rates.
- There is also greater flexibility for users because organizations pay only for the computing resources they actually use.
- Public clouds are highly scalable.
- Public clouds provide universal accessibility.
- Applications and data are automatically backed up and upgraded.

Disadvantages of public cloud deployment

- The main drawback of public cloud deployment is multi-tenancy. The services cloud service providers offer are deployed in the same physical infrastructure as that of multiple users through virtualization. So, although the workspaces of users are logically separated, they still share the same physical infrastructure and other fundamental software platforms. This leads to security issues.
- Outages can occur that affect the availability and reliability of hosted services.
- Public cloud deployment provides only restricted visibility and control.
- Any data stored in the public cloud is necessarily insecure. Users have no idea where their data are stored in the public cloud environment.
- Since the storage of data as a result of public cloud deployment is distributed across different geographical locations this may lead to the issue of non-compliance against the security and privacy regulations of the enterprise concerned.

2.3.2 Private Cloud Deployment

In private cloud deployment the cloud is owned and managed by a single organization that only offers services to its users (and maybe its partners) *over a private LAN on demand through a self-service portal*. Private clouds can be deployed either via cloud platforms, such as Eucalyptus and OpenStack, or by adding automation, orchestration, management, and self-provisioning capabilities to an already virtualized infrastructure. However, the resources of an enterprise should be pooled together into one centralized unit and made available to users on demand through a self-service portal.

Core features of private cloud deployment

- A private cloud allows consistent processes to be automated and includes a self-service interface and service catalog that allow internal developers to provision services on demand.
- A private cloud is highly automated in managing pools of resources including compute servers, storage, networks, platforms, development and deployment platforms, middleware, application servers, web servers, database servers, and middleware.
- A private cloud offers common services that improve the efficiency of the environment.
- A private cloud incorporates security and governance capabilities specially designed for a company's requirements.
- A private cloud should have a self-service portal that controls the way various users of the enterprise (divisions, departments, and partners) can access it.
- A private cloud controls the service level of the platform based on constituent needs and compliance requirements.

There are two possible ways of deploying in the private cloud: *(i) private cloud deployment within the organization concerned* and *(ii) private cloud deployment within a third-party cloud provider facility.* These two deployments are shown in Figs. 2.8 and 2.9, respectively.

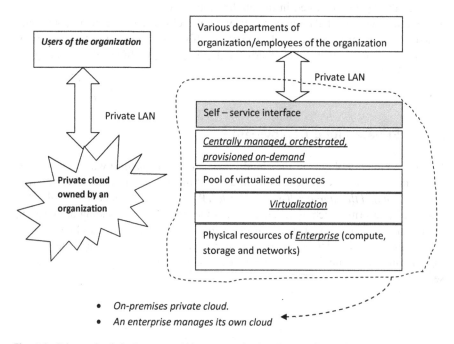

Fig. 2.8 Private cloud deployment within an organization (on-premises private cloud)

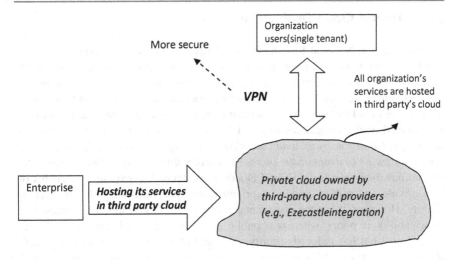

Fig. 2.9 Private cloud deployment using a third-party cloud

(i) *Private cloud deployment within the organization concerned*

In this model an organization establishes and manages its own cloud. As shown in Fig. 2.8 the cloud is established using the resources of the enterprise. The enterprise itself owns the resources. The resources are virtualized, pooled, orchestrated, managed, and provided to employees of the organization over a private LAN through a self-service portal.

(ii) *Private cloud deployment with third-party cloud provider*

In this model the physical resources are located in a third-party facility and provided by a third-party provider. However, the provider provides his resources only to a single customer. They are not shared among multiple customers as in public clouds. Private-cloud computing is defined by privacy and the service provider provides services via *secure connections such as a VPN over the internet.*

Overall, the cloud is located off-premises, managed by third-party service providers, and is accessible only to the enterprise concerned through a self-service portal over a VPN (as shown in Fig. 2.9). In contrast to public cloud deployment, either model of private cloud deployment allows only the users of a single enterprise and its partners to access the cloud. *There is no multi-tenancy.* A more important difference is the size of a private cloud, which is very small when compared with a public cloud (i.e., resources are limited to, say, around 1000 servers). A private cloud is meant for only one user (i.e., an enterprise). Partners of the enterprise may be allowed to access the private cloud. Since there are no external users security is preserved.

2.3.3 Hybrid Cloud Deployment

According to the National Institute of Standards and Technology (NIST) *a hybrid cloud is a combination of public and private clouds bound together by either standardized or proprietary technology that enables data and application portability*. Organizations tend to host all sensitive applications, services, and data in an on-premises cloud and other services in an external public cloud to avail themselves of unlimited computational resources. *A hybrid cloud is more suitable to meeting the unexpected or uncertain load conditions of an organization as it is not easy for any organization to dynamically increase its scalability quickly (let alone instantly) without advanced planning.* Hybrid clouds were devised to exploit the benefits of both private and public clouds. A private cloud provides a significant level of security. However, it has the disadvantage of suffering from limited resources (i.e., its scalability is poor), whereas a public cloud provides sufficient scalability at reduced cost but has reduced security. *A hybrid cloud aims to achieve high scalability, low cost, and high security by integrating a private and a public cloud. Integration results in high flexibility.* The objectives of a hybrid cloud and its underlying concept are given in Fig. 2.10. The overall concept of a hybrid cloud is shown in Fig. 2.11.

In a hybrid cloud the important technical aspect is to establish the connection between a private cloud and a public cloud facility.

Core connection points to be made between a private cloud and a public cloud

Integration: In a hybrid environment sensitive data and processes are typically carried out in a private cloud, while generic non-sensitive and common services are hosted in a public cloud. Now, in a hybrid cloud environment there is a need for appropriate seamless integration of data and processes across a private and a public

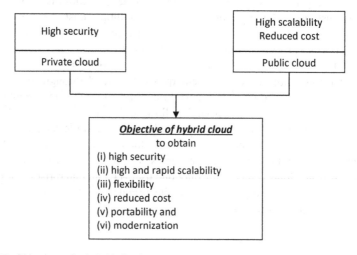

Fig. 2.10 Objectives of a hybrid cloud

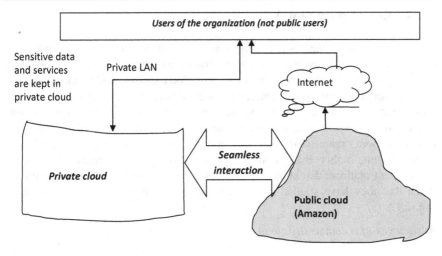

Fig. 2.11 Concept of a hybrid cloud

cloud to be done such that the users should realize consistent and prompt delivery of their services.

Data localization: It is often the case that enterprises do *not* want their data to be distributed. They need their data to be *localized*. The primary needs for data location include

• performance and manageability requirements; and
• security and compliance requirements.

Hence, data localization according to the policies of an enterprise has to be performed correctly in a hybrid cloud setup.

Operational visibility and management: To provide services that can be used consistently and predictably it is essential that there is unified management of the variety of resources provided by both private and public clouds. Hence a hybrid cloud should implement proper and unified management of all resources to facilitate global monitoring of all resources and clear visibility.

Security: Security in a hybrid cloud needs to be managed in conjunction with visibility and control. It must also be managed based on an open governance model.

Portability: A hybrid cloud facilitates the modernization of applications and the flexibility and portability of applications by providing containerization technology, which packages an application along with its dependencies so that it will run in a Linux (open-source) environment. A hybrid cloud also provides an OpenStack environment, which is an open-source cloud operating system and serves as the critical element in the cloud to achieve portability. Hence an enterprise can avail itself of these features while integrating a private and a public cloud.

2.3.4 Community Cloud

The main aim of businesses is to stay connected with their customers, employees, and partners. A community cloud can centralize all these individual stakeholders into one community. A community cloud is a cloud service model that provides a cloud computing solution to a limited number of organizations (or a few communities) that have similar security, privacy, governance, and management policies. The infrastructure and computational resources of a community cloud are exclusive to two or more organizations that have common privacy, security, and regulatory considerations, rather than a single organization. A community cloud is a multi-tenant platform that allows several companies to work on the same platform given that they have similar security and regulation policies. This is shown in Fig. 2.12.

Advantages of a community cloud

- The cost of setting up a community cloud versus and individual private cloud is often less as a result of being able to divide costs among all participants.
- Communities can incorporate the required level of security, privacy, and compliance requirements easily as they have those aspects in common.
- Communities can collaborate on projects easily.
- Like a private cloud a community cloud can be hosted in a third-party facility.

Disadvantages of a community cloud

A fixed amount of bandwidth and data storage is shared among all community members.

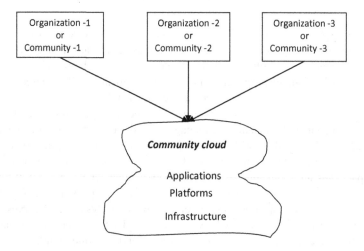

Fig. 2.12 Community cloud

2.3.5 Multi-cloud

Different public cloud service providers supply different kinds of services to cloud users. The services provided by different providers may have different costs, different quality attributes, etc. A cloud user (or an organization) may wish to avail himself of a particular service (say, an IaaS service from Amazon) and a PaaS service (say, from Azure). This scenario where the services of more than one public cloud are integrated to achieve a business goal for an individual or an organization is called multi-cloud. *One of the main criteria for multi-cloud is that it should mix* more than one public cloud. In addition, a multi-cloud can mix with an on-premises legacy asset/data center and a private cloud. The multi-cloud concept is shown in Fig. 2.13.

Multi-cloud computing, as noted above, commonly refers to the use of multiple public cloud providers. It is more of a general approach to managing and paying for cloud services in a way that seems best for a given organization.

Advantages of multi-cloud computing

– *Optimized return on investment*: Different cloud providers offer their services with a diverse range of characteristics, functionality, pricing models, and policies. With multi-cloud computing a cloud user can choose the best offer for each requirement. For example, for IaaS the user may choose Amazon, whereas for PaaS he/she may choose Azure. By combining these he/she will get a better return on investment.
– *Superior security*: A multi-cloud infrastructure allows organizations to maintain a hybrid cloud environment that enables a combination of security and cost savings at the same time.
– *Low latency*: With a multi-cloud infrastructure the data center closest to end users can provide the data requested with the minimum server hops.

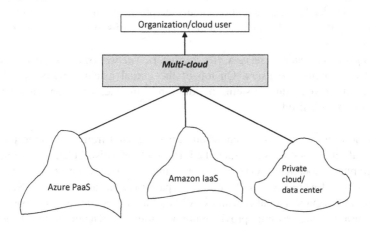

Fig. 2.13 Concept of multi-cloud

– *Autonomy*: A multi-cloud infrastructure empowers organizations to mix and match platforms and vendors such that their workloads are not locked into individual cloud providers. Switching vendors becomes easier and even automated at times since workload performance is never tied to individual vendors. As a result of lower vendor lock-in customers get the autonomy to address changing business needs for performance, security, and return on investment.

– *Less disaster prone*: A multi-cloud model offers almost 99.5% availability and hence maintains redundancy at multiple sites. This makes resources or data less disaster prone.

2.4 Service Class Models

Cloud service providers offer or deliver different kinds of services to users. There are three major categories: Infrastructure as a Service, Platform as a Service, and Software as a Service [3–5]. All the service models have the fundamental characteristics of cloud computing: elasticity, scalability, on-demand computing, multi-tenancy, metering service, and pay-per-use pricing model. Similarly, they have the same limitations such as data integrity, security, and vendor lock-in. These service classes are discussed in this section.

2.4.1 Infrastructure as a Service

Infrastructure as a Service (IaaS) allows distributed virtualized computational resources, such as servers, storage devices, network devices, and virtual machines, to be shared (Fig. 2.14). The IaaS environment can be likened to an on-premises infrastructure (as shown in Fig. 2.14). It can be seen that in an on-premises facility control entirely lies with the enterprise, whereas in an IaaS service model the provider completely controls and maintains the physical infrastructure. Cloud users can control the virtual machines and other platforms on top of the physical infrastructure.

IaaS providers offer (i) servers, (ii) storage, (iii) networks, (iv) hypervisors, and (v) virtual machines to users. On top of the virtual machine users install their required guest operating system, middleware, runtime, data, and applications according to their needs:

• IaaS cloud providers offer their resources on-demand from their large pools of physical infrastructure. Very often the infrastructure is distributed across different geographical locations. IaaS providers employ cloud *orchestration technology* using software such as OpenStack, Apache Cloudstack, or Open Nebula to create and manage virtual machines (VMs). Cloud orchestration involves carrying out automatic resource provisioning according to dynamic needs. It decides

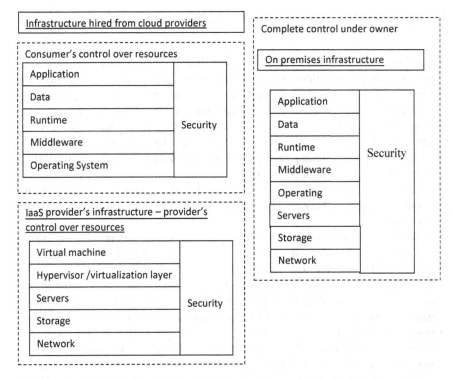

Fig. 2.14 Control and responsibilities of IaaS providers and consumers in contrast to an on-premises infrastructure

the most appropriate physical host to assign to VMs, performs VM migration from one host to another whenever required, allocates storage volumes to VMs, and provides usage information for billing.

- This kind of service is suitable for organizations that have difficulty funding the basic infrastructure to run their businesses. IaaS is the right choice for organizations looking for high levels of customization for their infrastructure.
- IaaS normally requires a high degree of technical proficiency to configure the infrastructure acquired from cloud providers. Hence IaaS is more suitable for enterprises with a highly skilled set of developers, network administrators, and database administrators who can work as a team to build applications from scratch, manage network traffic and storage traffic, and maintain and scale up or scale out requirements according to the needs of enterprise applications.
- Responsibilities are shared by both IaaS providers and consumers. With an IaaS model providers gain control over actual physical hardware resources. Users have control only over resources that are above the virtual machine. In the case of an on-premises infrastructure complete control, responsibility, and management lies with the owners. Among the most popular IaaS providers are Amazon Web Services (AWS), Cisco Metapod, Microsoft Azure, Google Compute Engine (GCE), and Joyent.

Common business scenarios suitable for Infrastructure as a Service cloud computing

- *Handling uncertain workload conditions and dynamic scalability*: When an enterprise has applications with uncertain workloads, it may choose IaaS for migration as IaaS provides excellent dynamic scale-up or scale-out options. IaaS is characterized by its rapid elasticity and pay-per-use pricing option.
- *Hosting web applications*: IaaS provides an infrastructure including servers and networks for hosting web applications that have a large number of users. With good resource provisioning the applications are likely to have high availability, high scalability, and high performance.
- *Handling big data*: Storing and processing big data requires vast storage and processing capacity. IaaS cloud can fulfill the need to store and process big data efficiently.
- *Running test and development cycles*: The computing and networking power behind IaaS cloud makes it suitable for running the different testing and development cycles of enterprise applications.
- *Providing disaster recovery*: IaaS cloud can offer a robust and scalable infrastructure for consolidating the disparate disaster recovery systems of an enterprise into one virtualized environment to handle data loss during disasters.
- *Hosting high-performance but not mission-critical applications*: Complex but not mission-critical problems, such as climate or weather predictions, financial modeling, and evaluation of products, requires many stages for calculations and analysis to be made. Such applications need huge computing power, which can be served well by IaaS cloud.

Benefits of Infrastructure as a Service cloud

- Eliminating the upfront cost of managing and setting up an on-site data center.
- Responding quickly to evolving business demands as a result of cloud elasticity.
- Improving business continuity and disaster recovery.
- Maintaining direct access to servers, networks, and storage.
- Deploying a new infrastructure in minutes and rapidly testing new ideas.

2.4.2 Platform as a Service

Platform as a Service (PaaS) providers *offer users both the hardware structure and software platform needed for applications development*. In general, PaaS providers offer both the underlying hardware infrastructure and software platform such as web servers, application servers, database servers, and a programming environment (e.g., J2EE, .Net, or Python).

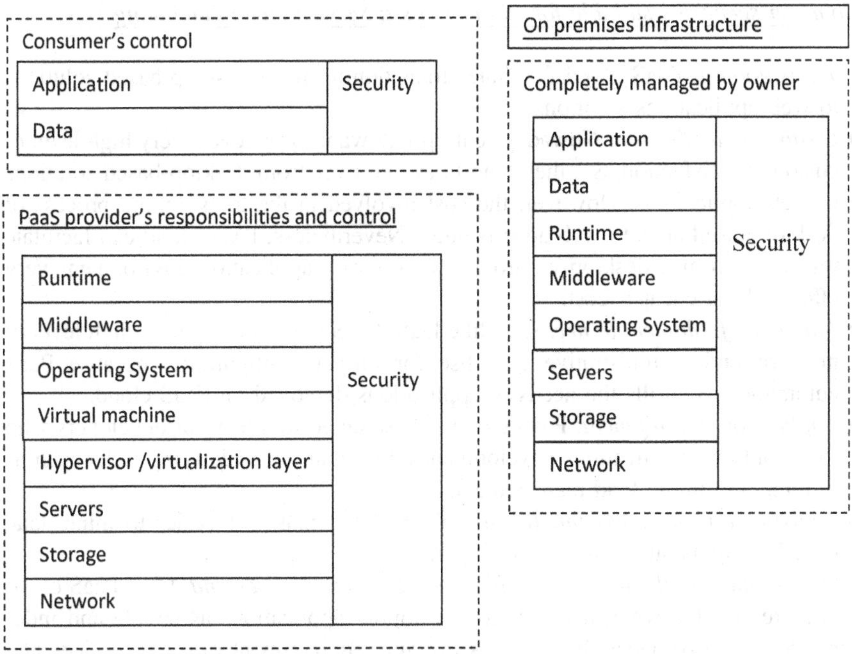

Consumer's control	
Application	Security
Data	

On premises infrastructure

Completely managed by owner

Application	
Data	Security
Runtime	
Middleware	
Operating System	
Servers	
Storage	
Network	

PaaS provider's responsibilities and control

Runtime	
Middleware	
Operating System	Security
Virtual machine	
Hypervisor /virtualization layer	
Servers	
Storage	
Network	

Fig. 2.15 Control and responsibilities of PaaS providers and consumers

- Developers can use PaaS as a platform or framework to develop and customize their applications.
- PaaS makes the development, testing, and deployment of applications quick and cheaper.
- PaaS models provide benefits such as increased developer productivity and short time to market for applications.
- However, in the PaaS model users gain control only over applications they install on the platform and data. They have no control over the underlying hardware and platform, which are completely managed by PaaS providers. This is shown in Fig. 2.15.

Popular PaaS providers include Google App Engine, Microsoft Azure, and RedHat OpenShift. Google App Engine and RedHat OpenShift provide a complete platform for the development of distributed web applications based on an open-source environment, whereas Microsoft Azure offers a platform for both Windows-based and open-source tools, such as .Net, Python, Ruby, and PHP, for applications.

Common scenarios suitable for Platform as a Service cloud computing

- *Transitioning*: PaaS cloud facilitates transitioning from desktop-based solutions to web applications solutions.
- *Customer satisfaction*: Nowadays enterprises want to achieve a very high level of customer satisfaction. So, they tend to switch over from desktop-based solutions to web applications. However, the cost involved in the transitioning process of desktop-based apps to web apps is huge. Nevertheless, PaaS cloud can facilitate transition from a desktop environment to a web application environment very effectively at cheaper cost.
- *Automatic fulfillment of needs*: Unlike IaaS, PaaS does not require a high level of network and administrative expertise for proper configuration because PaaS automatically fulfills the needs of applications deployed on PaaS cloud.
- *Application development*: PaaS cloud is best suited to a team of developers who focus only on applications development rather than on underlying tasks such as runtime and traffic load management.
- *Analytics and business intelligence*: PaaS cloud makes it easier to mine data, unlock insights, and improve predictive forecasting.
- *Development of the means of deployment of microservices and APIs*: PaaS cloud is more suitable when it comes to developing applications as simple and independent *microservices*. It facilitates the quick deployment of microservices and enables incremental delivery of Agile development.
- *Providing additional services*: PaaS is more suitable for enterprises in providing *additional services* such as security, scheduling, workflow, and directory.

Benefits of Platform as a Service cloud

- Eliminating the cost of software licensing and reducing the costs involved in maintenance, software updates, and patches.
- Reducing coding time by offering precoded and built-in frameworks and platforms.
- Providing multi-platform support so that applications can be developed very quickly across more than one platform (i.e., cross-platform applications) and providing support to include a wide range of users from desktop users to web browsers to mobile users.
- Providing the geographical and collaboration support needed by developers to work collaboratively on the platform and tools provided by PaaS cloud from different locations without any difficulty.
- Providing efficient life cycle management for building, testing, deploying, managing and updating web applications in the same integrated environment.

2.4.3 Software as a Service

Software as a Service (SaaS) allows cloud service providers to offer completely developed applications to users over the internet on a subscription basis. Users can simply log in and use applications completely provided by SaaS providers and run on the providers' infrastructures. In this model users have no control at all over anything. All layers are under the control of SaaS providers (as shown in Fig. 2.16). A couple of examples of SaaS applications are Salesforce's CRM and Workday's ERP.

Common scenarios suitable for Software as a Service cloud computing

- *Non-technical enterprises*: SaaS can offer completely developed software applications to non-technical companies that want to deploy their websites and applications rapidly with SaaS cloud managing such things as hosting, security, and server uptime.
- *Enterprises wanting to move from internally hosted exchange email to a cloud-based corporate email, calendar, or other office tools*: SaaS facilitates this by enabling the employees of the enterprise to gain access to email or calendar from any system that has access to the internet.

Benefits of Software as a Service cloud

- Eliminating installation and maintenance costs.
- Providing remote access to software applications over the internet.

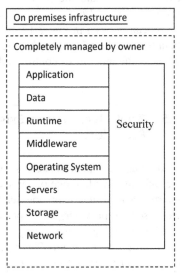

Fig. 2.16 Control and responsibilities of SaaS providers and consumers

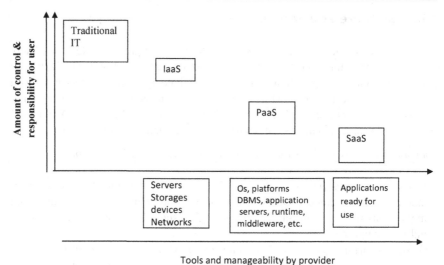

Fig. 2.17 Amount of control for IaaS, PaaS, and SaaS

- Providing anytime and anywhere access to SaaS applications.
- Employing enterprise-grade software and cutting-edge technology for applications.
- Providing simple pay-per-use pricing in which users only have to pay for actual usage.

   In a nutshell the above three service models demonstrate that the users' control over resources and the providers' manageability of models can be perceived as shown in Fig. 2.17.

   As can be seen in Fig. 2.17 the manageability of providers over SaaS is greater than PaaS and IaaS, and the manageability of providers from IaaS to SaaS increases whereas the amount of control and customization decreases from IaaS to SaaS.

2.5 Brief Overview of Existing Public Cloud Service Providers

Many major companies, such as Amazon, Salesforce, Microsoft, IBM, and Google, are offering a wide range of services on demand as utilities for public use over the internet with different pricing schemes. Table 2.1 lists some of the most popular cloud service providers and types of service models.

   The following sections briefly describe typical examples of each service type: Amazon Elastic Compute Cloud (IaaS server), Amazon S3 (IaaS storage), Amazon CloudFront (IaaS network), Microsoft (PaaS), and Google Apps (SaaS).

Table 2.1 List of popular public cloud service providers

Type of service model	Popular cloud service providers
Infrastructure as a Service (network)	Amazon CloudFront, Rackspace, Century Link
Infrastructure as a Service (storage)	Amazon S3, Rackspace, HP Objectstorage
Infrastructure as a Service (server)	Amazon EC2, HP Cloudcompute, Gogrid, Joyent
Platform as a Service	Microsoft Azure, IBM, Google AppEngine
Software as a Service	Google Apps, Salesforce, SAP, IBM

2.5.1   Amazon Elastic Compute Cloud (EC2)

Amazon Elastic Compute Cloud (EC2) is a web service that offers computing capacity or servers on demand with immediate availability over the internet. Amazon EC2 provides a web interface called the Amazon EC2 Management Console. Users can log into the Amazon Management Console and get access to EC2. Amazon EC2's infrastructure is worldwide: North America, Europe, and Asia. Broad-level locations of Amazon EC2's infrastructure are treated as *regions*. Each region contains more *availability zones* of infrastructures (as shown in Fig. 2.18). Figure 2.18 shows that users can access Amazon EC2 via the company's web interface (AWS). In addition, Amazon has its own general configured image called the Amazon Machine Image (AMI). It gives the image of generic server specifications with memory, processing speed, Operating System even including software like Application server, etc. Users can use preconfigured images, configure their own server requirements, and create *instances* (virtual computing servers) from the image. There are different types of instances such as those offered by AMI. The type of instance determines the hardware of the host computer (i.e., CPU, memory, storage, etc.) in which the instance gets deployed. Instance types include *general purpose instances, compute-optimized instances, memory-optimized instances, and storage-optimized instances.*

Features of Amazon EC2

- Amazon EC2 offers virtual computing servers called instances.
- Each instance can be accessed using secure login credentials called key pairs (AWS uses public key cryptography). In addition, users can configure security groups through which they can access instances.
- Users can configure their instances at different locations to avoid a single point of failure.
- Users can avail themselves of Amazon storage volumes to store their data.
- Users can create tags or metadata and attach those tags to EC2 resources.
- Amazon EC2 can be used with different pricing options: on-demand instance-based pricing, reserved instance-based pricing, and spot instance-based pricing. In on-demand instance-based pricing users have to pay for their instances on an hourly basis with no up-front or long-term payments. In reserved instance-based pricing users reserve instances by means of a nominal up-front

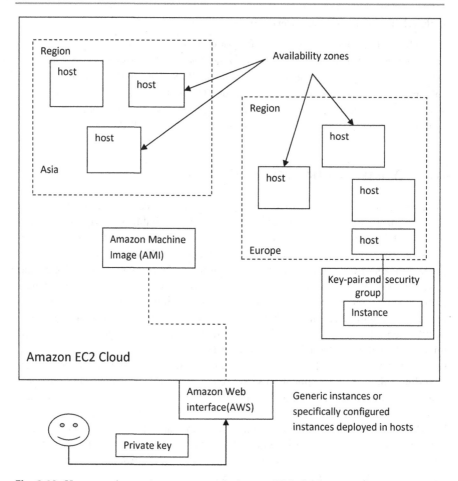

Fig. 2.18 User accessing an Amazon server via Amazon Web Services

payment for 1 year, after which they have to pay for use of reserved instances on an hourly basis. In spot instance-based pricing users set a maximum price for availing themselves of the instance and if the actual usage price crosses the maximum price set by the user the provider will shut down spot instances.

2.5.2 Amazon Simple Storage Service

Enterprise applications generally require the ability to store data on a massive scale. Amazon Simple Storage Service (S3) provides *object storage* for the storage and retrieval of any amount of data from anywhere and from any applications including mobile applications, large-enterprise applications, IoT-based applications, social

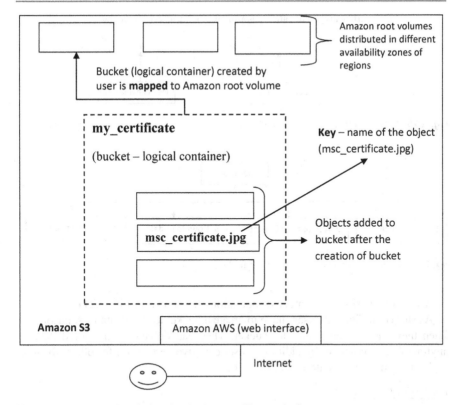

Fig. 2.19 Storing and retrieving data in Amazon S3 over the internet

networking–based applications, and real-time applications. Amazon S3 provides very good durability, comprehensive security, and compliance capabilities that meet even the most stringent regulatory requirements. It gives customers flexibility in the way they manage data for cost optimization, access control, and compliance. S3 provides query-in-place functionality, which allows the execution of powerful analytics directly on the data at rest in S3. Amazon S3 offers scalable storage space to users on demand over the internet using Web Services APIs and interfaces. In Amazon S3 data are stored as *objects* in containers called *buckets*. An object is the fundamental entity of S3 and contains data and metadata. As buckets are containers of objects users have to create buckets before storing objects in them. Users are not restricted to one bucket, they can create as many as they like. When creating a bucket users can choose suitable geographical locations for the bucket. Let us consider the case when a file (*object*) called *msc_certificate.jpg* is to be stored in Amazon S3. As the first step a bucket is created with, say, the name *my_certificate*. The bucket is logically mapped to Amazon root volume (as shown in Fig. 2.19).

Objects are addressed using URLs. Continuing with our case, the object *msc_certificate.jpg* is stored in the bucket *my_certificate*. The URL of the object is constructed as in Fig. 2.20.

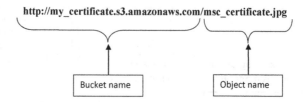

Fig. 2.20 URLs of objects in Amazon S3

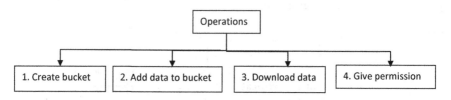

Fig. 2.21 Operations that can be carried out in Amazon S3

A user can perform a number of operations (as shown in Fig. 2.21).

As shown in Fig. 2.21 users have to create a bucket to store data in Amazon S3. Then they can add data into the bucket. They can download the stored data at anytime from anywhere. In addition, a user can give permission for others to store (upload) or download data from his/her bucket.

Features of Amazon S3

Amazon S3 boasts a number of features:

- *Storage class*: Each object in Amazon S3 has a storage class associated with it. There are two storage classes: *standard* and *reduced redundancy*. Standard storage is the default and more secure as data are stored with replication (i.e., backed up) among availability zones across different regions. However, in reduced redundancy storage data are stored in only one region. This may be suitable for data that are less important, old, or may no longer be required.
- *High scalability*: Any amount of data can be stored and retrieved.
- *Security*: Amazon provides the option of encrypting data both during rest and transit. In addition, many copies of data are maintained to provide backup in case of data loss. Amazon offers two kinds of encryption: (1) server-side encryption in which Amazon takes responsibility for encrypting the data before storage and decrypting the data before presenting the data to the user and (2) client-side encryption in which users take the responsibility for encryption and decryption.
- *Durability*: The provider (Amazon) ensures the integrity of data at regular intervals as well as during storage and retrieval processes. Should any issues occur consistency and integrity will be restored using replicated data.

- *Low price*: Data can be stored and retrieved at low cost using three pricing models: on-demand pricing, reserved instance-based pricing, and spot instance-based pricing.

2.5.3 Amazon CloudFront

Amazon CloudFront is a content delivery network (CDN) that securely delivers a user's static and dynamic web contents to viewers. The concept of Amazon CloudFront is shown in Fig. 2.22.

Let us consider a user called abc.com (as in Fig. 2.22). The user wants to deliver or distribute his contents to his viewer using Amazon CloudFront. Once he becomes a user of CloudFront, whenever a viewer submits a request to the website of abc.com (say, http://abc.com/products.html) the viewer request will be forwarded to the edge location of CloudFront which provides a higher bandwidth to fulfill the request. Then a response to the request will be sent either from the cache of the edge

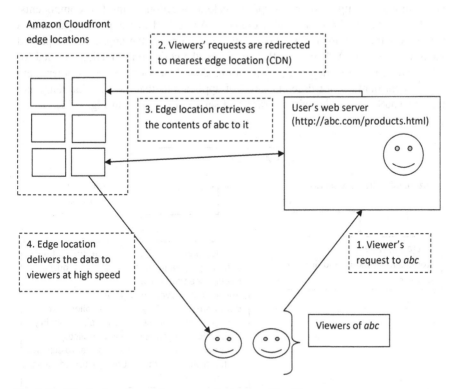

Fig. 2.22 Distribution of a user's contents via Amazon CloudFront

location if available or the edge location retrieves the requested content from abc.com and delivers it through high bandwidth and high speed to the viewer. This is shown in sequence in Fig. 2.22.

2.5.4 Microsoft Azure

Microsoft Azure offers an application-hosting environment on demand where developers can deploy and run their applications. This relieves developers from managing the environment and enables them to focus on developing the application alone. Microsoft offers Azure services in 19 centers located in different geographical regions. Hence any enterprise deploying its applications in Azure can choose the nearest service point and efficiently satisfy its customers. Azure is well known for providing its development, testing, runtime, and deployment platform for a variety of applications both promptly and at lower cost. Microsoft Azure offers services such as Service Bus, Access Control, Caching, Integration, and Composite App. It is compatible with all programming languages and development frameworks including .NET, Java, Ruby, and PHP.

Microsoft Azure supports the deployment and delivery of simple cloud-based applications right up to large enterprise–scale applications using two components: *Worker Role* and *Web Role*. Web Role is an Azure VM that is preconfigured as a web server that automatically provides the end point for the application deployed via a website or an API. Worker Role performs the computing functions needed for the operation of the deployed application. Azure provides a development and deployment platform for different kinds of applications that have a wide range not only of PaaS services but also storage and servers (as shown in Fig. 2.23).

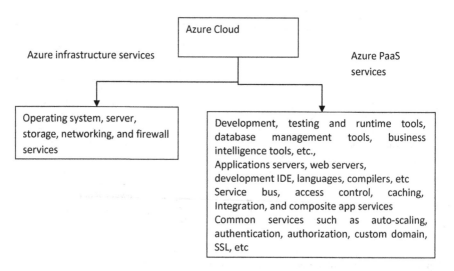

Fig. 2.23 The rich set of Azure services

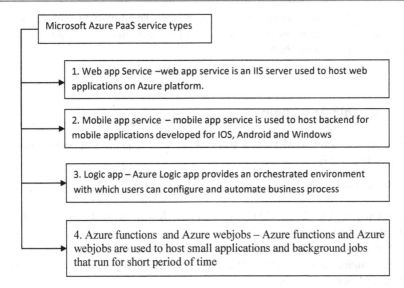

Fig. 2.24 Microsoft Azure PaaS service types

Azure PaaS services are of multiple types and are used according to the specific applications of developers. Major service types of Azure are given in Fig. 2.24.

Along with the standard service types Azure PaaS provides *Azure Event Grid* as an event-handling service for applications. Similarly, *Azure Service Bus* provides asynchronous messages *Queues* and *Topics* to applications. In addition, Azure offers various types of storage:

- blob storage to store large files (especially audio files, video files, and database backups);
- table storage in which data in rows and columns format can be processed asynchronously; and
- file storage that can be used as an extra hard disk or a high-performance disk.

In addition, the Azure platform provides other services such as cognitive services, the Azure content delivery network (CDN), cache services, and an API management service to manage the APIs of third parties.

Features of Platform as a Service

- PaaS offers increased developer productivity and reduces development time significantly by providing a complete platform infrastructure that has additional features such as directory services, search options, authentication, authorization, and other common services that can be integrated with applications.
- PaaS offers complete life cycle management for developing, testing, running, deploying, and maintaining applications in a cloud platform.

- PaaS offers support for multiple operating systems and multiple languages so that any kind of generic application from web applications to mobile applications can be deployed in Azure PaaS.

2.5.5 Google App Engine

Google App Engine (GAE) is a PaaS cloud with a high-level architecture (as shown in Fig. 2.25).

Features of Google App Engine

- As shown in Fig. 2.25, GAE has a set of low-level APIs to interact with underlying IaaS services.
- GAE completely hides the underlying infrastructure from applications and provides complete development and deployment support, primarily for the development of open-source applications.
- GAE provides a web server and applications server platform for deploying applications developed using languages such as Python, Java, and Go.
- GAE monitors the availability and performance of applications continuously and according to performance the engine will either scale up or scale down nodes in the runtime environment (as shown in Fig. 2.25).

2.5.6 Force.com

Salesforce.com offers a PaaS development platform called *force.com* for applications developed in *Apex*. It consists of four major components: database, business logic, user interface, and integration (as shown in Fig. 2.26).

Force.com offers the *Builder* tool for developing web applications quickly without writing large amount of code. Builder provides a user interface to create objects and fields. After creating objects Builder automatically creates a web interface and completes development of the application in less time. In addition, it offers a rich reporting environment.

2.5.7 Salesforce.com

Salesforce.com offers a customer relationship management (CRM) application that helps users organize customer information and manage the processing of sales. The high-level architecture of Salesforce.com is shown in Fig. 2.27.

As shown in Fig. 2.27 Salesforce.com offers a number of applications: *Sales Cloud* (CRM), *Service Cloud*, *Radian6*, *AppExchange*, and *Chatter*. CRM helps to

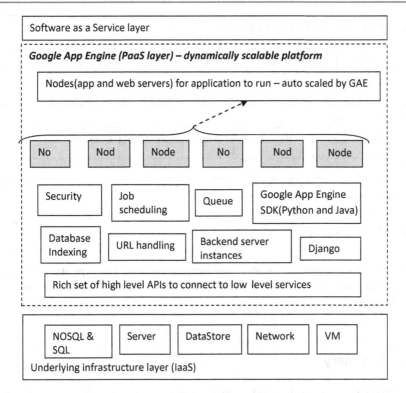

Fig. 2.25 Applications deployed in Google App Engine

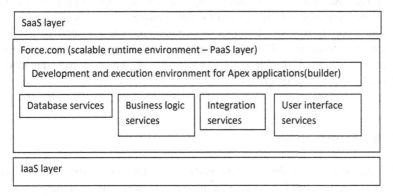

Fig. 2.26 Force.com (Platform as a Service)

organize and manage customer information and sales. Service Cloud helps communicating with customers via contacts and social media. Radian6 is a marketing application to promote sales. AppExchange stores the application data, and Chatter facilitates collaboration of staff and internal/private sharing of data within the user

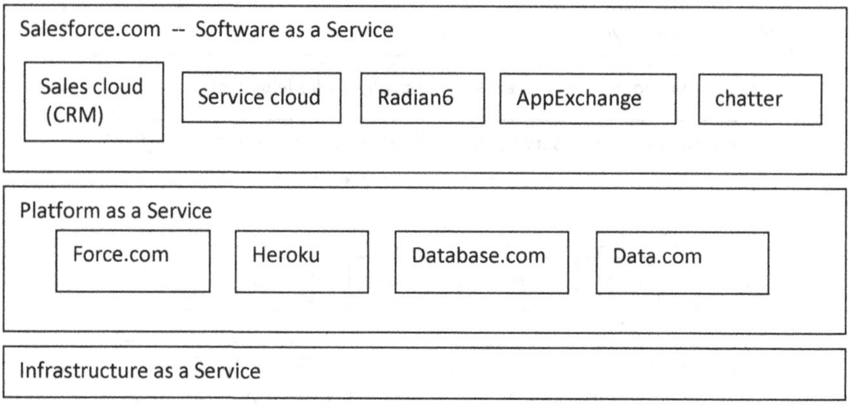

Fig. 2.27 Salesforce.com

enterprise. In addition to SaaS Salesforce.com offers PaaS products such as *Force.com* and *Heroku* for hosting applications along with *Data.com* and *Database.com* for storage.

2.6 Summary

This chapter presented the fundamentals of cloud computing. It covered features unique to cloud computing: rapid elasticity, on-demand computing, scalability, self-service based access, resource pooling and provisioning, and pricing schemes. It elaborated a number of deployment models: private, public, hybrid, community, and multi-cloud. It discussed different service class models and depicted them with rich schematic diagrams. To improve our understanding of cloud computing the chapter gave a brief description of public cloud providers accompanied by high-level architectural diagrams.

2.7 Exercises

1. Imagine you are a senior scientist working on climate modeling in a very small R&D firm. You need to work with 10-year-old data. The modeling algorithms need to work in a parallel fashion with all the data to give precise results. The firm decided to go for cloud migration? As a senior scientist what sort of cloud model should you opt for to ensure precise climate modeling?
2. Imagine you are a simple e-content creator with a web server that has limited capacity. What is the best way to manage the distribution of e-content to a large number of viewers (write an assignment)?

3. Discuss in detail the various service class models provided by cloud providers.
4. Compile a list of some of the more common public cloud providers for IaaS, PaaS, and SaaS.
5. As a corporate owner of a major textile enterprise comparing public and private cloud deployment what sort of deployment should you opt for? Justify your idea.

References

1. Goyal S (2014) Public vs Private vs Hybrid vs Community—cloud computing: a critical review. Int J Comput Netw Inf Secur 3:20–29
2. Zaharia-Rădulescu A-M, Radu I (2017) Cloud computing and public administration: approaches in several European countries. Proc Int Conf Bus Excell 11(1):739–749. ISSN 2558-9652
3. Rani D, Ranjan RK (2014) A comparative study of SaaS, PaaS and IaaS in cloud computing. Int J Adv Res Comput Sci Softw Eng 4(6):158–161
4. Mosbah MM (2013) Current services in cloud computing: a survey. Int J Comput Sci Eng Inf Technol (IJCSEIT) 3(5)
5. Nazir M (2012) Cloud computing: overview & current research challenges. IOSR J Comput Eng (IOSR-JCE) 8(1):14–22. ISSN 2278-0661, ISBN 2278-8727

Technological Foundations of Cloud Computing

3

Learning Objectives

Many people wonder how cloud computing is capable of providing *resource sharing with elasticity* using the same physical hardware infrastructure for different users who deal with different kinds of computing tasks. *What is it that facilitates the offering of infrastructure or a platform or software to many users in a multi-tenancy environment? What are the key technologies that enable the cloud to take its solid shape?* The objective of this chapter is to present answers to these questions. By the end of this chapter the reader should have an understanding of the key technological foundations of cloud computing.

Motivational Questions

1. How does cloud computing acquire scalability and multi-tenancy?
2. How can consumers avail themselves of lots of resources irrespective of heterogeneity among platforms, operating systems, and hardware?
3. What is the key that drives cloud computing?
4. What are the technological foundations behind cloud computing?
5. What is virtualization and containerization?
6. What are service-oriented architecture and micro-services architecture?

Preface

In the previous chapter the reader was introduced to how the requirements of recent applications, such as *uncertain load condition resolution, rapid development and release deployment, reduced capital and operational cost, rapid provisioning of*

© Springer Nature Switzerland AG 2019

S. Chellammal and C. Pethuru Raj, *Essentials of Cloud Computing*,
Texts in Computer Science, https://doi.org/10.1007/978-3-030-13134-0_3

resources, are fulfilled using the core features of cloud computing, cloud architecture, different service models, and different cloud deployments. Further, the reader was introduced to the public cloud service providers for IaaS, PaaS, and SaaS clouds. Moving to the next level, in this chapter the reader is introduced to the *key technological foundations of cloud computing*. As mentioned in the first chapter cloud computing is not a new type of computing that stands alone as a separate computing paradigm, instead it is firmly rooted in its predecessors: *grid computing* and *utility computing*. Evolving computer hardware and software technologies, such as *multi-core processor technology, virtualization, containerization, parallel programming models, service-oriented architecture (SOA), microservices architecture (MSA), Web 2.0 tools, software-defined networking, software-defined security*, etc., are facilitating the evolution and rapid growth of cloud computing. In this chapter these technological drivers are discussed in detail.

3.1 Basic Foundations of Cloud Computing

In most businesses customer demands change frequently. Quick delivery of customer demands are essential to achieving a competitive edge in business. Business organizations face many challenges in delivering customer demands quickly. They need to resolve a number of urgent and critical needs that involve both *time and cost factors*:

- Startup businesses need to set up the required infrastructure in as short a time as possible. This involves prohibitive capital and operational costs for many small and medium-sized enterprises.
- Organizations need to have skilled sets of network administrators, database administrators, developers, testers, etc., to develop the required networks and application code.
- Time and cost in establishing common services such as load balancing, fault tolerance, and firewalls.
- Time and effort to establish the required scalability, performance, security, reliability, and other non-functional quality attributes.
- Different infrastructure to perform different test runs.
- Time to establish the required application architecture.

In a nutshell, on the one hand, businesses want their *critical needs*, such as reduced capital cost, reduced operational and maintenance costs, short time to market, customer satisfaction, business agility, and quality attributes (such as scalability, availability, security, manageability, and flexibility), to be solved by making use of technologies that they are unable to develop in-house. On the other hand, major enterprises, such as Amazon, Microsoft, and Salesforce, are interested in renting out their underutilized software and hardware resources, applications, etc. to other businesses and users who are in need of the same. By renting out their

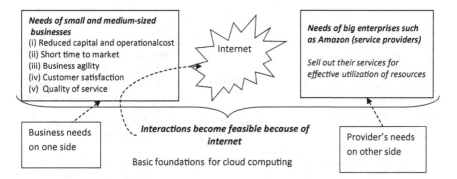

Fig. 3.1 Basic foundations of cloud computing

underutilized resources they not only utilize their resources efficiently, but also earn good profits. There are of course two entities involved in such an arrangement: *organizations like Amazon who rent out or offer their services* (these organizations are service providers) and *enterprises who consume the required services from providers.* Such an interaction between the above two entities only becomes feasible because of the *internet.* Thus the business needs of small and medium-sized enterprises, the needs of service providers wanting to rent out their resources, and the internet form the basis of cloud computing (as shown in Fig. 3.1).

3.2 Technological Drivers of Cloud Computing

Cloud computing has developed very rapidly as a result of various technological drivers: multicore technology, parallel programming, virtualization and containerization, grid and utility computing, WAN, internet, Web 2.0, service-oriented architecture, microservices architecture (MSA), DevOps, Agile software development, open-source software tools, software-defined networks, and software-defined security. These drivers are shown in Fig. 3.2.

How different technological drivers fit into different layers of the cloud architecture and play critical roles are shown in Fig. 3.3.

In the cloud infrastructure there are three kinds of services: Infrastructure as a Service, Platform as a Service, and Software as a Service. IaaS providers theoretically offer any number of hardware resources, such as servers, storage devices, and networks, for use according to the dynamic demands of users. PaaS providers offer almost all kinds of platforms along with infrastructure to users wanting to deploy their applications without worrying about the resources needed for load balancing, scalability, performance, etc. Similarly, SaaS providers offer completely developed cloud-deployed software applications that users can consume on a subscription basis. It is worth pointing out that these services are provided simultaneously to many consumers. The huge resources of cloud service providers are shared among multiple users. Clearly, there is something or some technology that enables this

Open source tools and APIs
MSA, Devops, Agile
Technological drivers of cloud computing
Software defined security
Software defined networking
Virtualization and containerization
Grid and utility Computing
Multi-core technology
Parallel programming
WAN, internet, SOA, Web 2.0

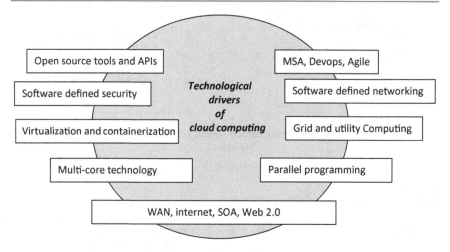

Fig. 3.2 Technological drivers of cloud computing

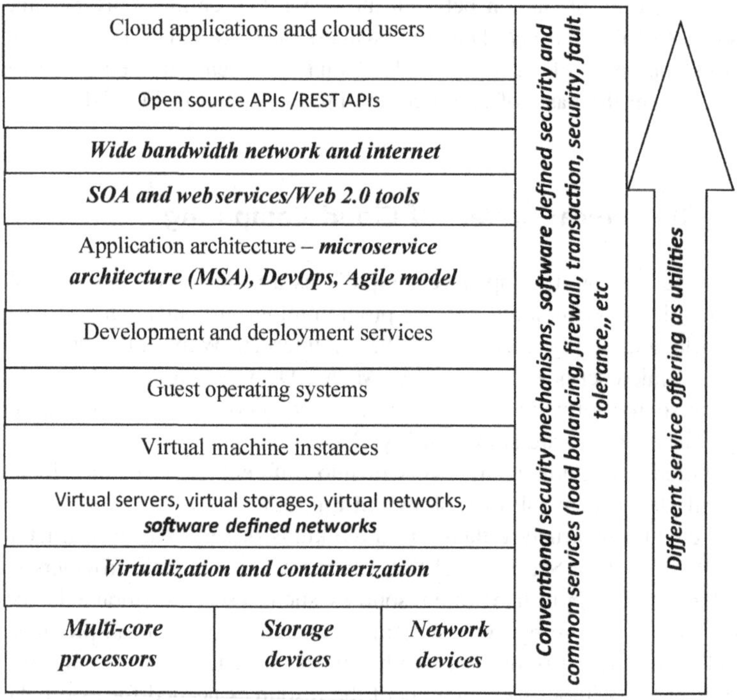

Cloud applications and cloud users
Open source APIs /REST APIs
Wide bandwidth network and internet
SOA and web services/Web 2.0 tools
Application architecture – microservice architecture (MSA), DevOps, Agile model
Development and deployment services
Guest operating systems
Virtual machine instances
Virtual servers, virtual storages, virtual networks, software defined networks
Virtualization and containerization
Multi-core processors
Storage devices
Network devices
Conventional security mechanisms, software defined security and common services (load balancing, firewall, transaction, security, fault tolerance,, etc
Different service offering as utilities

Fig. 3.3 How technological drivers fit into different layers of the cloud architecture

kind of sharing of resources among multiple users simultaneously and enables each user to have varying demands: that technology is *virtualization* [1]. Since cloud service providers offer servers, storage, and networks the concept of virtualization is applied at different levels (such as servers, storage, networks, memory, data, applications, and desktops) so as to yield virtualized servers, virtualized storage, virtualized networks, virtualized memory, virtualized data, virtualized applications, virtualized desktops, etc. Hence virtualization is key to the implementation of cloud computing. Along with virtualization another technique called *containerization* has recently appeared on the scene. Containerization is more efficient than virtualization when it comes to the efficient utilization of resources. Recent advances in hardware technologies have led to the *production of multi-core processors* at mass scale. Corresponding with advances in hardware, software programming models have been developed to support *parallel programming* and simultaneous execution of programs. In addition, since cloud computing has its roots in *grid computing* and *utility computing*, both of which cast light on how computing resources could be shared similar to domestic utilities using a *pay-per-use pricing model*, it too can be used in like manner. Wrapping technologies (such as service-oriented architecture) and application architecture (such as microservices architecture) form other major pillars supporting cloud computing. The internet, IP WAN, MPLS WAN, software-defined networks, and software-defined security have significantly influenced the growth of cloud computing. The different technological drivers are discussed in detail in subsequent sections.

3.3 Multi-core Technology and Parallel Programming Models

The cloud computing environment is primarily built on top of multi-core technology. The vendors of microprocessors, such as Intel, AMD, IBM, and Sun, produce multi-core processors. For example, *Intel dual-core processors* are integrated in personal computers and laptops. Recently Intel introduced *quad-core technology* and *64-core architecture*. As the name implies, a multi-core processor contains more than one core on a chip. A core refers to a complete computational unit (CPU unit) that has either one or two levels of cache. For example, a typical Intel quad-core technology is shown in Fig. 3.4. Each core contains a CPU with dedicated two-level caches: L1 and L2. They all share primary main memory. Other examples of multi-core processors manufactured by AMD and Sun are AMD quad-core Phenom II processors and SUN 8-core Ultra Sparc T2 Plus Niagara processors. As multi-core processors are essential for high-performance computing they form one of the core elements of the cloud infrastructure.

To fully utilize the computation power of multi-core processors two programming models—*Message Passing Interface* (MPI) and *OpenMP*—are used to bring about parallelization in programming. MPI is a standardized message passing communication protocol for programming parallel computers. MPI has

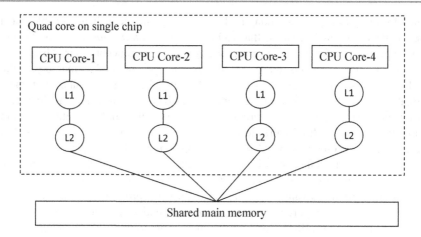

Fig. 3.4 Typical quad-core technology of Intel

specifications for both point-to-point and collective communication methods. The goals of MPI include performance, scalability, and portability. OpenMP is an implementation of a multi-threaded API for providing parallel programming for multiple processors that have shared memory across multiple platforms. Both MPI and OpenMP play crucial roles in the cloud environment.

3.4 Virtualization

Motivational Example
Virtualization is not a new concept. The concept of virtual memory was introduced in the 1960s by IBM. IBM introduced the virtualized operating system and called it *time sharing*. In this system the mainframe hardware is partitioned and shared by multiple virtual machines simultaneously. However, due to the high cost of time-sharing systems the concept did not gain popularity.

In the 1970s Intel developed the *X86* processor and personal computers. These were very cheap to buy. Personal computers used *virtual memory* to execute programs whose size was larger than the size of physical memory. For example, the available physical memory might consist of only 4 pages, say, whereas a program might actually consist of 8 pages. In general, most programs did not require all the pages to be present in memory at a given time. This meant that only those pages needed for execution at a given time were brought to main memory. Virtual memory is based on this concept. In this technique only those pages that are needed currently are allowed to remain in main memory and other pages will be in secondary memory. Whenever those pages that are in secondary memory are required

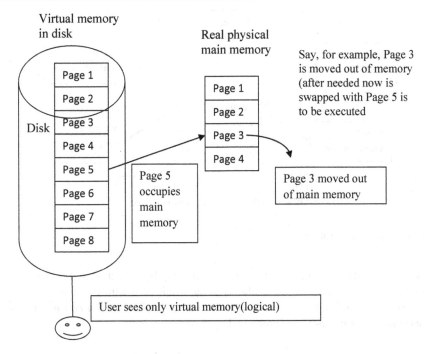

Fig. 3.5 Concept of virtual memory

for execution, then they are brought to main memory and the previously loaded pages are taken to secondary disk memory, a process called *swapping* (as shown in Fig. 3.5).

The concept of swapping the required pages of a program between disk and RAM helps in multi-programming too. As shown in Fig. 3.5 *virtual memory can only be seen as logical memory, which is larger than physical memory, and can be shared by more than one program at a given time.* Basically, the physical main memory is shared by more than one program simultaneously without any conflict.

Virtualization can be applied to any physical resource such as servers, storage devices, and networks. After virtualization, physical resources can be viewed as logical resources at a higher level of abstraction. When virtualization is applied to servers, then more than one virtual machine can be operated. Multiple virtual machines share the same physical server infrastructure. When virtualization is applied to storage devices, then the different heterogeneous storage devices can be seen as a single logical storage device. Similarly, when virtualization is applied to a physical network, then a single network can be seen as different virtual networks configured by different virtual machines. Cloud computing employs different types

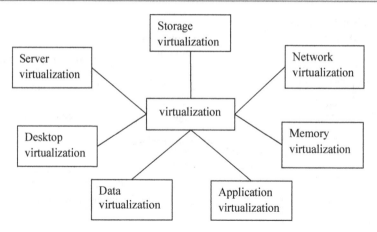

Fig. 3.6 Types of virtualization

of virtualization and provides virtual resource pooling by allocating and reallocating virtualized resources according to the dynamic needs of multiple tenants.

Depending on the way in which virtualization is implemented *it can be broken down into various types* (as shown in Fig. 3.6).

3.4.1 Server Virtualization

Server virtualization provides the capability to create many virtual servers on top of the real physical server by separating and abstracting the real server (i.e., a machine with CPU, RAM, hard disk, etc.) from the rest of the system. The primary objective of server virtualization is to increase resource utilization by partitioning a single physical server into many virtual servers where each virtual server has its own operating system and applications. Moreover, each virtual server is unaware of the presence of other servers. Each virtual machine is logically separated from other virtual servers. Conventionally, each server is tied to a particular operating system and, typically, a particular application is deployed in a server. To understand the concept of virtualization better a conventional system with no virtualization and an infrastructure with virtualization are shown in Figs. 3.7 and 3.8, respectively.

Fundamentally, *the architecture of Intel X86 is designed to work with one particular operating system.* This is the basic limitation that allows much of the processing power of computers to remain underutilized. In conventional systems computer hardware is generally manufactured and typically configured so that a single commercial operating system will be utilized at any given time. That is, even in computers that have been installed with more than one operating system *only one operating system will be run at a given time with the help of a boot option. They will not run simultaneously.* Required applications are deployed on top of the

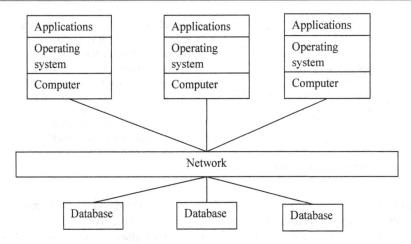

Fig. 3.7 Conventional infrastructure (without virtualization)

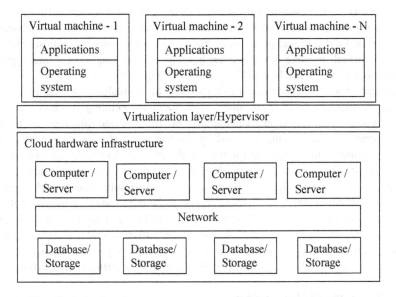

Fig. 3.8 Virtualized cloud environment

operating system. The network serves as the fundamental agent for any machine to connect with other computers or databases that are available at different sites. Although the network helps in establishing connections among different machines and databases, every machine is tied to its own operating system and applications.

There are two key points to be noted here: *not every machine is fully utilized and most of the time they may be idle or underutilized*, and *if more and more machines are added to cope with the growing number of applications, then an enormous*

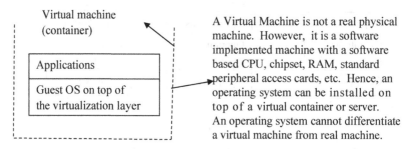

Fig. 3.9 Concept of virtual machine

amount of heat will be produced by the machines. Provision of an appropriate heat-dissipating facility takes up a lot of space and is expensive.

Introducing virtualization into the above picture allows a virtualized infrastructure to be seen (as shown in Fig. 3.8). In a virtualized environment all databases and all machines are combined to form the cloud infrastructure. The virtualization layer (software) is implemented on top of the cloud infrastructure. This layer is called a *hypervisor* or *virtual machine monitor*. This virtualization layer abstracts the physical hardware and provides as many virtual machines as requested by the users. A virtual machine is a container holding an operating system and applications. It is not a real machine. This is shown in Fig. 3.9.

Compared with a conventional infrastructure the virtualization layer in a virtualized infrastructure helps in installing more than one operating system on a given physical hardware. This layer fools each virtual machine into thinking that it is the only operating system being operated by the hardware. However, more than one virtual machine will actually be running on the physical hardware simultaneously. So, the processing power of the machine is fully utilized without wasting it. Virtualization is similar to running multiple processes simultaneously with a single CPU time-sharing them. These processes will share the available hardware without conflict *under the control of a hypervisor*. Similar to the concept of multiple processes sharing the hardware and CPU concurrently over time in a virtualized cloud environment different virtual machines share the same physical hardware concurrently over time without any conflict with the *help of a virtualization layer*.

3.4.1.1 Types of Hypervisors

There are two types of hypervisors: *type 1 or native or bare metal hypervisors* and *type 2 or hosted hypervisors* (as shown in Fig. 3.10).

In native or bare metal hypervisors (type 1 hypervisors) the hypervisor will be built as firmware within the hardware itself by the hardware vendors. This kind of hypervisor gives better performance than a hosted hypervisor. In hosted hypervisors the hypervisor is installed on top of the host operating system (as shown in Fig. 3.10). Type 1 hypervisors are faster than type 2. However, the host operating system supervises and manages the underlying hardware in type 2 hypervisors. Hence type 2 hardware supports both a wide range of hardware as well as hardware

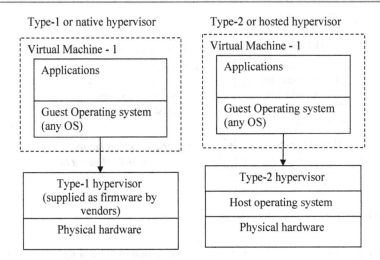

Fig. 3.10 Two types of hypervisors

produced by different vendors. In addition, the installation of type 2 hardware is easier done than type 1.

3.4.1.2 Types of Server Virtualization

Different types of server virtualization in use (as shown in Fig. 3.11). Which virtualization method is the most suitable depends on such requirements as application and cost.

Full Virtualization

In full virtualization the guest operating system does not require any changes to be made for it to interact with the hardware. The guest operating system imagines that it is the only operating system running on top of the underlying hardware. It is

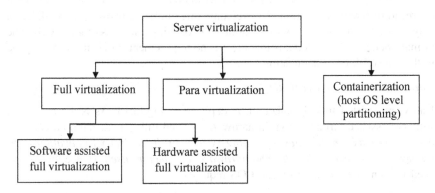

Fig. 3.11 Different types of server virtualization

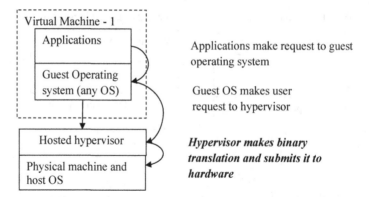

Fig. 3.12 Software-assisted full virtualization

completely unaware of other virtual machines that are running on top of the hypervisor. This characteristic of full virtualization is implemented in two ways: *software-assisted full virtualization* and *hardware-assisted full virtualization*. No changes need to be made in the guest operating system in either case.

Software-assisted full virtualization

Software-assisted full virtualization is depicted in Fig. 3.12. In software-assisted full virtualization user applications interact with the guest operating system, which in turn makes calls to a hypervisor. In this model type 2 hypervisors are typically used. The hypervisor makes an appropriate binary translation of the request and submits the request to the physical hardware. Any guest operating system can be used such as Windows, Linux, or Mac OS. Hence the hypervisor should consist of device drivers that are compatible with any commercial OS, make an appropriate binary translation according to the type of guest operating system, and submit a lower level request to the hardware.

The limitation of software-assisted full virtualization is that it has the additional overhead of binary translation. To overcome this limitation hardware virtualization may be used. This model of virtualization can host different types of guest OSs. The primary benefit of this model is that there is no requirement for changes to be made in the guest OS or in applications.

Hardware-assisted full virtualization

Hardware-assisted full virtualization is depicted in Fig. 3.13. As is the case with software-assisted virtualization, in hardware-assisted full virtualization *no changes need to be made in the guest operating system. In this model virtualization technology is integrated within the X86 hardware architecture itself.* Hence there is no need for binary translation of guest OS requests.

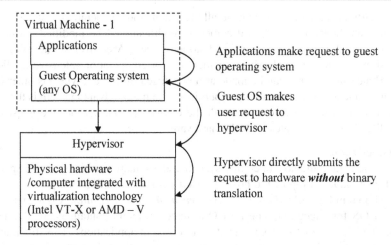

Fig. 3.13 Hardware-assisted full virtualization

Para Virtualization

Although hardware-assisted full virtualization provides better performance, it is still subject to a standard flow of calls. That is, the application will make calls to the guest OS which in turn makes calls to the hypervisor. Communication with the hardware is through the hypervisor. Para virtualization was developed to further improve performance. As shown in Fig. 3.14, *para virtualization allows guest OSs to be modified so that they can make direct hardware calls (but under the control of the hypervisor) and they are aware that they are running in a virtualized environment*. Typically, proprietary operating systems like Windows will not permit modification of an OS.

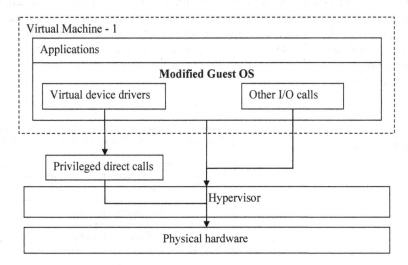

Fig. 3.14 Para virtualization

Para virtualization developers generally use open-source operating systems, such as Linux and Sun Solaris, when it comes to modification. The modified guest OS contains virtual drivers for network and storage access. Moreover, a guest OS can be modified to have virtual drivers of memory for computation-intensive applications. Hence such access can be made as a privileged direct call, whereas other I/O calls are made as usual through the hypervisor. The major advantage here is that the hypervisor does not need to contain all the device drivers; instead, the guest OS itself directly communicates with the hardware.

Containerization

In containerization the host operating system creates many partitions or user spaces called *containers* on top of the host OS itself (as shown in Fig. 3.15).

As shown in Fig. 3.15 *there is no hypervisor in containerization.* Containers use the host OS for execution. The host OS creates different containers for different users. The host OS distributes its function to different applications. This distributed nature of operating systems eliminates the system calls and overhead associated with hypervisors. Hence it gives a better performance than virtualization.

3.4.2 Storage Virtualization

Storage virtualization is the concept of abstracting or hiding heterogeneity among different storage devices from the applications that manage them. Different techniques may be used to get the different physical storage devices to aggregate in a pool of logical storage that can be accessed and managed in a unified way from a centralized console. In conventional storage management with no storage virtualization, storage management has to deal with the varying characteristics of different storage devices as well as vendor-specific features. Conventionally, storage management has dealt with each device as a discrete unit (as shown in Fig. 3.16).

The primary difficulty with conventional storage is how to deal with heterogeneous storage devices. Another difficulty is that the devices are manufactured by different vendors.

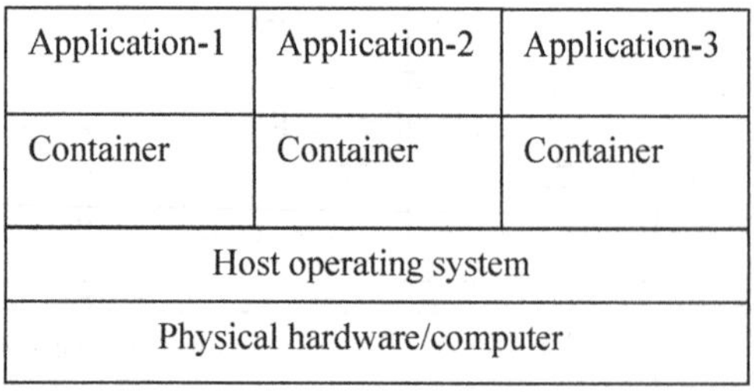

Fig. 3.15 Concept of containerization

Application-1	Application-2	Application-3
Container	Container	Container
Host operating system		
Physical hardware/computer		

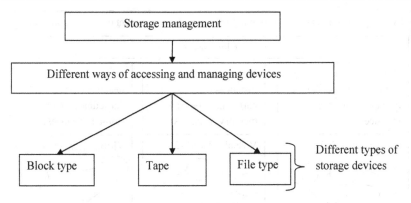

Fig. 3.16 Conventional storage with no virtualization

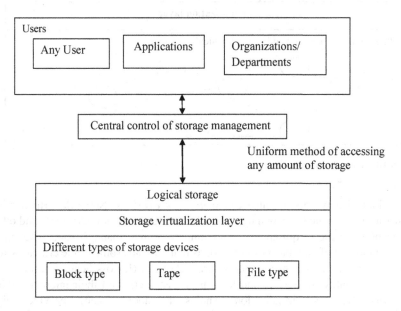

Fig. 3.17 Virtualized storage

In *virtualized storage* (as shown in Fig. 3.17) various devices are aggregated into a single pool of logical storage by the storage virtualization layer. This layer hides the heterogeneity of devices and provides a uniform way of managing them.

3.4.3 Network Virtualization

Network virtualization [2] refers to the creation of more than one logical and virtual network that work simultaneously and share the same single physical network.

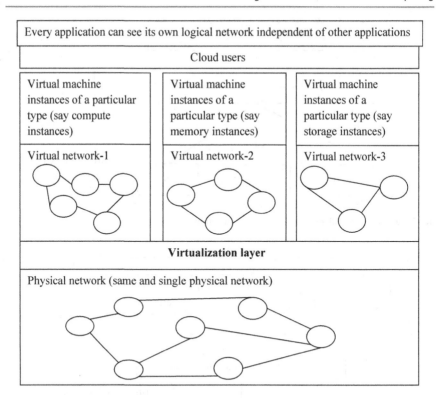

Fig. 3.18 Network virtualization

These logical networks are also called *network overlays*. Network virtualization allows users to create their own network with their own topology, routing, and other application-specific requirements including resource management. The most important aspect of network virtualization is that it avoids some of the critical issues associated with the current internet: Internet Protocol (IP) ossification, issues with end-to-end quality of service, and lock-in of customers with their internet service providers. Network virtualization handles the above issues, provides high throughput for data transmission, and delivers control over end-to-end quality of service. An overview of network virtualization is shown in Fig. 3.18.

As shown in Fig. 3.18 the virtualization layer helps to create virtual networks according to the requirements of the top layer of VMs and their applications. Hence any application can configure its required topology, routing, and the other network stuff with virtual networks instantly and gain network connectivity. Network virtualization restricts the movement of data and information across networks and enhances security. The most important aspect is that each virtual network is isolated and independent of the other networks.

3.4.4 Memory Virtualization

The physical primary memory across different servers is aggregated into a single large primary memory that is accessible by applications deployed in virtual machines. In general, there are three memory addresses (as shown in Fig. 3.19): a machine address that represents the actual physical address sent on the bus to memory, a guest physical address that represents the virtual address of memory as seen by the guest OS, and a guest virtual address that represents the virtual address as seen by the guest application.

As memory is very closely involved with compute logic, enterprises need to add memory to achieve higher performance of applications. However, adding memory is very expensive. Memory virtualization helps to share existing memory across many servers as a single larger memory. Hence it helps in achieving higher performance at lower cost.

3.4.5 Desktop Virtualization

In desktop virtualization the hardware, operating system, applications, data, and user profile of a real desktop can be abstracted from a client machine to a remote server (as shown in Fig. 3.20).

As shown in Fig. 3.20, after desktop virtualization a user will work with a virtual desktop in a cloud server. When a client accesses a desktop all applications and corresponding data are accessed from a central server.

3.4.6 Data Virtualization

Data virtualization is the concept of aggregating data from heterogeneous data sources at different locations into single items of data and logical data that can be accessed easily by applications (as shown in Fig. 3.21). Data virtualization

Fig. 3.19 Different addresses in the virtualized memory of a cloud environment

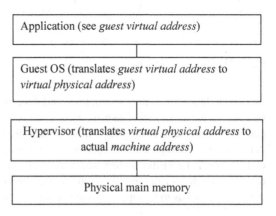

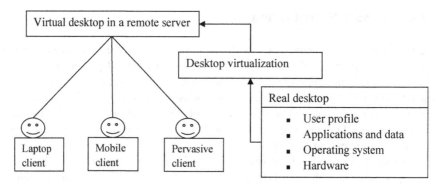

Fig. 3.20 Desktop virtualization

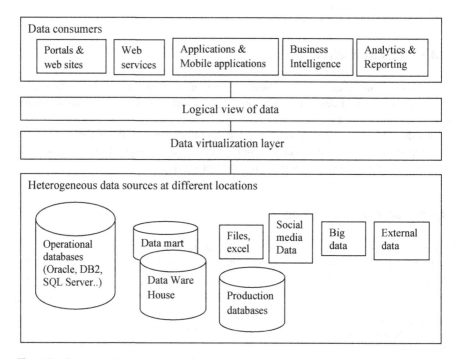

Fig. 3.21 Data virtualization

facilitates data access, data integration, and data management by providing a single data management model. The primary advantage is that data consumers can retrieve and manipulate data from one or more data sources without knowing the technical details of data storage such as API, access language, storage structure, or its format or location. Data virtualization facilitates real-time access to data. Data virtualization reduces data errors and helps to combine the results of data sets from multiple data sources so as to produce *federated data* and make such data available to users.

3.4.7 Application Virtualization

In application virtualization a given application in a particular operating system is made to execute in a virtual way on any operating system. Application virtualization abstracts applications from underlying operating systems. Deploying an application in traditional systems means packaging parts of the application and installing the application according to the requirements of the target operating system and machine. As shown in Fig. 3.22 the application virtualization layer in the cloud environment fools applications into getting deployed in any virtual guest operating system.

In hardware-assisted full virtualization *no changes need to be made in the guest operating system since virtualization technology is integrated within the X86 hardware architecture itself.* Hence there is no binary translation of guest OS requests.

In a nutshell, *virtualization is the creation of virtual resources, such as servers, storage devices, networks, and desktops, by abstracting the heterogeneity in hardware. This is being pursued by cloud service providers to effectively use their computational resources and maximize their profits.* The benefits and limitations of virtualization are considered in the following subsections.

Advantages of virtualization

- *Server consolidation*: Virtualization was first put into practice in the 1960s to allow the partitioning of large IBM mainframe machines. Virtualization allows many virtual machines with different operating systems to run the same hardware simultaneously. All physical servers are consolidated here into a large logical server that runs several virtual environments. This enables effective utilization of resources. Processing can be done using a reduced number of servers, which reduces the physical rack space required, heat produced, and cost.

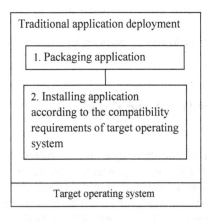
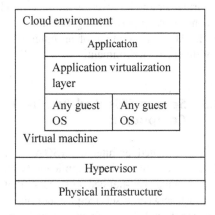

Fig. 3.22 Application deployment in traditional and cloud environment

- *Maximizing uptime*: Virtualization helps in providing a guaranteed uptime of servers and applications and dynamic resource provisioning.
- *Improved disaster recovery*: Virtualization helps in backing up critical data quickly and in automated recovery during disaster. Virtualization can also be used to test a disaster recovery failover by setting up a mock-up disaster so that appropriate safety measures are always kept in place ready for use.
- *Faster deployment*: Server virtualization allows servers that have the required configuration to be deployed in just a few minutes.
- *Increased productivity*: As virtualization reduces the number of servers and the amount of hardware, managing the physical infrastructure becomes easier. In addition, as the configuration and provisioning of resources can rapidly be carried out the productivity of the software professional is enhanced. Moreover, cloud platform services enable developers to concentrate only on real core application development rather than spending time in establishing the platform and developing an integrated development environment (IDE).
- *Increased flexibility*: As there are no constraints to availing themselves of resources from a virtualized environment users can do so with increased flexibility.
- *Predictable cost*: A virtualized cloud environment facilitates evening out the costs of resources consumed by users.
- *Protection from server failure*: Virtualization provides a means of implementing redundancy without purchasing real hardware. If a virtual machine fails in a virtualized environment, another virtual machine takes care of the failure instantly.

Disadvantages of virtualization

- The upfront cost involved in implementing virtualization (which is expensive).
- Although virtualization provides several advantages not all hardware and software vendors support it.
- Virtualization involves a number of elements and all of them need to work cohesively to perform a given task.
- The IT staff members of an enterprise need to receive training to work in the virtualized environment.

3.5 Service-Oriented Architecture (SOA) and Cloud Computing

Service-oriented architecture (SOA) is an architectural style that promotes the development of business applications by reusing existing interoperable services (which have well-defined interfaces) that can be accessed over the internet. The contract between a service provider and a service consumer or user is defined in a document called the *Service Level Agreement* (SLA). With SOA a business application need not be developed from scratch and can be built by assembling different services provided by a service provider. With SOA an application can interact with another application (application-to-application or business-to-business interaction) using a set of XML-based open protocols. These protocols include Web Service Description Language (WSDL), Simple Object Access Protocol (SOAP), and Universal Description, Discovery and Integration (UDDI).

Advantages of service-oriented architecture

• SOA allows business applications to be developed by reusing existing services.
• SOA allows enterprises to take high-level decisions and achieve business intelligence by integrating different applications.
• Using SOA wrappers allows legacy applications to be made internet aware.

In Fig. 3.23 the concept of SOA is exemplified using a travel plan service.

Let us consider a travel plan service that allows users to plan package tours by automating different tasks such as flight booking from source and destination locations for users on given dates, hotel booking for those dates, and cab booking to see the sights on those dates. Note the services are provided by different providers. However, according to SOA these services are interoperable irrespective of the operating system and programming language used to develop them. The travel plan service can be simply implemented by just invoking the *flight service* provided by service provider *A* and then invoking the *hotel service* provided by service provider *B* and then invoking the *cab service* provided by provider *C*.

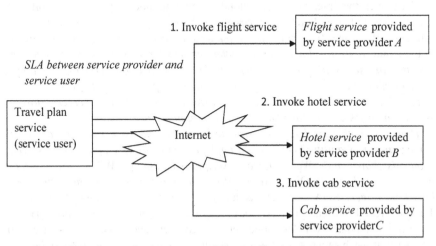

Service Providers and consumers are following Service Oriented Architecture & hence the services are interoperable and accessible over Internet

Fig. 3.23 Concept of SOA

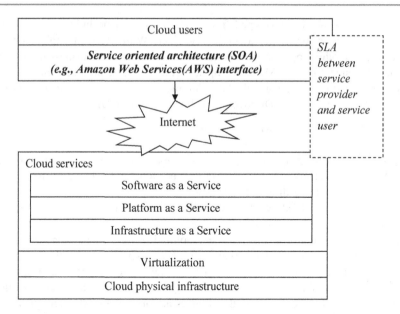

Fig. 3.24 Cloud computing uses SOA (say, REST) to deliver services to users

The concept of SOA can be utilized in the cloud environment (as given in Fig. 3.24).

For example, let us consider Software as a Service (SaaS) since it is similar to SOA. SaaS providers offer software applications to users on a subscription basis. The software application is here deployed in a cloud server. Users simply use services over the internet. Hence cloud computing not only provides software applications, but also platform services and infrastructure services. In other words, a full range of services from hardware to platform to software applications are offered in the cloud. *Both the cloud and SOA offer services but their focuses are different. The primary focus of SOA is to offer business application services (functional services of business applications), whereas cloud computing aims to provide a wide range of services starting from the basic hardware infrastructure: servers, storage devices, networks, and platforms to software applications.*

However, both paradigms are oriented toward reusing existing IT assets to achieve business agility. SOA is often implemented using XML-based web service protocols that include Web Service Description Language (WSDL) for interface description and Simple Object Access Protocol (SOAP) for communicating XML-based messages. SOA applications are now employing Representational State Transfer (REST) instead of SOAP for communication between applications. Hence there is no standard API that cloud service providers and cloud users can use to interact with each other. *Cloud providers often use web service protocols in their communications.* For example, *Amazon service providers offer their service interfaces as Amazon Web Services (AWS).*

3.6   Grid and Utility Computing Technologies

In grid computing, computing resources that belong to different administrative domains are shared to achieve a unified, common goal. In general, the resources are of heterogeneous types and dispersed at different geographical locations. Basically, grid computing aggregates the computing power distributed across different networks of computers to form a *grid*, which holds massive computer power and is used to solve complex problems using the parallel programming paradigm. In general, grid computing also uses the virtualization concept. Utility computing rents out computing resources, such as hardware and software, on demand. That is, computing resources are rented much like public utilities such as electricity, water, and gas.

Cloud computing has evolved into an amalgam of grid computing and utility computing. It consolidates resources distributed at different locations, employs virtualization to create a huge resource pool, and then offers different kinds of services to users just like a public utility such as electricity. Consumers are charged as per their use of resources using a pay-as-you-go pricing model. Hence cloud computing can be seen as:

$$Cloud\,computing \;=\; Grid\,computing \;+\; Utility\,computing$$

3.7   Web 2.0 for Cloud Computing

Web 2.0 is a collective term used to represent a set of web technologies that includes wikis, blogs, social bookmarking sites, podcasts, video sharing, instant messaging, internet telephony, audio/videoconferencing, really simple syndication (RSS) feeds, content generators, and other forms of social media. The basic idea behind Web 2.0 tools is to enhance the interconnectivity of web applications and enable users to interact with the Web instead of passively obtaining information from the Web. Web 2.0 tools emphasize online collaboration and sharing of information. For example, wiki is a collaboration tool that allows many users to prepare and organize documents and resources related to a particular theme. Similarly, RSS helps various social media interact with one another. Internet telephony, like Skype, allows real-time communication of audio between two or more people over the internet. Netmeeting or audio/videoconferencing enables real-time communication of audio and video between two or more people. A cloud computing model uses the internet as its platform to deliver its services to users on demand. As a natural evolution, cloud computing has adopted Web 2.0 tools to provide its services to users.

3.8 Microservices Architecture (MSA), DevOps, and Agile

Microservices architecture (MSA) is a design pattern that provides a new approach to creating applications by breaking them down into simple, small, independent, interoperable, and self-deployable services that have well-defined interfaces.

Important features of microservices architecture

- Microservices exchange data and procedural requests with one another.
- Each microservice is accessible using APIs such as REST.
- Microservices can be implemented using any programming language.
- An important aspect of microservices is that they use lightweight communication protocols *and are highly focused on providing single capability.*
- MSA can be perceived as a modern method of implementing SOA. Because SOA and MSA share many characteristics applications are developed in the form of independent service modules. They are accessible over the internet. They have well-defined interfaces. SOA employs an enterprise service bus (ESB) that combines services to provide a complete business process. Deployment takes a long time using an ESB. Even if a small change is made to a particular service the entire process has to be stopped for rebuilding and redeployment, all of which of course consumes time. *However, in MSA each and every microservice is self-deployable, a unique feature to MSA. MSA is anti-ESB in nature. A central ESB is often replaced by distributed specialized microservices that can hold their own business data should there be a need for the services to be more efficient.*
- Microservices are deployed in containers. A containerized environment for deploying microservices will be provided through proper DevOps (development operations) implementation. This involves microservices working with the modernized concepts of SOA, a software development model (like Agile), containerization, and DevOps (as shown in Fig. 3.25).

Fig. 3.25 Concept of MSA working together with Agile, DevOps, SOA, and containers

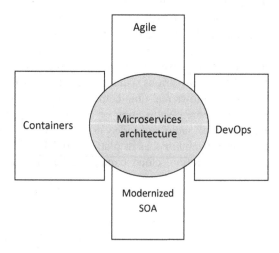

- Unlike SOA, MSA does not specify any constraints on the way in which interfaces are described nor does it mandate a protocol like SOAP. Microservices typically use REST APIs, which are lightweight, simple, and URL based.
- Another important aspect of MSA is that each service can have its own connection to the database table concerned (not the entire database). This enhances the performance of applications significantly.
- Businesses are in need of a software development model, like Agile, and continuous delivery (CD) to meet the dynamic demands of customers. MSA serves as the right choice for Agile [3, 4] and CD. Agile development has its focus on the talents and skills of individuals, modeling the process to specific people and teams. Agile gives importance to four core values: individuals, interactions regarding processes and tools, working software regarding comprehensive documentation, customer collaboration regarding contract negotiation and responding to changeover following a plan. An Agile software architecture could be described as a system of microservices that could be created, modified, tested, replaced and easily maintained in isolation.
- MSA requires the implementation of DevOps. DevOps represents a set of processes that highlight the importance of development and operations teams collaborating together so as to complete the development and release of software products in an Agile manner. The structure of an organization frequently has to be modified so that MSA and DevOps can work in unison to achieve agility.

3.9 Software-Defined Networking and Software-Defined Security

The cloud computing environment deals with a huge network consisting of several networking devices. Manually configuring these devices is tedious and time consuming. As a result the concept of software-defined networking (SDN) was developed. SDN is used to configure network devices by means of programmable interfaces. SDN does so with the help of an SDN controller, which provides a global and unified view of the entire network from the network itself to the applications that stay on the top.

As is the case with servers and storage devices, networks are also virtualized. Virtual networks consist of several virtual switches and links. In addition to having a virtualized network, cloud computing uses networking functions that can be implemented using software (not hardware). This policy is being followed to avoid the expense involved in hardware switches and routers. The technique by which networking functionalities are implemented using software is called network function virtualization (NFV). What happens with virtualized networks and NFV concept is that there exist many virtual end points, virtual switches, virtual links, etc. Hence conventional security on its own is not enough to ensure security in such a virtualized environment as a result of invisible boundaries. This has led to the concept of software-defined security (SDS) for SDN. SDS aims to provide security at both the physical and virtual boundaries of data, resources, and tenants and to detect security breaches through violations of boundaries. Boundaries are defined by security policies. Security violations by attackers are predicted, continuously monitored, and detected. Both proactive and reactive security mechanisms are incorporated to keep the infrastructure safe against security threats. Thus SDN and SDS enable cloud service providers to implement the secure networking stuff required.

3.10   Summary

This chapter essentially discussed the various technological foundations of cloud computing. It elaborated on the various technologies and tools—such as virtualization, multi-core processors, distributed file systems, Web 2.0 tools, SOA, and web services—*that were the forerunners of cloud computing*. It described in detail how these technologies are exploited to meet the features of the cloud computing paradigm. It highlighted how these technologies enable cloud service providers to deliver different service offerings—such as Infrastructure as a Service, Platform as a Service, and Software as a Service—to users. It described how the internet remains the backbone of cloud computing. It gave special emphasis to the concept of virtualization, which serves as the central and critical enabler of cloud computing. It described how cloud computing employs virtualization in different areas such as server virtualization, storage virtualization, network virtualization, desktop virtualization, application virtualization, and data virtualization. It explained using rich schematic diagrams how virtualization helps in abstracting physical infrastructure and enables cloud computing to provision resources logically to a wide range of users according to their demands. It gave an account of how cloud computing took advantage of the advent of multi-core processors to establish its physical infrastructure. It discussed the significance of parallel programming models and highlighted how SOA and Web 2.0 tools can be used to reveal the different services of cloud providers. The modern trend of making use of MSA, Agile, and DevOps in cloud computing was also emphasized.

Finally, the chapter discussed how cloud computing has been extensively influenced by modern networking trends: software-defined networking, network function virtualization and software-defined security. It highlighted the use of SDN to automatically configure cloud networks. It highlighted the role NFV plays in replacing networking functions that had up to now been implemented in hardware using software. It also outlined the presence of invisible boundaries and virtual links/switches in the cloud environment that needs software-defined security along with conventional security mechanisms.

In a nutshell, the chapter illustrated how cloud computing as a modern computing trend took on its current, solid shape by exploiting various technologies and techniques. It is not unreasonable to say that the cloud only became very popular in such a short time span as a result of these technologies.

3.11 Exercises

1. Compile a list of Web 2.0 tools. Explain how these tools can be used to build an e-learning web application in the cloud environment (case study question).
2. What kind of virtualization do you think Amazon EC2 might use? Explain why?
3. What role do web services play in cloud computing?
4. How does multi-core technology help cloud computing?
5. Compile a list of technological enablers for cloud computing.
6. Explain the different categories of virtualization in detail.

References

1. Chaufournier L, Sharma P, Shenoy P, Tay YC (2016) Containers and virtual machines at scale: a comparative study. In: Proceeding Middleware '16, Proceedings of the 17th international middleware conference. ACM. Article No. 1. ISBN 978-1-4503-2138-9
2. Carapinha J, Jiménez J (2009) Network virtualization—a view from the bottom, VISA '09. ACM, Barcelona, Spain, 17 Aug 2009
3. Mišić B, Novković M, Ramač R, Mandić V (2017) Do the microservices improve the agility of software development teams? In: XVII international scientific conference on industrial systems (IS '17). Novi Sad, Serbia, pp 170–175, 4–6 Oct 2017
4. Di Francesco P, Malavolta I, Lago P (2017) Research on architecting microservices: trends, focus, and potential for industrial adoption. In: IEEE international conference on software architecture (ICSA). IEEE

Cloud Networking

4

Learning Objectives

The cloud computing environment is huge and consists of several computational resources dispersed across different geographical locations. Obviously one knows that the resources are connected with one another with the help of networks. This chapter aims to show how networks evolved from the simple design of a flat network model to a software-defined networking model for the cloud. By the end of this chapter the reader should have an overall idea about enterprise networking, cloud networking, and how they best work together to achieve business goals.

Motivational Questions

1. How do enterprises network their branches?
2. What are the basic networking requirements of any enterprise?
3. How do enterprises go about designing their networks? Are there any standard models?
4. What is enterprise internetworking?
5. What kind of networking model is followed in cloud networking?
6. There are a huge number of devices in the cloud. But how do we configure them? Is it done manually? Or by programs?
7. We came across the term software-defined networking and security in the previous chapter? Do you recall what they are?

Preface
In previous chapters the reader was taken through the origin of cloud computing, its unique characteristics, different service models, different deployment models, core techniques, and technologies that enabled cloud computing to take on its current

© Springer Nature Switzerland AG 2019
S. Chellammal and C. Pethuru Raj, *Essentials of Cloud Computing*,
Texts in Computer Science, https://doi.org/10.1007/978-3-030-13134-0_4

form. An inherent feature of cloud computing is that its resources are physically distributed across different locations. The obvious questions then become: How are dispersed resources connected? What kinds of networking models are being used in cloud networking? To gain a deeper understanding of what is involved here this chapter at first describes such factors as the basics of networking concepts, how enterprises connect their networks using LANs and WANs, and networking goals and requirements. Secondly, it describes the fundamental networking models: flat networking and hierarchical networking. It then presents the recent need for more and more communications within the enterprise itself (so-called east–west communication) rather than communication between client and server (north–south communication). Using this communication concept the chapter introduces the leaf spine networking model, which is the state-of-the-art model in cloud networks and large data centers. After describing the leaf spine model the chapter goes on to point out that this model alone is not sufficient because the configuration of each networking device is a dominating factor when making decisions on networking performance in the case of very large enterprise networks and cloud-based data centers. It is at this point in the chapter that the concept of software-defined networking is discussed in detail. Further, to meet the constraints of shorter time to market and lower cost many networking functions, which earlier were implemented using expensive and specialized hardware, are now being implemented with software using *network function virtualization* (NFV). This chapter gives an overview of NFV too.

4.1 Fundamental Concepts of Networking

Computer networking enables *sharing* of hardware and software resources [1]. Computers in a network are connected one to another using cables or wireless media, and resources are shared using standard communication protocols. There are two popular network reference models: Open Systems Interconnect (OSI) and Transmission Control Protocol/Internet Protocol (TCP/IP). They provide general guidelines for constructing networks and protocols. The OSI model consists of seven layers: *application, presentation, session, transport, network, data link*, and *physical*. The TCP/IP architecture consists of four layers: *application, transport, internet*, and *link*. The OSI model serves as a theoretical reference architecture, whereas the TCP/IP architecture is adopted when adding to the existing global internet. Various networking devices, such as hubs, switches, bridges, routers, and gateways, are used to construct a network. Before turning to enterprise networking a brief description of these networking devices is now given.

4.1.1 Basic Networking Devices (Hubs, Switches, Bridges, Routers, Gateways)

Hub

A hub is one of the basic networking devices used to connect multiple hosts. It is used to transfer data and has many input and output ports. A hub works in half

Fig. 4.1 Hub and collision
domain hub

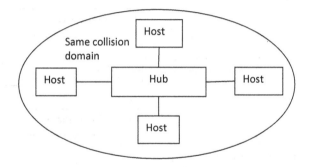

duplex mode (i.e., at a given time only one device can send data to a hub). When data arrive at any one of its input ports it will copy the data to *all output ports* (i.e., it broadcasts incoming data). It *does not have the intelligence to forward the incoming data to only one particular* receiver. It is working in layer 1 of the OSI model. With this model whenever more than one host sends data simultaneously a collision will occur. All the hosts connected to a hub have the same collision domain. It is the responsibility of the transmitting host to detect the *carrier* (a signal that exists in the connecting wire) and then to transmit the packets. Even if devices detect the carrier and send the signal more than one host can sense the carrier and send the data simultaneously. In such situations a collision will occur. When a collision occurs the transmitting host will send a jam signal informing all the hosts of a hub that a collision has occurred. The host will resend the data after some time. The collision domain in a hub is shown in Fig. 4.1.

Switch

A switch is a networking device used to connect devices by forwarding received packets to the destination intended using a packet-switching method. It is a layer 2 (link layer of OSI model) device. It is more intelligent than a hub. A hub forwards the incoming data to all output ports. But a *switch forwards the packet only to the receiving port for which the data is intended.* When compared with a hub a switch gives better network performance because each device connected to a switch can independently send data to any other device in the switch. Since a switch is intelligent in forwarding packets, only the receiver intended can receive them, but any host can transmit the data to other devices without waiting for others. A switch has many ports to which devices are attached. For example, a switch with four ports is shown in Fig. 4.2. Each attached device becomes a microsegment. A switch maintains a table of media access control (MAC) addresses of the devices. Data in layer 2 are transmitted as frames. Each frame contains source and destination MAC addresses. When a frame arrives at a switch the switch will forward the received frame only to the segment that contains the destination MAC and not to all other segments. In layer 2 a network is segmented into more than one collision domain.

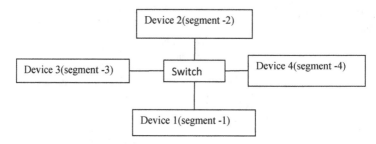

Fig. 4.2 Switch with four ports

Each port in a switch forms a collision domain, which differs from a hub where all devices connected to a hub form a collision domain. Another term related to packet forwarding is the broadcast domain. A broadcast domain consists of all devices that can reach each other at the data link layer (OSI layer 2) by broadcasting. All ports on a hub or a switch are by default in the same broadcast domain (this is shown in Fig. 4.3).

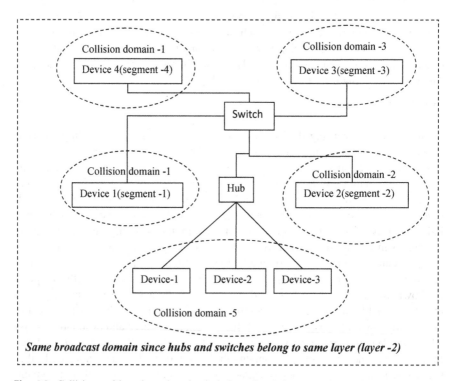

Fig. 4.3 Collision and broadcast domains in hubs and switches

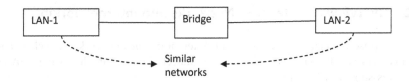

Fig. 4.4 Bridge connecting two similar LANs

Bridge

A bridge is a layer 2 networking device. It is used to connect two similar networks. For example, a bridge connecting two LANs working on the same protocol is shown in Fig. 4.4. It has a single input and single output port thus making it a two-port device. It also adds functionality, like filtering of traffic, by reading the MAC addresses of the source and destination.

Router

A router is a layer 3 networking device that routes data packets based on their IP addresses. A router normally connect LANs and WANs together and has a dynamically updated routing table it uses to make decisions on routing data packets. A router divides the broadcasting domain as shown in Fig. 4.5.

A router analyzes data being sent over a network, changes how they are packaged, and sends them to another network. A router receives data packets, evaluates the network addresses of incoming packets, and decides which address and which router it needs to use to forward packets. This is performed with the help of local routing tables. Routing tables can be computed either statically or dynamically.

Gateway

A gateway is used to connect two networks together that may work on different networking models with different protocols. It can operate on any network layer. A gateway is generally more complex than a switch or a router.

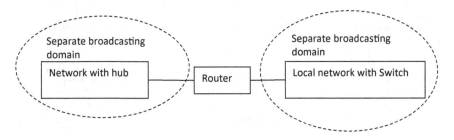

Fig. 4.5 How a router divides the broadcasting domain

4.2 Overview of Enterprise Networks and Internetworking

An enterprise typically has a number of different campus networks, branches, and data centers at different locations that are connected one to another using *LAN or WAN* (as shown in Fig. 4.6).

Computers within the same building are typically connected one to another using a local area network (LAN). Campus networks may consist of one or more LANs that are connected one to another using a router. Different networking elements, such as hubs, switches, bridges, and gateways, are used for networking. For example, within a campus different machines and devices are connected using switches. Twisted copper cables and shielded copper cables are used to connect computers. LAN networks can be used up to a distance of 1 km. Ethernet and Wi-Fi are the two primary ways to enable LAN connections. Ethernet is a specification

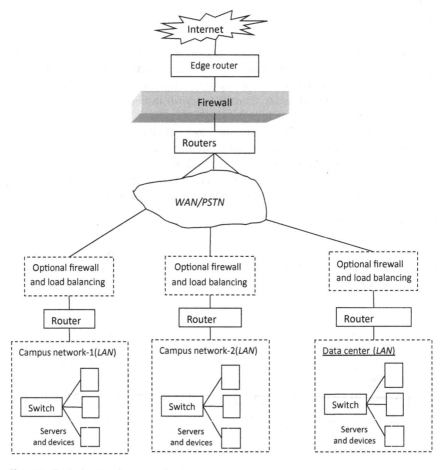

Fig. 4.6 Typical enterprise network

that enables computers to communicate with each other. Wi-Fi uses radio waves to connect computers to a LAN. Networks more distant than 1 km are connected using WANs. Fiber-optic cables are used to enable long-distance networking as there is no loss in fiber-optic communication. In addition to branches and campus networks enterprises also have data centers. A data center is a repository that houses a large number of the networked servers, storage devices, routers, switches, firewalls, load balancers, and other computing infrastructure of an enterprise. It is used for remote processing, storage, and distribution of various services to applications and users. When a client submits a request from a location remote to the enterprise via the internet, an edge router will route the requests to the access routers concerned through firewall security policies. Each campus network can have its own firewall and load balancer according to the requirements of applications. The access router will route the requests to respective local routers of campus level networks. Then the request received by the local router concerned is forwarded to the relevant switch in the LAN.

Overall, the main objective of enterprise networking is to *provide an integrated backbone for communication among individual workgroups, LANs, data centers, and users. **Various enterprise internetworking techniques, such as private WAN, IPVPN, and MPLS WAN**, are used to interconnect different LANs and WANs.*

Enterprise private WAN

Enterprise private WAN networks interconnect the branches, data centers, and head office of an enterprise that are separated by more than 1 km (as shown in Fig. 4.7).

Internet Protocol Virtual Private Network

Enterprises can extend their private networks using encrypted connections over the internet. An employee of an enterprise who works outside the enterprise (say, at home) can securely connect to the enterprise network via VPN tunnels (as shown in Fig. 4.8).

VPNs provide secure connections using encryption protocols to generate virtual P2P connections. For added security the actual IP address of users is replaced by a temporary IP address.

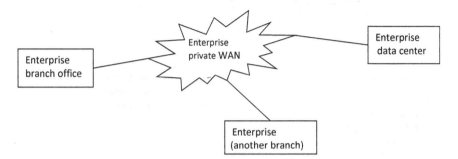

Fig. 4.7 Enterprise internetworking using a private WAN network

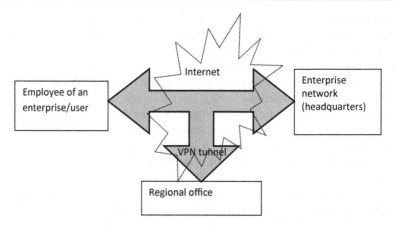

Fig. 4.8 Internet virtual private network

Multiprotocol Label Switching (MPLS WAN) for High-Performance Applications

MPLS WAN is an IP VPN that allows using a single network for data, voice, video, and business applications. MPLS WAN is used to connect data centers, corporate headquarters, and branch offices according to the needs of various applications of enterprises. The MPLS WAN network is a guaranteed and secure network that offers a dedicated MPLS service. Using this protocol an enterprise can prioritize traffic, so important applications like voice and video are not compromised by applications like email. Ethernet access is used to connect to the MPLS WAN

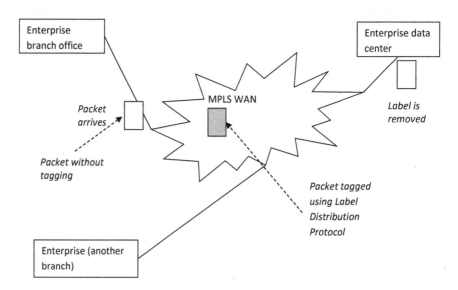

Fig. 4.9 MPLS WAN for high-performance applications

network. Consolidating all types of data packets, such as voice, video, data, and other applications, into one MPLS-enabled VPN allows an enterprise to have a single point of control for all critical functions. MPLS uses classes of service that allow enterprises to put time-sensitive applications, like VoIP, in a priority class (i.e., data packets are tagged with labels as in Fig. 4.9) and batch traffic, like email, in a "best-effort" class. MPLS IP VPNs are popular because a single network is used for all voice, video, and data traffic. MPLS networks provide various benefits such as improved uptime, improved bandwidth, and reduced network.

4.3 Network Design Requirements and Design Goals

Designing an enterprise network is based on the number of devices comprising the network and size of the network. Networks are of three types:

- small networks consist of up to 200 devices;
- medium-sized networks consist of 200 to 1000 devices; and
- large networks consist of more than 1000 elements.

Networks should be designed carefully according to the size, applications requirements, and non-functional parameters such as performance and latency. The performance, reliability, and security of all systems have to be at least sufficiently satisfactory. Different network models, communication protocols, operating systems, strategies, mobile devices (such as smartphones, laptops, and palmtops), and sensor devices are integrated with the unified goal of delivering the services of the enterprise effectively. *In general, enterprise networks should be designed to meet the following fundamental requirements*:

- network should be reliable and highly available;
- network should be manageable;
- network should be scalable;
- network must be secure;
- network should follow a simple design;
- network latency should be low;
- network should have high throughput;
- network should stay up even under overloaded conditions; and
- network should be easy to modify.

Design Goals

The fundamental goals of network design are (as shown in Fig. 4.10):

Fig. 4.10 Goals of network design

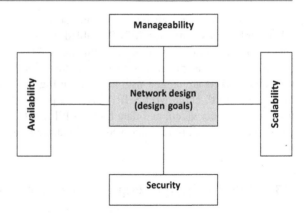

- *Scalability*: A network should be scalable. This means that a network should be designed in such a way that it is capable of including increasingly more applications and users without affecting the quality of service delivered to existing users.
- *Availability*: A network should be highly available. This means that a network should be so designed that it delivers *expected, consistent, and reliable* functionalities and performance 24 h a day, 7 days a week, and 365 days a year. Even if part of a network fails it should not affect business.
- *Security*: Since security is an essential feature network design should include suitable security policies and devices (such as filters, firewalls, and intruder detection systems) wherever required.
- *Manageability*: Network design should be simple so that it can be easily managed and maintained.

4.4 Standard Network Models

Three standard networking models are used to design an enterprise network (as shown in Fig. 4.11):

- flat networking model;
- hierarchical networking model; and
- leaf spine networking model.

These models are briefly explained in the following subsections.

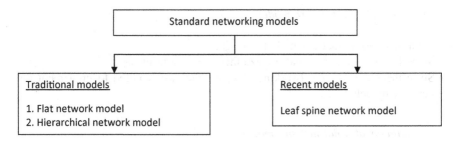

Fig. 4.11 Standard network models

4.4.1 Flat Networking Model

Small networks can be designed using the flat networking model. A flat network is a very simple design in which all the hosts of a small network are connected to either a single switch or to a limited number of switches and hubs. It does not use a router, but does use a single broadcasting domain.

The flat networking model is shown in Fig. 4.12. In the flat network model (subject to the application requirements, network load, and number of users) the switching element will be chosen for connecting devices. Switches are more expensive than hubs. When there are high-bandwidth requirements (e.g., when applications have many users or there is heavy network traffic) systems can be connected using switches. Since a switch divides the collision domain into as many devices as are connected to it, it gives better network performance by allowing all the ports to simultaneously transmit to other ports. Hubs are only used for very small networks with less traffic. In addition, switches use MAC addresses for data transfers. Hubs are unaware of MAC addresses since they work in the physical layer. Hosts connected to a hub simply use Ethernet's *carrier-sense multiple access collision detect* (CSMA/CD) to control access to shared bandwidth.

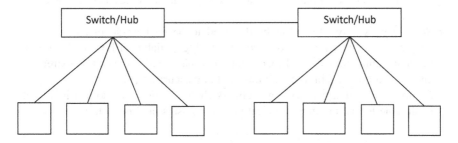

Fig. 4.12 Flat network model

Advantages of a flat network model

- A flat network model is simple to design.
- Since flat networks are small in size they are easy to manage.
- Since there are fewer networking elements the cost required to implement flat network models is low.

Disadvantages of a flat network model

- A flat network model does not allow for division of the broadcasting domain. Instead it a has single broadcast domain. A single broadcast domain should be limited to only a few hundred devices; generally, up to 200 devices can be connected. If the number of devices exceeds more than a few hundred the network becomes unusable.
- A flat network model does not help in filtering undesirable traffic.
- When more devices are added to the network the response time can be very long.

4.4.2   Hierarchical Networking Model

Design Principles of a Hierarchical Network Model

As mentioned earlier the four goals of network design are availability, scalability, security, and manageability. To achieve these goals network design is undertaken using a set of *structured design principles*:

- *Hierarchy and modularity*: When network design follows a hierarchical structure, network complexity is reduced. Using hierarchical layers network complexity can be divided into manageable layers. In hierarchical design each layer has a defined set of functions. Dividing the network design into modules makes the design easier.
- *Resiliency*: A network should be designed to be resilient so that the network remains available with its expected functioning (reliability) both under normal (normal traffic and expected load) and abnormal conditions such as extreme or unexpected traffic, failure conditions, and any security threat.
- *Flexibility and modifiability*: The network should be designed so that it is easily modifiable to include more applications, more users, and more traffic.

Architecture of Hierarchical Networking Model
A hierarchical networking model is made up of three layers: access layer, distribution layer, and core layer.

- *Access layer*: The access layer is used to gain entry/access to the network of an enterprise. Access layer switches are also called end-of-row switches (EoR switches connect all rows of the rack in a data center/server room) or top-of-rack switches (ToR switches) since the layer is usually located at the top of the rack.
- *Distribution layer*: Also called an aggregation layer this layer provides policy-based connectivity. Routing, filtering, and quality of service (QoS) policies are managed by this layer as are individual WAN connections.
- *Core layer*: The core layer provides the high-speed forwarding services needed to move packets among different devices of the distribution layer in different regions of the network. The core layer is also called the network backbone. It is capable of aggregating traffic from many distribution layer devices and forwarding large amounts of data quickly. Each layer has its own network devices and protocols.

Advantages of hierarchical networking model

- *The major advantage of the hierarchical network is that each layer has its own broadcast domain* (as shown in Fig. 4.13). *In a hierarchical network the local traffic of a particular layer will remain within the layer and will not travel to a higher layer,* but traffic that has to travel to a higher layer can do so. This improves network performance significantly. As shown in Fig. 4.13 an access layer device (say, an access switch) receives data after crossing the firewall and load balancer, identifies the switch or router to which the data is to be sent, and sends the data to the device concerned. The high-end switch or router of the core layer that received the request identifies the destination and routes/sends it to that device/another WAN. The core layer typically deals with layer 3 routing or layer 2 switching. In such a transmission it is only when there is a specific need that data can cross the other layers. Otherwise the local traffic of any layer remains within the layer.
- Another important advantage concerns the network traffic and objectives of hierarchical networking models. Such models have been developed with **client-to-server communication** (*or north-to-south communication*) **in mind** and hence do not focus on east–west communication. In small and medium-sized enterprises east–west communication is less because there are fewer devices and interconnections. Small networks rarely opt for virtual LANs.

Further, to illustrate the concept of a hierarchical layer network model Fig. 4.14 shows how an enterprise network and its data center are connected. As shown in Fig. 4.14, there are two LANs (LAN-1, LAN-2) situated in different campuses of the enterprise. These two campuses are networked to form an enterprise branch. There is a data center at another remote location. The enterprise branch and data center are connected using private WAN.

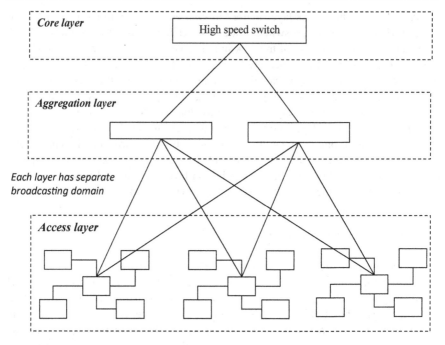

Fig. 4.13 Hierarchical layer network model

Disadvantages of hierarchical networking model

- Since the hierarchical networking model was basically developed to support client-to-server communication (or north-to-south communication) it does not deal well with east–west communication.
- *When it comes to enterprise applications there is too much traffic within enterprise networks themselves to fulfill the needs of various applications.* That is, other than *north–south*, which refers to *client–server communication, there are many server-to-server or east–west traffic* patterns. These traffic patterns are not handled with a fixed number of hops in the hierarchical layer design. For example, in Fig. 4.14 if S1 wants to send some data to S2 (i.e., to a server that belongs to the same LAN as S1), the access switch itself will transmit the communication. There is no need to go to the aggregation layer. But if S1 wants to send some data to say S5, which belongs to LAN-2 of the enterprise (both the source server and destination server belong to the *same enterprise campus network*), then *data will hop through the aggregation layer*. If S1 wants to send data to say S10, which belongs to another WAN network (i.e., the data center), then *the data will hop through the core switch*. Hence the number of hops involved in data transfer varies according to the source and destination.

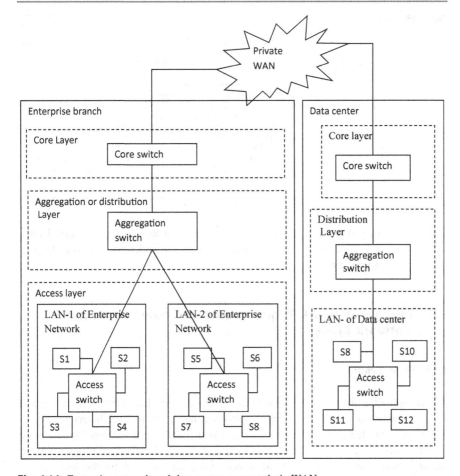

Fig. 4.14 Enterprise network and data center connected via WAN

- Since there are not many devices in small networks the latency due to east–west communication is predictable, but in large networks network latency becomes unpredictable.
- Since large enterprises employ virtualization to abstract the physical network, virtual LANs are used to logically group physical devices of the same layer; however, this still increases latency. For example, local area networks of the core layer may span more than one floor in a building (as shown in Fig. 4.15). Trunk lines are now used to keep traffic within the VLAN concerned.
- Although traffic is confined within a VLAN in large enterprises, since there are several server devices that need to communicate with one another server-to-server or east–west traffic increases. This implies that there will be more VLAN traffic, which in turn creates *loops* in networks. The Spanning Tree Protocol (STP) can be used to avoid loops. However, it *does not allow parallel forwarding paths*,

Fig. 4.15 Concept of VLAN

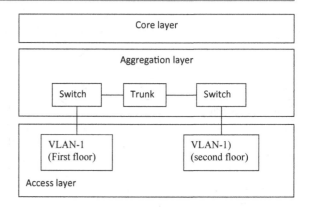

which are very important to achieving high performance and throughput. Hence increased east–west traffic affects uplink performance badly, and network latency becomes unpredictable.

4.5 Modern Network Requirements and Need for Suitable Network Model

East–West Traffic

As mentioned earlier, modern enterprise networks and data centers are large and span a number of buildings. They employ virtualization to hide heterogeneity in hardware. This led inevitably to huge east–west traffic within enterprise networks. Traffic within large enterprises needs to be effectively handled with deterministic latency (note that this requirement is not efficiently handled by the hierarchical model as it was developed with north–south communication in mind).

Scalability

The number of servers and devices keep on increasing as do the number of virtual servers. For example, around 20 virtual servers can be configured on a single physical server. Data centers typically contain around 100,000 physical servers. Hence a huge number of virtual servers are involved in data centers. To support multiple tenants data centers adopt network virtualization [2]. Each tenant has his/her own virtual network, which must be logically separated from other virtual networks.

Digitization of Data

Everyday digitization of data drives tremendous changes in customer demands and hence enterprises have to evolve to satisfy a wide variety of use cases:

- videoconferencing applications;
- video sharing and video games;
- video surveillance applications;
- real-time processing of streaming data;
- situational awareness applications with robotics;
- big data applications;
- IoT applications; and
- natural language applications.

Typically, most use cases either require

- huge storage of data;
- huge computing power to process data; and
- huge networking capabilities to send and receive data.

Automation of Networking Configuration

The need for business agility drives the automation of networking. For example, after testing a code in the development environment let us consider the code is to be moved to the integration and production environments. When software is moved to different environments, configuring the required security policies, access policies, and routing policies in each environment becomes essential. In addition, the movement of software among different environments will happen on a daily or weekly basis in an Agile enterprise. In such a scenario manual configuration of the policies required in each environment will become impractical. This drives the automation of networking configuration.

High Performance

Network performance includes such features as high bandwidth, low latency, low jitter, and no packet loss. On the one hand, external customers expect very low latency when they interact with enterprise websites. On the other hand, such business processes as manufacturing and monitoring require very frequent data exchange with very low latency. Hence it is essential to include various enterprise networking solutions such as WAN optimization, static routes, migration of servers to nearest points, and caching contents.

Manageability

As the enterprise network spans across different locations, visibility and control of network devices has to be met with a global view of devices.

Availability of Network Links

It is up to enterprises to ensure that services are offered in line with agreed services levels (as per the SLA) and have sufficient path redundancy. Suitable load balancing has to be ensured for peak loads.

Secure Networking

Security is brought about by making use of a number of security mechanisms such as authentication and identity management, access control, firewalling, single sign-on, data loss prevention, fraud detection, malware detection, intrusion detection and prevention, and audit records. Security is an important concern as enterprise networks span multiple domains and different service provider sites.

These requirements make it clear that enterprise networking has to offer quality of service not only in bandwidth or performance but in many other areas as well. Enterprise networks cannot stand alone from computing or storage technologies. Networking techniques should grow in line with the speed of computing and storage because the use cases of business processes are becoming increasingly agile and dynamic. The digitization of data drives three major tasks: data storage, data transformation, and data transfer. All three tasks essentially need networking capabilities. Ensuring networking capabilities are optimized is essential when data and processes are not in same location. Since data get distributed the processing of data is done in a distributed manner along with parallel processing techniques. This is essentially responsible for bringing a very large amount of internal traffic to the enterprise network. Hence large enterprises and data centers prefer another network architecture called *leaf spine architecture.*

4.6   Leaf Spine Architecture

In leaf spine architecture (also called *flat tree* architecture or *CLOS* architecture for Charles Clos who developed it) there are only two layers: the spine layer and leaf layer (as shown in Fig. 4.16).

In leaf spine architecture servers are connected to leaf switches. Each leaf is connected to every spine. There is no direct spine-to-spine or leaf-to-leaf connection in this architecture. The leaf layer consists of access switches that connect to devices such as servers. The spine layer is the backbone of the network and is responsible for interconnecting all leaf switches. The path is randomly chosen so that traffic load is evenly distributed among the switches of the spine layer. If oversubscription of a link occurs (i.e., more traffic is generated than can be aggregated on the active link at any one time), the process for expanding capacity is straightforward. An additional spine switch can be added, and uplinks can be extended to every leaf switch, resulting in the addition of interlayer bandwidth and reduction in oversubscription. If device port capacity becomes a concern, a new leaf switch can be added by connecting it to every spine switch and adding network configuration to the switch. The ease of expansion optimizes the IT department's process of scaling the network. *The important aspect of this architecture is that every server can reach every other server with the same number of hops. This makes network latency predictable and consistent.* In this architecture the spine

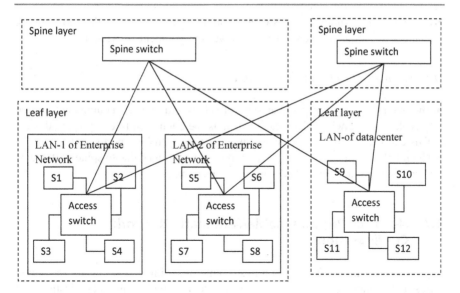

Fig. 4.16 Leaf spine architecture

layer is the backbone of the network and is responsible for interconnecting all leaf switches.

Advantages of leaf spine architecture

- *Improved redundancy*: In leaf spine architecture [3] each leaf switch is connected to multiple spine switches. That is, leaf spine topologies provide many paths between two points, typically implemented using protocols such as Transparent Interconnection of Lots of Links (TRILL) or Shortest Path Bridging (SPB). TRILL and SPB allow traffic flow across all available routes, which offers improved redundancy and at the same time still prevent loops.
- *Improved performance*: The ability to use multiple network paths at the same time improves performance. As a result of TRILL and SPB being capable of using multiple routes congestion is less of an issue. Having only a single hop between any two points gives a more direct network path, which can also improve performance.
- *Improved scalability*: Leaf spine topologies are also inherently scalable. Providing so many paths between any two network points, all of which are available to carry traffic, reduces the possibility of congestion even in a large network. Adding switches to a leaf spine network provides additional traffic routes, thus increasing scalability.
- *Enterprise adaptability*: Although leaf spine architecture was originally designed for data center networks to address the east–west nature of traffic between servers and storage systems, the architecture can also be extended outside the data center to the enterprise network at large.

- *Fixed switch configuration*: Switch configuration is fixed so that no network changes are required even when the server environment is dynamic.

Disadvantages of leaf spine architecture

- The main disadvantage is the amount of cables and network equipment required to scale the bandwidth since each leaf must be connected to every spine device. This can lead to more expensive spine switches with high port counts.
- The number of hosts that can be supported can be limited due to spine port counts restricting the number of leaf switch connections.

4.7 Need for Programmable/Automatic Network Configuration

As enterprises move from on-premises enterprise infrastructures to the cloud infrastructure there is a need not only to consider the architecture of applications but also network architecture models. Traditionally, enterprises provided the typical tiers of an application—client tier, business logic tier, and database tier—in different servers and interconnected those servers by means of the network infrastructure. In the 2010s enterprises adopted the service-oriented architecture (SOA) model to develop business applications and achieve business agility. One of the tenets of this development was to promote reusability and interoperability. SOA provides application-to-application interactions with the help of an enterprise service bus (ESB). An ESB serves as the central location to integrate applications using a loosely coupled, asynchronous, reliable, and secure messaging model. Although an ESB provides centralized integration of applications, it is inflexible. An ESB is basically used to integrate different applications, whereas recent microservices architecture (MSA) provides the architecture to develop applications in the form of *microservices*. Microservices are autonomous, self-contained, and self-deployable. This makes deployment much easier. Whenever there is a change in a service, only that particular service is redeployed. In contrast to a traditional monolithic or SOA-based application, which treats all functions as a single process, MSA treats each service as a process. These services can communicate with one another using HTTP. Moreover, a microservice can be manipulated through its application programming interface (API). In much the same way as they have modernized their application architecture, enterprises primarily focus on the recent software development process model—namely, Agile—in contrast to the old waterfall or other models. They do so because the *Agile model accepts changing and dynamic customer demands and emphasizes continuous integration and continuous delivery of software development. When an application is developed in a traditional manner, continuous delivery becomes difficult.* For example, when an application is developed the first thing to be done is to freeze the requirement features of the project. Then the web design/GUI development team and database team take on the project from the development team and carry out that part of the project they are tasked with. In this model continuous delivery is difficult. *In addition, from a network point of view various tasks have to be carried out according to the requirements of the application*:

(i)   IP address ranges for applications have to be provided;
(ii)   quality-of-service factors and security policies have to be provided for the application;
(iii)   load balancing has to be provided;
(iv)   switching and routing have to be provided for the application; and
(v)   various network devices have to be configured.

When these tasks are carried out manually—depending on the size and complexity of applications—the time taken to configure is high and continuous delivery is difficult. Manual device-level provisioning or configuring the devices through a command line interface (CLI) is inflexible and time consuming. But enterprises want their applications to be highly available and reliable. If the network configuration is made programmable, the needs of enterprises can be met easily and quickly. Continuous delivery and the Agile model can be introduced without any issues.

4.8   Different Methods of Configuring Network Devices

To provide clear insight into the way in which network devices are configured we outline three methods:

(i)   manual and conventional configuration method;
(ii)   early automatic configuration methods; and
(iii)   modern software-defined networking.

4.8.1   Manual and Conventional Method for Configuring Network Devices

In general, each networking device has three components it can use to manage its operations: the control plane, data plane, and management plane (as shown in Fig. 4.17). These planes are implemented in the firmware of the networking device.

Management Plane

The management plane of a device allows a network operator or administrator to access and manage the device. A network operator or administrator can log into the

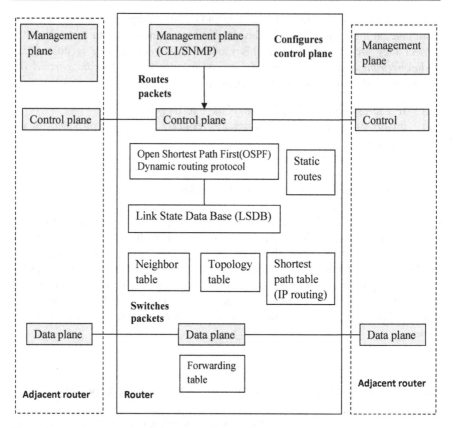

Fig. 4.17 Three planes of a networking device

device and manage the device via a command line interface (CLI), a Simple Network Management Protocol (SNMP), or some other methods. The management plane is used to control and monitor a device.

Control Plane

The control plane performs all functions related to data routing. The control plane uses different routing protocols such as Routing Information Protocol (RIP), Open Shortest Path First (OSPF), Interior Gateway Routing Protocol (IGRP), Enhanced Interior Gateway Routing Protocol (EIGRP), Exterior Gateway Protocol (EGP), Border Gateway Protocol (BGP), and Intermediate System to Intermediate System (IS-IS). These protocols produce various dynamic tables. For example, OSPF is a link-state dynamic routing protocol. It maintains three different tables: (i) a neighbor table (contains a list of neighbors), (ii) a topology table (also called a link-state table) (gives complete link details in the same network), and (iii) shortest path table (gives the best and shortest route). OSPF is an open-source protocol that supports routers of any vendor. Compared with other distance vector-routing protocols OSPF is suitable for large and heterogeneous networks. OSPF computes more quickly than the others and whenever topology changes it is the most effective at computing routing information.

Data Plane

The data plane is also called the *forwarding plane* as it forwards data to an adjacent device according to the path determined by the control plane. The data plane creates a forwarding table (or MAC table). It updates the forwarding table according to changes and updates received from the control panel.

Limitations of Conventional Configuration of Devices

Large enterprise networks and data centers need more flexible, programmable, API-driven, and virtualization-aware networking services. Since data communication is growing at a faster rate new networking devices constantly need to be connected and configured. In general, network configuration is done manually. When many devices have to be configured manually, the likelihood of introducing configuration errors is greater. In traditional networking each device tries to make its own decision about routing and switching since each device has a control plane (as shown in Fig. 4.18). Control is decentralized among all devices.

Another major issue with traditional networking is that the devices are manufactured by different vendors who use their own networking protocols (as shown in Fig. 4.19). As the network grows more heterogeneous, communications among all devices become increasingly complex. A number of efforts have been made to facilitate automating the networking of data centers and enterprises.

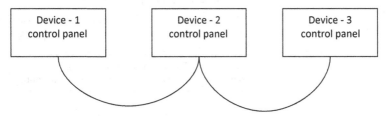

In traditional networking, every device has independent control panel.
It leads to decentralized control.

Fig. 4.18 Decentralized control among all devices

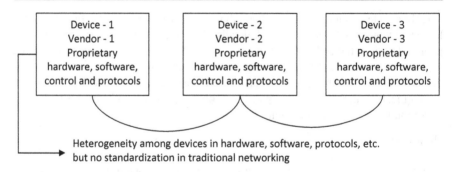

Heterogeneity among devices in hardware, software, protocols, etc. but no standardization in traditional networking

Fig. 4.19 Heterogeneity among devices

4.8.2 Early Methods for Automatic Configuration of Network Devices

Some of the early networking paradigms for automatic configuration include Remote Authentication Dial In User Service (RADIUS), Forwarding and Control Element Separation (ForCES), 4D Centralized Network Control, and Ethane.

Remote Authentication Dial In User Service (RADIUS)

RADIUS was the first to introduce automation to the creation and configuration of networks. A RADIUS network controller serves as an orchestrator for all networking devices. With RADIUS, network administrators need not know vendor-specific details. They develop the network requirements of applications in the form of scripts. These scripts are transformed into vendor-specific code and this code is configured in the device (as shown in Fig. 4.20).

Fig. 4.20 RADIUS serves as an orchestrator

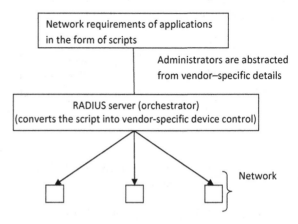

Forwarding and Control Element Separation (ForCES)

ForCES has defined an open, programmable, distributed router architecture based on the physical separation of routing and forwarding tasks (as shown in Fig. 4.21). Control elements in ForCES prepare the routing information for forwarding elements. Each control element may interact with one or more forwarding elements. Control elements are managed by the control element manager and forwarding elements are managed by the forwarding element manager. Control elements and forwarding elements interact with one another using the ForCES protocol.

The architecture defines a number of different interfaces:

- Fp interface—the interface between the control element and the forwarding element;
- Fi interface—the interface between one forwarding element and another forwarding element;
- Fr interface—the interface between one control element and another control element;
- Fc interface—the interface between the control element manager and the control element;

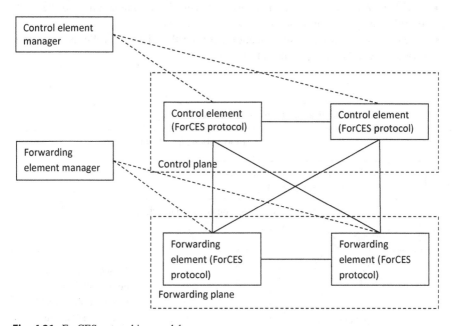

Fig. 4.21 ForCES networking model

- Ff interface—the interface between the forwarding element manager and the forwarding element; and
- Fl interface—the interface between the control element manager and the forwarding element manager.

4.8.3   Software-Defined Networking

The Open Networking Foundation (ONF), a non-profit organization, promotes software-defined networking [4, 5] as being capable of fixing issues with the traditional networking model and with the configuration of devices. The software-defined networking architecture at the highest level is as shown in Fig. 4.22 and comprises five components:

- *Application plane*: SDN applications reside on the application panel.
- *Control plane*: The SDN architecture provides a central controller that provides high-level control and routing functions for individual networking devices using software.
- *Data plane*: The data panel consists of low-cost network switches that only have data-forwarding capability.
- *Northbound interface*: Communication between SDN applications and the SDN controller is via the northbound interface.
- *Southbound interface*: Communication between the SDN controller and network devices is via the southbound interface.

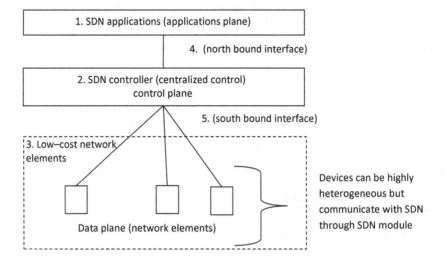

Fig. 4.22 Components of SDN architecture

The southbound interface (SBI) defines the standard way in which an SDN controller interacts with network elements. To create a standard method of SBI the vendors of network devices should support standardization. OpenFlow is being extensively used as the standard way of implementing SBI. Various vendors of networking devices—such as Cisco, Juniper, Big Switch Networks, Brocade, Arista, Extreme Networks, IBM, Dell, HP, and NEC—also provide support for OpenFlow. There are other SBI protocols such as Open Virtual Switch DataBase (OVSDB), Yang, or NetConf.

The northbound interface defines the standard way in which an SDN controller and SDN application interact. Since the SDN architecture is being implemented by different vendors more than 20 types of SDN controllers are available on the market. Different controllers provide different types of NBI APIs. The main reason for different varieties of NBI APIs is that the needs of applications vary from application to application. Most NBI APIs are either ad hoc or REST APIs.

An SDN controller provides a means to dynamically control the behavior of network devices as required by the application layer. An application implements its application-specific network requirements through an SDN controller with the help NBI APIs. The orchestration function of an SDN controller provides automated control and management of network devices. Different SDN controller companies —such as Cisco, HPE, NEC, Lumina, and Juniper—offer a range of SDN controllers. An SDN controller typically consists of a collection of pluggable modules that can provide different network services and tasks.

The application plane specifies the SDN applications that can define the behavior of network devices in a programmatic manner. How devices behave depends on the needs of applications. These applications convey their network requirements to an SDN controller using NBI APIs.

4.8.3.1 Features of Software-Defined Networking

Separation of Control Plane from Data Plane

The actions of the forwarding plane depend on different tables and logic such as whether *to forward the incoming packet, drop the packet, filter the packet, consume the packet, or replicate the packet.* The logic and algorithm underlying the actions of the forwarding plane need global knowledge of the network. Actions in a conventional network model are performed in the individual control planes of devices and the state of each and every device remains synchronized so that the entire network can continue working. But with the introduction of network virtualization and multi-tenancy, several virtual devices need to be configured according to the requirements of the application. Hence SDN totally deactivates the control planes of individual devices and replaces them with a centralized controller that manages all forwarding planes. *The first task of SDN is to separate the control plane of individual devices.*

Low-Cost Network Devices

Since intelligence is removed from devices in SDN it is not necessary to use costly network devices in the infrastructure layer. SDN promotes using low-cost network switches. An SDN controller manages the network using higher level policies as defined by applications. It performs all the control logic and gives instructions to network devices, which forward the packets or perform actions in accordance with instructions from the controller.

Network Abstraction and Automation

SDN aims to provide network operators with a global view by hiding the internal workings of the network. SDN provides complete abstraction, so much so that the network programmer can easily obtain a global view without being aware of hardware-specific details. He can program the network requirements of applications simply by using NBI interfaces. Network programmers no longer need concern themselves with individual device configuration, physical vendor-specific hardware details, or proprietary interfaces.

Openness

SDN emphasizes open and standard protocols for communication between the controller and network devices (SBI) and communication between applications and the controller (NBI). Open interfaces allow interoperability among devices manufactured by different vendors. Open interfaces will also reduce the cost of networking devices.

4.8.3.2   How Does a Software-Defined Networking Controller Help Software-Defined Networking Applications Manage a Network?

This section describes how an SDN controller helps SDN applications to manage their network efficiently and easily. Using a high-level schematic this concept is explained in Fig. 4.23. An SDN controller *provides a global view of the network* for applications residing in the top layer and fulfills the network requirements raised by SDN applications by abstracting the internal workings of the network.

SDN applications here refer to applications in the network layer such as load-balancing applications, applications that set up firewall policies and access control, fault tolerance applications, provisioning of networking devices, removal of networking devices, detection of network failures, network status monitoring, detecting events, and responding to events in the network.

An SDN controller helps SDN applications carry out their tasks by abstracting the physical network. It provides these SDN applications with a global view of the network. These applications control the network with the help of a controller. For example, after obtaining a global view of the network the SDN applications prepare

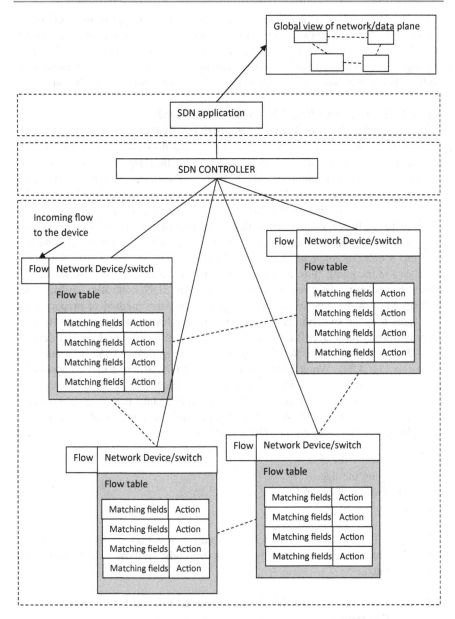

Fig. 4.23 How an SDN controller helps SDN applications manage networks

what is known as a flow table for SDN switches. When a packet arrives at the
network layer it is the responsibility of the network layer to decide what is to be
done with it. Possible operations on the packet include sending the packet to the
destination, accepting the packet, performing some filtering action, and discarding

the packet. Depending on application requirements the SDN application will create a flow table for each network switch/router with the help of the SDN controller. An SDN controller sits in between SDN applications and SDN devices. It has an intelligent networking operating system with open interfaces inside to communicate with SDN applications at the north end and SDN devices at the south end.

4.8.3.3   Software-Defined Networking Controllers and Software-Defined Networking Switches

As shown in Fig. 4.23 an SDN controller prepares flow tables for SDN switches according to the needs of SDN applications. Here flow represents a sequence of packets with a set of common or same headers. *For example, flow refers to a set of packets with the same source IP and same destination IP. The action defined for all such packets will be the same. Hence actions are defined for each flow.* The combination of flow (i.e., all packets that share a set of common header values) and its corresponding action make up an *entry* in a flow table. *A flow table ultimately contains a table of flow entries.* When a flow arrives at an SDN switch the switch matches the incoming flow against each entry in the table. If the switch finds a match it performs the corresponding action. An SDN controller abstracts the heterogeneity in the type of switch and gives a uniform method of preparing the flow table for each switch in any layer. This means that it simply prepares the flow entry uniformly for a layer 2 Ethernet switch, a layer 3 router, or a layer 4 TCP port. *An SDN switch compares the flow against matching fields of the flow entry* (as shown in Fig. 4.24). When a flow arrives at an SDN switch it first compares the ingress port of the header with the address of the SDN switch. If the ingress port matches, then the switch compares the header values against matching fields of each flow entry in the flow table. When a match is found the corresponding action will take place. The functions of an SDN switch include

(i)   forwarding the data;
(ii)   dropping the data;
(iii)   filtering the data; and
(iv)   accepting the packet.

If a match is not found the switch will send the flow back to the controller. The controller creates a rule for the flow and accordingly the flow will be sent to the relevant switch.

4.8.3.4   Functional Modules of a Software-Defined Networking Controller

To carry out different functions with SDN applications and SDN devices an SDN controller typically makes use of a number of functional modules, a southbound interface, and a northbound interface (as shown in Fig. 4.25).

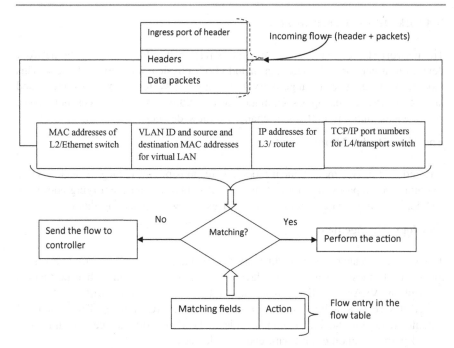

Fig. 4.24 Functions of an SDN switch and how it interacts with an SDN controller (comparing the header values of flow against matching fields in the flow entry)

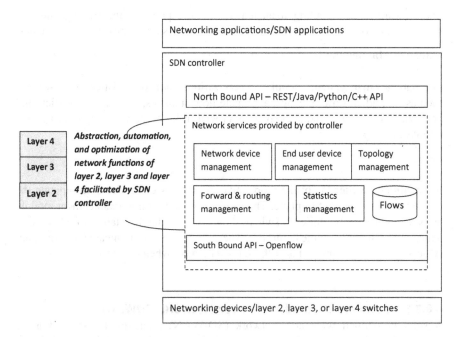

Fig. 4.25 Functional modules of an SDN controller

Network Device Management

The network device management module is responsible for managing the network devices in a network. Devices can include both physical and virtual devices. This module manages a wide range of switches: layer 2 switches, layer 3 routers, and layer 4 switches. It manages such matters as the addition of new devices, deletion of new devices, and any updates or changes in new devices.

End User Device Management

The end user device management module is responsible for managing such devices as computers, laptops, and mobile devices. It is tasked with identifying additions, deletions, or any changes in end user devices and with managing them.

Topology Management

The topology management module involves sending Link Layer Discovery Protocol (LLDP) messages to network devices to gather information such as port name, description, VLAN ID, IP address, capabilities of device (i.e., whether the connected device is a switch, router, or server), and MAC address. This functional module maintains the information details of how network devices are interconnected with one another and with end user devices.

Forwarding and Routing Management

The forwarding and routing management module prepares the routing and forwarding functions for switches. It prepares flow tables and sends them to switches.

Statistics Management

The statistics management module collects various kinds of statistics from switches such as individual flow statistics, aggregate flow statistics, flow table statistics, and port statistics. These statistics play a crucial role in network monitoring and troubleshooting.

Flows

As mentioned earlier the primary objective of an SDN controller is to separate the data plane from the control plane. The forwarding and routing management module prepares the flow table for each switch. Flows refer to the flow tables of all devices, which are maintained in the controller. These flows are communicated to individual switches. A switch simply takes the relevant action when it receives a flow.

4.8.3.5 Software-Defined Wide Area Network (SDWAN)

A software-defined wide area network (SD-WAN) refers to the application of software-based network technologies to WAN connections and is used to more

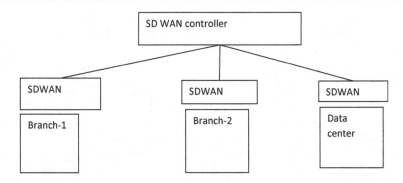

Fig. 4.26 Software-defined WAN

effectively route all network traffic between headquarters, data centers, remote and branch offices, and the cloud (as shown in Fig. 4.26).

An SDWAN controller controls and manages all network branches and data centers using software. Back in the day enterprises used conventional WAN with specialized hardware, which was expensive. However, nowadays an SDWAN controller provides many network functions and device configurations through software. The customers of enterprises are demanding more flexible, open, and cloud-based WAN technologies, rather than installing specialized WAN technology that often involves expensive, fixed circuits or proprietary hardware. SDWAN technology is constantly evolving, has been found to be more flexible, and can be controlled via cloud software.

4.9   Network Function Virtualization

Much like SDN there is another network-related technique called network function virtualization (NFV). The primary objective of NFV is to virtualize network functions such as load balancing, implementing firewall policies and routing, WAN optimization, and deep packet inspection. Back in the day these functions were implemented using specialized expensive hardware. With the advent of NVF these functions are now implemented in software. This reduces the costs involved in setting up the network infrastructure of large enterprises. Because these functions are implemented using virtual machines and commodity hardware the network provisioning process is simplified. NFV plays a crucial role in simplifying network management and provision in the transport, session, presentation, and application layers. The European Telecommunications Standards Institute (ETSI) defined the architecture of NFV and broke it down into three components: NFV infrastructure, virtualized network functions (VNFs), NFV management and orchestration (NFV MANO) (as given in Fig. 4.27). Further, NFV helps operations support systems (OSS) to provide internal network requirements and business support systems (BSS) to deal with end users.

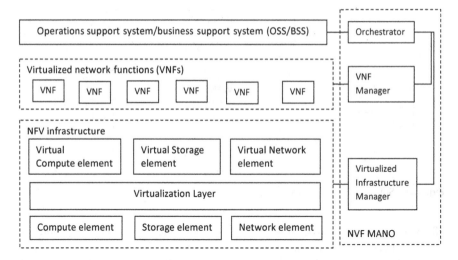

Fig. 4.27   Architecture of NFV

Network Function Virtualization Infrastructure

The NFV infrastructure comprises physical hardware made up of computing servers, storage devices, and network devices that are distributed across different geographical locations. This physical infrastructure is virtualized into a single logical virtual resource with the help of a virtualization layer on which different virtualized network functions are deployed.

Virtualized Network Functions

Different networking functions that back in the day were implemented using specialized hardware—such as routers, firewalls, load balancers, switches, access control mechanisms, network address translation (NAT), content delivery network (CDN), and radio access network (RAN)—are now implemented using software, virtual machines (VMs), and commodity hardware. These VNF elements are deployed on top of the NFV infrastructure.

Network Function Virtualization Management and Orchestration (MANO)

NFV management and orchestration consists of three components: *NFV orchestrator, virtualized infrastructure manager, and VNF manager.* MANO provides orchestration and life cycle management for virtualized software resources and other virtualization-related management tasks.

4.10 Summary

This chapter gave a complete overview of enterprise networking. It started by presenting network design requirements and network design goals. Conventional enterprise networking infrastructure and various enterprise internetworking techniques were outlined. It discussed two network tradition models: the flat networking model and the hierarchical networking model. The chapter also highlighted the inadequacy of the hierarchical model in meeting server-to-server and server-to-storage (east–west traffic) needs that predominate in modern networks. As a consequence the chapter introduced another type of architecture: the two-layered leaf spine architecture. In addition, the chapter emphasized how the arrival of digitization and Agile business trends compelled enterprises to migrate to the cloud where the virtualization technique is extensively applied such as at servers, storage devices, and network devices. The chapter outlined the difficulties encountered in manually configuring both physical and virtual networks and the time involved in so doing is such that the quick provision of resources to clients is practically prohibited. To address this, the chapter introduced SDN, which configures all networking devices programmatically and automatically. It described in detail the strength of SDN and how it hides the internal workings of vendor-specific network details from applications. Ultimately, it describes how SDN extends WAN as SD-WAN which connects different networks at different geographical locations using software controlled configuration.

4.11 Exercises

1. Explain the need for SDN.
2. Compile a list of the limitations of a leaf spine network and explain why we need SDN.
3. Write a short essay on NFV.
4. Write a short essay on SDWAN.
5. Give an account of how enterprise networks evolved from small networks to cloud-enabled enterprise networks (write an assignment).

References

1. Chao L (2016) Cloud computing networking—theory, practice, and development. CRC Press, Taylor & Francis Group
2. Baroncelli F, Martini B, Castoldi P (2010) Network virtualization for cloud computing. Annales des Télécommunications 65:713–721. https://doi.org/10.1007/s12243-010-0194-y
3. Akella A, Benson T, Chandrasekaran B (2015) A universal approach to data center network design. In: Proceedings of the 2015 international conference on distributed computing and networking. ACM

4. Culver T, Black C, Goransson P (2016) Software defined networks, 2nd edn. Morgan Kaufmann Publisher
5. Software Defined Networking (SDN) and its role in automating the provision and scaling of cloud native architectures in the data center through network programmability, Cisco document (2017)

Storage Fundamentals and Cloud Storage

5

Learning Objectives

Data are one of the major and core assets of every organization. Obviously there is a need for the data of any organization to be stored. There are different types of storage devices catering for different characteristics such as capacity, scalability, reliability, performance, and cost. Navigating and selecting a suitable storage device for a given purpose requires a good understanding of the different storage devices available. The objective of this chapter is to describe the various storage devices, how they have progressed from being conventional storage devices to cloud storage devices, and how data and the need for digitization have evolved.

Motivational Questions

1. What kinds of storage devices are there?
2. What protocols are being used to retrieve data?
3. What are file-level, block-level, and object-level data access models?
4. What do the acronyms DAS, NAS, and SAN stand for?
5. Why are there two types of SAN?
6. What is so special about FC SAN?
7. Are storage protocols different from generic TCP/IP traffic?
8. Is there a better way of handling data storage? If so, what is it?
9. Why is cloud storage gaining in popularity?
10. What is *software-defined storage*?

© Springer Nature Switzerland AG 2019
S. Chellammal and C. Pethuru Raj, *Essentials of Cloud Computing*,
Texts in Computer Science, https://doi.org/10.1007/978-3-030-13134-0_5

Preface

The first few chapters should have given the reader an understanding of the origin/purpose of cloud computing, the features or capabilities of cloud computing, different service models, different deployment models, and key technological drivers —especially when it comes to virtualization. The previous chapter discussed different enterprise network models and their concepts. It was shown that small and medium-sized networks adopt flat networking models or hierarchical network models, whereas large networks generally adopt leaf spine network models to cope with huge server–server traffic and storage–server traffic. Along with modern networking models, enterprises adopt cloud networking and software-defined networking to meet high-performance networking requirements and huge internal and external traffic.

This chapter takes a look at the concepts that underlie storage devices, which though secondary to networking represent another major aspect. To get a better understanding the reader is advised to go through the concepts of storage keeping two different aspects in mind: first, advances in hardware technology and the evolution of different storage devices and, second, evolving business requirements, explosive data growth, and digitization of data. Keeping these aspects in mind this chapter looks closely at both conventional storage devices and recent storage devices. Special emphasis is given to the need for cloud storage and software-defined storage (SDS). By the end of this chapter the reader will have a good idea on how to choose from the many storage devices based on such requirements as scalability, capacity, type of access, and performance.

5.1 Taxonomy of Storage

Data storage is high on the list of general requirements of enterprise applications. As technological changes and digitization have evolved, data are ubiquitously being generated almost everywhere at all instants of time. Industry, devices, social networking websites, smartphones, sensors, and the various domains of information technology, such as healthcare, financial, banking, education, weather, and e-governance, all generate data so much so that the current era of computing could be dubbed the era of data. As an asset of enterprises data have to be properly stored and managed for later retrieval, analytical processing, and decision support. Similar to the way in which data have evolved storage devices themselves have undergone revolutionary change resulting in many different types of storage (as shown in Fig. 5.1).

Initially servers were directly connected to storage devices (hard disks) using input/output controllers. Such devices are called *direct attached storage* (DAS) devices. They suffer from the serious drawback that a disk tied up with one server cannot be shared with other servers. Hence a second model of storage called *network-attached storage* (NAS) was developed. In this model the storage device is associated with an intelligent dedicated file-sharing operating system, called the NAS gateway. An important aspect of NAS is that it is assigned a unique IP address. This means this model of storage is network sharable. Typically, NAS

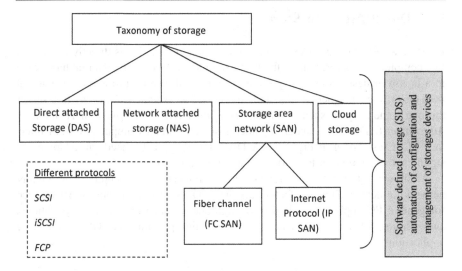

Fig. 5.1 Types of storage devices

consists of an array of storage disks shared by different servers. This model suffers from an important issue: NAS shares the enterprise LAN, which is supposed to carry general LAN traffic, with transport storage traffic. This means that the enterprise LAN is shared for both general application LAN traffic and storage traffic. Hence, under peak load conditions bandwidth-related issues and network congestion will occur. To overcome this a dedicated *storage area network* (SAN) was developed. *SAN is a dedicated storage network that uses a Fiber Channel for communication to provide high-performance data access*, which is one of the common and critical requirements of enterprise and real-time applications. Another way in which SAN has evolved is in exploiting the existence of generic IP networks to provide dedicated data access. So, there is a similarly dedicated native SAN with a Fiber Channel fabric called *Fiber Channel SAN* (FC SAN) in addition to an *Internet Protocol SAN* (IP SAN). Corresponding to the different ways of implementing SAN there are different storage protocols that can be used for data access, such as *internet Small Computer System Interface SCSI* (*iSCSI*) and *Fiber Channel Protocol* (*FCP*).

On the one hand, enterprises can choose between different types of data storage devices according to their requirements such as performance, capacity, type of access, scalability, backup facility, and budget. On the other hand, the explosive growth of huge data from various sources, such as business, social networking, Internet of Things (IoT), smartphones, satellites, and digitization of data, has been the catalyst for industry and enterprises to consider cloud storage. In addition, enterprises are more interested in availing themselves of storage services from cloud service providers as they provide storage as a service with reliable data access, high-performance, and optimized storage operations but at very low cost. The various types of storage devices are detailed one by one in the subsequent sections.

5.2   Direct Attached Storage

Direct attached storage (DAS) is a *digital storage device* that is directly connected to a computer or server. One of the best examples of DAS is the internal hard drive in a laptop or desktop PC. Very often DAS is used to refer to internal or external hard disk drives, magnetic disks, and an array of *disks attached directly* to a server through some adapter, such as a *host bus adapter* (*HBA*) or *Advanced Technology Attachment* (*ATA*), and standard protocols such as Small Computer System Interface SCSI (as shown in Fig. 5.2). A DAS device typically needs an adapter and significant configuration to work with a computer/server.

As shown in Fig. 5.2 the storage device is connected to a computer without any networking device. This is a feature unique to DAS. DAS is an appropriate choice for generic PC applications, high-end, high-performance mainframe applications, and certain other computer-intensive and high-performance OLTP database applications.

5.2.1   Architecture of DAS

Clients in a LAN used by small enterprises typically access DAS through a server. In so doing the three-tier architecture shown in Fig. 5.3 is followed.

Client Tier
Clients using a DAS architecture form a client tier that accesses applications in a server. Clients are typically connected to servers via Ethernet or a LAN network.

Server Tier
The server is another tier that runs applications. The server is connected directly to storage devices using a host bus adapter. As shown in Fig. 5.3 applications running on the server will initiate a data access or retrieval request from a higher level: *file I/O access to the operating system of the server.* The file system of the operating system handles the file I/O access request from the server application. The file system manages the file and directory structure. The file system maps the files into

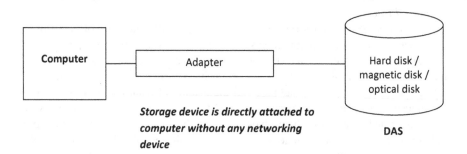

Fig. 5.2 Directly attached device

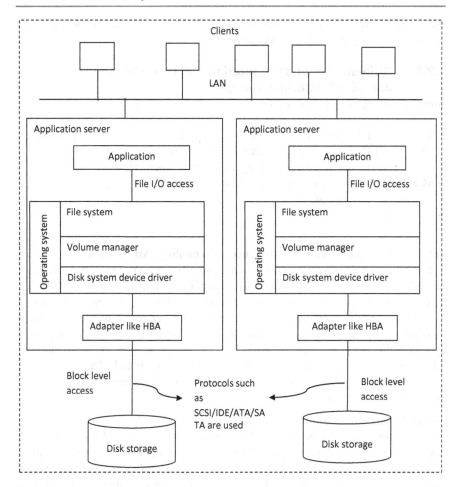

Fig. 5.3 Architecture of DAS

disk blocks in an abstract logical disk space (i.e., the file system converts the file I/O access request to a block-level request). The volume manager maps the block address into a real physical address (volume/cylinder/sector) on the disk. The volume manager sends the data request to the device driver. Thus, the file-level I/O initiated by the client application is mapped on to block-level I/O transfers that occur over such interfaces as SCSI and ATA between the client computer and the disk system.

A device driver connects the operating system and adapter. An HBA is typically used to refer to the Fiber Channel interface card between the computer and storage device. There are different kinds of adapters. For example, an SCSI adapter connects a computer to an SCSI device, whereas ATA host adapters are integrated into the motherboards of PCs. Motherboards are the conventional parallel interface between the computer and the storage device.

5.2.1.1 Different Adapters or Interfaces Between Computer and Direct Attached Storage

Important adapters that connect the computer and the DAS device:

- IDE/ATA: Integrated Device Electronics/Advanced Technology Attachment (also called PATA, Parallel Advanced Technology Attachment)
- SATA: Serial Advanced Technology Attachment interface
- SCSI: Small Computer System Interface
- SA: Serial Attached SCSI
- FC: Fiber Channel.

Integrated Device Electronics/Advanced Technology Attachment
IDE/ATA or PATA was the dominant desktop computer storage interface from the late 1980s until recently, when the SATA interface took over. The term IDE/ATA actually represents a dual-naming convention. The IDE component in IDE/ATA denotes the specification of the controllers that are connected to the computer's motherboard for communicating with the devices attached. The ATA component specifies the interface that is used for connecting storage devices, such as CD-ROMs, disk drives, and tape drives, to the motherboard. The most recent version of IDE/ATA is called Ultra DMA (UDMA) and it supports data transfer rates of up to 133 MB/s.

Serial Advanced Technology Attachment
SATA is the official successor to PATA. There have been two basic versions of SATA: SATA-150 and SATA-300. The numbers 150 and 300 represent the number of megabytes per second that the interfaces can support. One SATA port permits one device to connect to it. As SATA only permits one device to connect to it performance is better. The downside is that it is much more expensive to buy an eight-port SATA controller than an Ultra-320 SCSI controller that allows 15 devices to connect to it.

Small Computer System Interface
SCSI was developed by the American National Standards Institute (ANSI). SCSI connectors/interfaces are mainly used to connect disk drives directly to servers or client devices. SCSI connectors can also be used to establish connections to other peripheral devices such as printers and scanners. The source (server/client device) communicates with attached storage devices using the SCSI command set. The most recent version of SCSI (SCSI ultra 320) provides data transfer speeds of 320 MB/s and can handle up to 15 hard drives:

- *Serial-attached SCSI (SAS)*: SAS is the latest storage interface. It combines elements of both SCSI and SATA interfaces since it still uses SCSI commands while remaining pin compatible with SATA (i.e., SAS hard drives, SATA hard drives, or CD/DVD ROM can all be connected using the SAS interface). SAS can support a data rate of at most 1,200 MB/s. It is designed for the high-end server and storage market, whereas SATA is mainly intended for personal computers. Unlike SATA, SAS can be connected to multiple hard drives through expanders, but the protocol used to share an SAS port has lower overhead than SCSI. Coupled with the fact that the ports are faster to begin with, SAS offers the best of SCSI and SATA in addition to superior performance.

- *Fiber Channel* (*FC*): FC is a direct connect storage interface used on hard drives and storage area network (SAN) technology. It offers speeds of up to 400 MB/s. Native FC interface hard drives are found in very high–end storage arrays used in SAN.

5.2.1.2 Popular Direct Attached Storage Devices

Disk Drives

Disk drives are block-type storage devices. Each disk is divided into logical blocks (collection of sectors). Blocks are addressed using their logical block addresses (LBAs). Reading from the disk or writing to the disk is done using an LBA. LBA is a common logical scheme that simply specifies a number to fetch a block of data from storage. LBA is a simple linear addressing scheme. Internally, the disk controller converts the logical address into a physical address that gives the physical *cylinder–head–sector* (*CHS*) address of the data. Basically, a disk is composed of two surfaces called platters. Each platter is composed of concentric circles called tracks. The track number starts at zero at the outer side of the platter and then increases by one the nearer it gets to the inner side. Each track is further broken down into smaller units called sectors. A sector is the basic unit of data storage on a hard disk. A single track typically can have thousands of sectors and each sector can hold more than 512 bytes of data. Each track can hold a large amount of data reaching thousands of bytes. The cylinder value is the number of tracks on one side of each platter. There are the same number of cylinders on each side of a platter. The sector value is the number of sectors in each track.

When an LBA is given to the *volume manager*, it identifies the physical address and positions the correct sector of the required track of the disk under the head for read/write.

Disk drives allow random access operations on data stored in them and support access by multiple users/applications simultaneously. Disk drives also have more storage capacity:

- *Redundant Array of Independent Disks* (*RAID*): The basic objective of RAID is to combine multiple, small, inexpensive disk drives into an array to achieve

RAID storage with striping

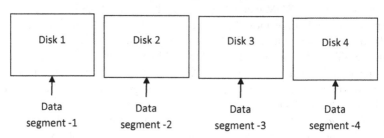

Fig. 5.4 Striping

performance or fault tolerance that is not attainable with one large, expensive drive. This array of drives appears to the computer as a single logical storage unit or drive. The underlying objective of RAID is achieved using two techniques: striping and mirroring.

- *Striping*: Striping refers to the task of splitting the data to be written across multiple disk drives to improve the performance of disk drives by balancing the load across them equally. Consider a RAID with four disk drives in which the given data are split into four segments. The striping technique allows the RAID controller to store different segments of data in different disks (as shown in Fig. 5.4). Since all the disks are simultaneously accessed striping results in high performance. However, it does not allow for redundancy. There is only one copy of data that is partitioned into segments.

- *Mirroring*: Mirroring refers to the task of storing more copies of data in multiple disks to ensure that even if one disk fails data in the other disk can serve as a backup copy. The primary advantage of disk mirroring is that it provides 100% data redundancy. Because the contents of the disk are completely written to a second disk, data are not lost if one disk fails. In addition, both drives contain the same data at all times, so either disk can act as the operational disk. If one disk fails, the contents of the other disk can be used to run the system and reconstruct the failed disk. For example, consider that the given data consist of four segments. They are mirrored in two RAID disks (as shown in Fig. 5.5).

Fig. 5.5 Mirroring

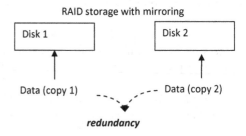

Advantages of direct attached storage

- DAS results in high performance and is the correct choice when there is no need to share data.
- Storage resources are dedicated to a particular server.
- DAS architecture is simple to configure.
- It is cheap to establish.

Disadvantages of direct attached storage

- Storage is decentralized (i.e., each server has its own dedicated data resource). Since servers are directly connected to data sources sharing of data among servers cannot be achieved with DAS architecture (i.e., without networking). This is one of the major limitations of DAS.
- Storage is not consolidated and hence is not effectively utilized.
- Availability and performance are low.

5.3 Network Attached Storage

5.3.1 Architecture of Network Attached Storage

NAS involves a dedicated shareable file server with a network address (IP address) that allows storing, retrieving, and accessing files for applications or clients in a network. *NAS is simply a node (like other computers in a network) that has its own IP address.* The architecture of NAS is given in Fig. 5.6.

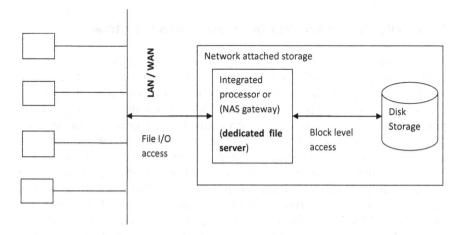

Fig. 5.6 Architecture of network-attached storage

As soon as an NAS device is connected to the network all other computers on the network can very easily access it. It allows multiple users to access data. NAS is accessed over an IP network and offers simple but high-level file I/O access for sharing files. Hence it is a preferred file-sharing option. Moreover, it has minimum storage overhead. NAS helps to offload the task of file sharing from expensive application servers that can then be used to perform other critical operations.

NAS consists of two components: *an integrated and dedicated file-serving processor called the NAS gateway* and *disk storage.*

Network Attached Storage Gateway

The NAS gateway is a *dedicated file server* whose core parts are:

- NAS CPU with memory;
- dedicated file-sharing operating system;
- network interface cards (NICs);
- hardware and software infrastructure to support various file-sharing protocols; and
- various I/O controllers, such as SCSI, IDE, and ATA, to manage disk storage.

The NAS gateway is not a general-purpose server. The operating system facilitates file sharing by providing high-level file I/O access. This means that client requests for data or information are in the form of files. A client application simply specifies which file is to be accessed or stored. It is the responsibility of the gateway to maintain the blocks of disks in which the requested file is stored. Using the block information it prepares the block address for file I/O access and facilitates block-level I/O access to the disk. Similarly, when data are retrieved from the disk they are returned to client applications in file I/O format.

5.3.2 File-Sharing Concept in Network Attached Storage

A file system is a structured way of storing and organizing data in the form of files. A file system is associated with a file access table that is used to find the block in which the file is located and access the file. File sharing is the concept of sharing files over a network. Typically, the person who creates the file sets up access privileges for users. Various levels of access with different privileges can be set up for a file. They are read permission, write permission, and execute permission. In addition, file sharing should ensure the integrity of the contents of a file in case it is used by more than one user at a time. There are different file-sharing protocols, such as File Transfer Protocol (FTP) and Distributed File System (DFS), as well as traditional remote client–server file-sharing protocols. FTP is a client–server protocol that enables transfer from an FTP server and FTP client over the TCP/IP network. DFS is a file system that is distributed across several hosts. The two most popular models of remote file sharing use a client–server model over the TCP/IP

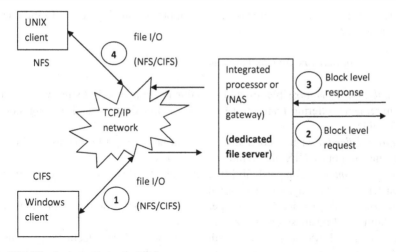

Fig. 5.7 File-sharing concept in NAS

network: the Network File System (NFS) for the Unix OS and the Common Internet File System (CIFS) for the Windows OS. Hence a Unix client accesses data in NAS using the NFS protocol and a Windows client accesses data in NAS using the CIFS protocol (as shown in Fig. 5.7).

These protocols are high-level file I/O access protocols. Clients will mount these file systems into their machines before they access files in NAS devices. These protocols are very simple to use. A user can simply store, browse, retrieve, and access files in a remote NAS device as though they were stored locally.

There are two ways of looking at file sharing in NAS: a high-level view and an internal view.

High-Level View of File Sharing

1. Clients mount the remote file system into their machines (a Windows client has to mount CIFS and a Unix client mounts NFS).
2. Clients can view files, create files, retrieve files, change files, etc.

Internal View of File Sharing

Internally, when clients make a request to retrieve a file they use an NFS or CIFS request.

1. Clients submit a high-level file I/O request to the NAS gateway.
2. The NAS gateway converts the high-level file I/O request into a block-level request with details of the actual blocks where the file is stored, can be written to, or retrieved from the disk.
3. The disk produces a block-level I/O response.
4. The NAS gateway again converts the block-level I/O response into a file-level I/O response and returns it to the client. It is the NAS gateway that performs all

the internal operations and allows very simple file-sharing access to the clients in a network.

Advantages of network attached storage

- *Scalability*: It is possible to add additional storage non-disruptively as per requirements, offering many cost benefits for organizations and helping storage consolidation.
- *Improved flexibility*: It is compatible and can be accessed by clients and servers running on both UNIX and Windows platforms.
- *high performance*: Using 10-Gb Ethernet media for data transfer offers high data transfer rates and improved performance.
- *Low cost*: NAS devices are cheaper and hence more suitable for small and medium-sized business organizations.
- *Redundancy*: NAS devices offer redundancy when RAID technology is used. Hence, clients can use multiple hard drives to back up their data, enhancing reliability.
- *Supports collaboration*: NAS allows multiple users to access data simultaneously, facilitating collaboration in project development.

Disadvantages of network attached storage

- NAS devices make use of the TCP/IP network for file sharing, which means a considerable amount of the bandwidth available will be utilized by NAS devices.
- NAS cannot offer any storage service guarantee for mission-critical operations.
- NAS is less efficient since data transfer is on top of the TCP/IP.

5.4 Storage Area Network

5.4.1 Why Do We Need Storage Area Networks?

Generally, most applications nowadays demand

- larger storage capacity;
- fast and efficient storage access;
- high availability of data; and
- scalable storage according to the dynamic storage requirements of applications.

Although network attached storage facilitates file sharing in a network, it is still unable to fulfill the growing needs for data storage requirements of large enterprise applications or the high-speed data transfer requirements of applications. This is because the storage needs of modern applications are typically scalable in nature. The Storage Area Network provides a scalable and high-performance storage facility that is typically tied into the network through a standard Ethernet connection. That is, it mixes server–storage communication with other application-related TCP/IP traffic. Hence the network is shared between storage traffic and other application traffic. This reduces the speed and effectiveness of data access. Moreover, NAS supports file-level access allowing conversion from file I/O access to block-level access and vice versa while reading and writing data. *SANs were invented to resolve issues surrounding performance and sharable data storage. SANs are high-speed, dedicated networks that connect the networks of servers to a large pool of storage devices via a Fiber Channel fabric. What sets SANs apart is that they segregate storage traffic from LAN traffic by using a dedicated Fiber Channel fabric, thus providing high application availability and performance.* SANs facilitate the pooling of storage among data centers. They detach isolated storage arrays from application servers and reduce the capacities required. The result is easier centralization of storage management, which is responsible for redistributing storage resources to other servers. Because SANs simplify the addition of storage they contribute to the virtualization of data centers.

5.4.2   Concept of a Storage Area Network

As mentioned earlier a storage area network is a high-speed dedicated network that connects servers typically linked in an enterprise LAN to a pool of storage devices through a Fiber Channel fabric (as shown in Fig. 5.8).

Typically, a LAN connects clients to servers and a SAN connects servers to storage devices. Application servers access storage devices through a dedicated SAN network. A SAN network is established with a Fiber Channel fabric. The two main transmission protocols used by most SANs are (i) Fiber Channel (FC) protocol and (ii) Transmission Control Protocol/Internet Protocol (TCP/IP). SANs are further broken down into FC SANs and IP SANs based on the protocol and the type of network used by them (as shown in Fig. 5.9).

5.5   Fiber Channel Storage Area Networks

5.5.1   Architecture of Fiber Channel Storage Area Networks

The architecture of FC SANs is shown in Fig. 5.10. It consists of three layers: (i) host layer, (ii) fabric layer, and (iii) storage layer.

Host Layer
Servers that provide support for SAN storage have adapters that allow them to connect to a SAN network. These adapters are called host bus adapters (HBAs). They are pieces of hardware that connect to the motherboard of the server via a slot on the motherboard. A server can communicate with a SAN fabric layer using an

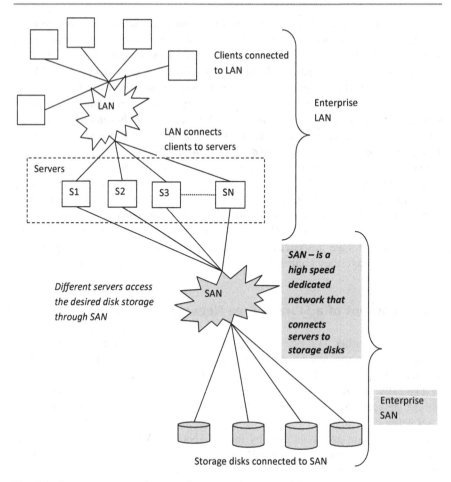

Fig. 5.8 Storage area network connecting servers to storage disks

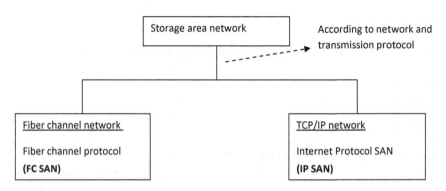

Fig. 5.9 Types of SAN

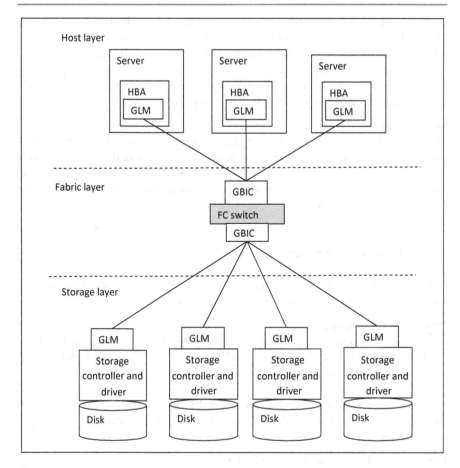

Fig. 5.10 Architecture of FC SAN

HBA. When a server wants to send data to SAN storage, it communicates with the HBA through its driver. The HBA moves the data to a gigabit link module (GLM), which converts digital bits into corresponding optical pulses.

Fabric Layer (Fiber Channel)
A fabric layer consists of different networking elements, such as hubs, switches, and bridges, for moving data between senders and receivers. SANs use the Fiber Channel architecture and the Fiber Channel Protocol (FCP) to transfer data in a server–storage system or from one storage system to another. The main reason for using a fiber optic channel is to make data communication highly reliable, as there is no loss in fiber optic communication. The Fiber Channel architecture offers fast and effective data access, which is essential for real-time applications.

A Fiber Channel (FC) cable connects the HBA of the host to FC switches. These FC switches make use of a Gigabit Interface Converter (GBIC), which converts optical pulses into corresponding digital pulses and vice versa. Nodes communicate via different FC topologies. The concepts underlying FC topologies, different types of ports in FC architecture, and Fiber Channel Protocol (FCP) stack and services are described in detail in the subsequent section.

Storage Layer

The storage layer consists of one or more storage systems with their input/output controller, drivers, and supporting ports. Storage devices are of different types such as disks, tapes, and RAID arrays. Every storage device is associated with a unique Logical Unit Number (LUN). A node that wants to access a storage device should do so by accessing this LUN.

5.5.2 Fiber Channel Topologies

Nodes communicate via different topologies: FC point to point, FC arbitrated loop (FC-AL), and FC switched fabric (FC-SW) (as shown in Fig. 5.11).

Point-to-Point Topology

In point-to-point topology (as shown in Fig. 5.12) two nodes are connected through the Fiber Channel. One is the server with an HBA and the other is the storage system. This is primarily used in DAS.

Point-to-point topology provides a dedicated Fiber Channel between the server and storage device. A maximum of two devices can be connected and hence scalability is very low.

Fiber Channel Arbitrated Loop Topology

FC-AL topology is formed by *connecting hosts to a Fiber Channel hub* (as shown in Fig. 5.13).

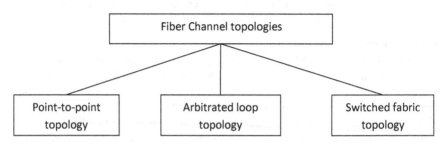

Fig. 5.11 Fiber channel topologies

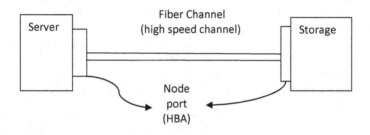

Fig. 5.12 Fiber channel in point-to-point topology

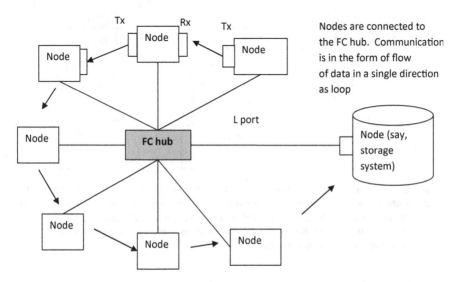

Fig. 5.13 Fiber channel arbitrated loop

Drawbacks of Fiber Channel Arbitrated Loop

Although an FC hub is capable of connecting 126 devices as a result of all devices sharing the same loop, performance is poor. Further, in this topology the bandwidth available is shared by all devices. Hence when a new device is added the bandwidth available to a node at that time is reduced. The maximum speed supported by an FC hub is 100 MB/s. This topology has been little used since 2010.

Fiber Channel Switched Fabric

FC-SW topology is the most resourceful and flexible topology. It provides multiple simultaneous data flows (as shown in Fig. 5.14). FC-SW topology uses FC switches, which are more intelligent than hubs. In this topology every node is connected to every other node. These switches do not time-share the available channel, instead they provide servers with individual channels as storage devices.

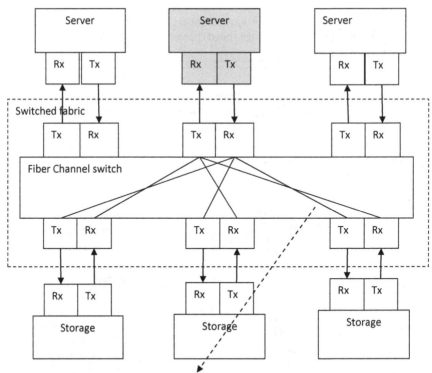

The way in which the Rx of a node is connected to the Tx of every other node and how the way in which the Tx of a node is connected to the Rx of every other node is shown for one node (shaded in gray). In this way a link is provided for every possible path determined by the switch. Hence the switch provides multiple data communication over individual links simultaneously.

Fig. 5.14 Fiber channel switched fabric topology

Consider the shaded server node in Fig. 5.14. The Rx of this server node is here connected to the Tx of every storage disk. Moreover, the Tx of this server node is connected to the Rx of every storage disk. Since every node is connected to every other node, they can all communicate with each other at any time. Switches permit simultaneous data flow among servers and storages. This significantly enhances the performance of data communication.

5.5.3 Fiber Channel Port Types

Basically, a port is a hardware pathway or connection that has two links: one for transmission and the other for reception. The different topologies of FC technology require different kinds of ports with specific functional characteristics:

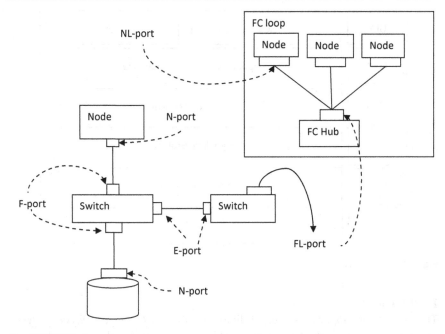

Fig. 5.15 Different port types

- *Node port (N-port)*: The N-port is used to connect a node (host or storage) to another node or fabric switch.
- *Fabric port or switch port (F-port)*: The F-port is a switch port that is connected to a node.
- *Node loop port (NL-port)*: The NL-port is a node port with the capability of loop functions and connected to a loop.
- *Fabric loop port (FL-port)*: The FL-port is a switch port with the capability of loop functions and connected to a loop.
- *Expansion port (E-port)*: The E-port is a switch port that connects to another switch.

These ports are shown in Fig. 5.15, which is a simple schematic that should aid understanding.

5.5.4   Fiber Channel Storage Area Network Protocol

A storage area network uses the *Fiber Channel Protocol* (*FCP*). The FCP consists of five layers: FC-0, FC-1, FC-2, FC-3, and FC-4 (as shown in Fig. 5.16).

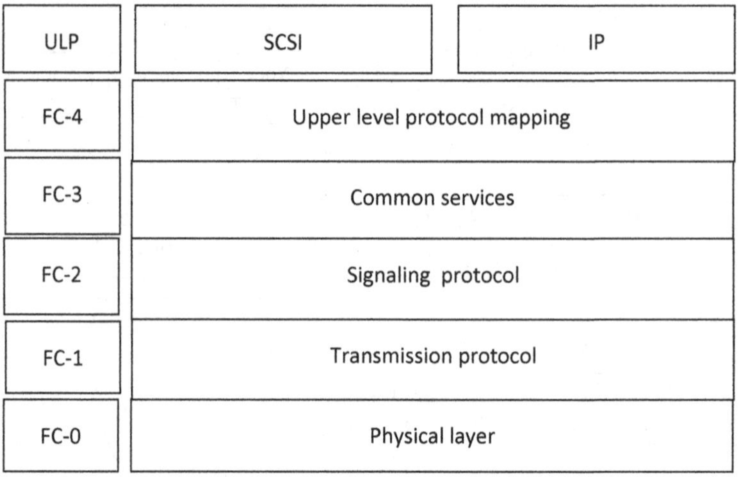

ULP
SCSI
IP
FC-4
Upper level protocol mapping
FC-3
Common services
FC-2
Signaling protocol
FC-1
Transmission protocol
FC-0
Physical layer

Fig. 5.16 FCP layers

FC-0 Layer

The FC-1 layer supplies a stream of digital bits to the *FC-0 layer* (*physical layer*). These bits are transmitted via copper cable or fiber-optic cable according to the distance and data rate involved. In FC optical communications the transmitter is a laser LED that emits laser light to represent a 1 (digital pulse) and no light to represent a 0 (digital pulse). Similarly, the receiver is a photosensitive diode that produces digital 1 s and 0 s according to the light it receives. FC-0 corresponds to transmitters, receivers, and the medium used to transmit the data (as shown in Fig. 5.17).

Digital bits
Transmitter
(laser LED)
Digital bits
Receiver (photodiode)
FC-1
FC-0
Fiber optic cable

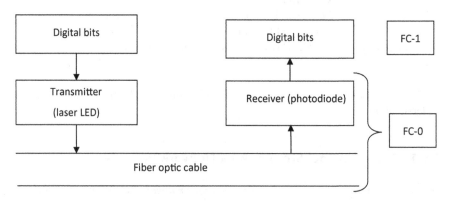

Fig. 5.17 FC-0 layer (physical layer)

FC-1 Layer
The FC-1 layer receives data from the FC-2 layer. The data received from FC-2 is in 4-byte format (i.e., 32 bits). FC-1 converts the data into a format that is compatible with FC-0 for transmission. As a standard, 4-byte information is encoded using *8B/10B encoding*. This encoding converts 32-bit transmission words into 40-bit format. The bits are serialized and sent to FC-0.

FC-2 Layer
The signaling protocol defined at this layer specifies the rules involved in transferring data blocks end to end. It defines *the frame format, various classes of services, flow control, sequences, exchanges, and error detection*. The FC-2 layer defines the structure of the FC frame (as shown in Fig. 5.18).

FC-2 sends the *Start of Frame (SoF) ordered set* to the FC-2 layer. It then sends frame header and the payload as a 4-byte data word. After sending the payload it finishes the transmission by sending a *Cyclic Redundancy Check* (CRC) and the *End of Frame (EoF) ordered set*. CRC is used for error detection. An *SoF ordered set* interprets all following data as the payload until it receives an *EoF ordered set* (*note that different classes of services, flow control, and sequences and exchanges are all provided by the FC-2 layer—for clarity, subsection numbers are given*).

5.5.4.1 Different Classes of Services
The FCP offers different kinds of services according to different topologies. A node can opt for a particular service. *The FCP defines six service classes.* They are *Class 1, Class 2, Class 3, Class 4, Class 6*, and *Class F*. Classes 1, 2, and 3 are generally used by all topologies, whereas the other service classes are rarely used.

Class 1 Service (Connection-Oriented, Dedicated Service)
In this service class the FC provides a *dedicated connection* (*circuit*) between the sender and receiver. It allocates full bandwidth for this circuit. It establishes a circuit that can only get removed if the sender or receiver requests its removal. The data

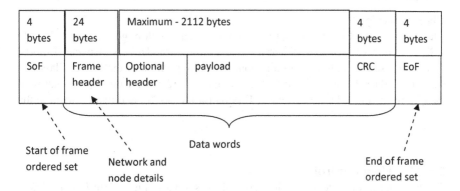

Fig. 5.18 FC-2 frame format

sent are acknowledged by the receiver. In addition, the sender and receiver cannot engage in any type of communication until the current circuit between them is active.

Class 2 Service (Connectionless, Acknowledged Service)
In this class the FC provides a connectionless service. Data are transferred without establishing a circuit between ports. There is no dedicated connection, as a result of which there is no dedicated connection and multiple ports can transmit and receive data frames simultaneously. Node ports share the available bandwidth. Even though a circuit is not established between the sender and receiver the reception of data is still acknowledged by the receiver.

Class 3 Service (Connectionless, Unacknowledged Service/Datagram)
In this model no acknowledgement is sent by the receiver. Hence there is no guarantee that the data are received by the receiver. This class is also called as *datagram connectionless service*. Although it optimizes the use of fabric resources it is up to the upper-layer protocol to ensure that all frames are received in the correct order. This class is well suited for SCSI and is a commonly used service class in FC networks.

Class 4 Service (Connection-Oriented, Virtual Circuit-Based, and Multiplexed Service)
In this class the FC offers multiple, connection-oriented "virtual circuits." Each of these circuits is set up individually, possibly with different destination nodes, and reserves a fraction of the available bandwidth of the link.

Class 6 Service (Multicast Service)
If an N-port request s a *Class 6* service for one or more destinations, a multicast server (FFFFF5) in the fabric establishes *connections* from the source N-port to all destination N-ports, receives an acknowledgment from all the destination ports, and sends it back to the originator. When a connection is established, it is retained and guaranteed by the fabric until the initiator ends the connection. *Class 6* was designed for applications, such as audio and video, that require multicast functionality.

Class F Service
Class F is used for *switch-to-switch* communication through *inter-switch links* (ISLs). It is a connectionless service that notifies non-delivery between E-ports, which are used for control, coordination, and configuration of the fabric. Class F is similar to Class 2. The main difference is that Class 2 deals with N-ports that send data frames, while Class F is used by E-ports for the control and management of the fabric.

5.5.4.2 Flow Control
The FCP defines two levels of flow control (as shown in Fig. 5.19): *link-level flow control* and *end-to-end flow control*.

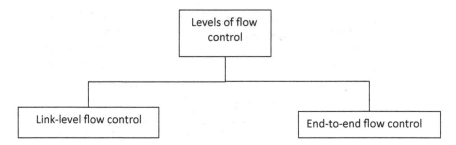

Fig. 5.19 Different levels of flow control in FC

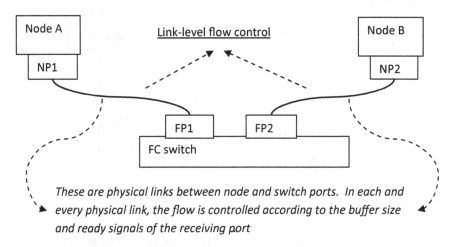

Fig. 5.20 Link-level flow control

Link-Level Flow Control
Link-level flow control deals only with the link between an N-port and an F-port or between two N-ports. Consider the data transfer between two nodes in Fig. 5.20.

Node A transfers frames to Node B. Node ports are prefixed with "NP" and fabric ports are prefixed with "FP." Consider that data are traveling through the physical links *NP1–FP1* and *FP2–NP2*. When data are transferred from *NP1–FP1*, flow control is ensured by the *buffer-to-buffer credit method*. Both ports exchange information on how many frames each port is happy to receive at a time from the other port (i.e., the number of frames set by the receiver will become the *buffer-to-buffer credit value for the sender and* vice versa). The credit values remain fixed until communication ends.

End-to-End Flow Control
End-to-end flow control is another level of flow control (as shown in Fig. 5.21) where the flow of frames is controlled by *end devices* (not at physical-link level).

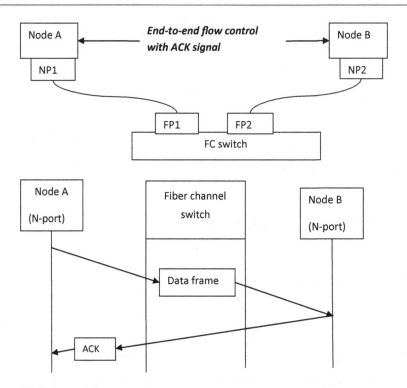

Fig. 5.21 End-to-end flow control

End devices use *end-to-end credit* and an *ACK* signal to control the flow. Prior to transmission, end devices set their *end-to-end credit* based on the receiver capability. The receiver sends an *ACK* to the sender with which the sender tracks *end-to-end credit*.

5.5.4.3 Sequences and Exchanges

A sequence is a set of one or more related frames. For example, transfer of a large file would be accomplished in a sequence consisting of multiple frames. Frames within the same sequence have the same *SEQ_ID* field in the header. The *SEQ_CNT* field shows how frames are ordered within a sequence. A sequence also defines the error recovery boundary. If an error occurs in a transmitted frame, the sequence to which that frame belongs will be retransmitted. An exchange contains one or more sequences. It is comparable to a SCSI I/O process and is the mechanism used to coordinate the exchange of information between two nodes.

FC-3 Layer

The FC-3 layer is not currently used, but has been made available to provide common services to implement advanced features such as striping, hunt groups, and multi-cast in future applications.

FC-4 Layer

The FC-4 layer defines the high-level application interfaces that can communicate over the FC. It specifies the mapping rules of upper-layer protocols (ULPs), such as *Small Computer System Interface* (*SCSI*), *Intelligent Peripheral Interface* (*IPI*), *High Performance Parallel Interface* (*HIPPI*), *Internet Protocol* (*IP*), and *Single Byte Command Code Set Mapping* (*SBCCS*), used at lower levels of the FC. Each ULP supported by an FC requires a specific mapping, which is available in an FC-4 document. For example, the Fiber Channel protocol for SCSI is known as FCP. It defines the FC mapping necessary to use the lower levels of FC to transmit SCSI command and data between a SCSI initiator and a SCSI target.

5.5.5   How the Fiber Channel Storage Area Network Works: An Overview

Consider a typical scenario in which an SAN network consists of one or more servers connected to an array of storage systems through a dedicated, high-speed network (as shown in Fig. 5.22):

- Consider a host that wants to access a storage device (say, Storage A in Fig. 5.22) on the SAN. It sends a SCSI request to gain access to the storage device. The SCSI commands are encapsulated into FC packets. The request is accepted by the HBA of the host. The data are converted from high-level information units into a sequence of frames compatible with the FC.
- The GLM of the HBA converts data from its current format to an optical format. Optical pulses are transmitted through a fiber-optic cable (FC) and reach the fabric switch.
- It is in this switch that data are converted from optical to digital format.
- The switch retrieves the frame header, finds the destination, and places the data in the relevant output port.
- Once again the data are converted to optical format, travel through the optical FC, and reach the destination.
- At the destination the data are once again converted from optical to digital format (a task carried out by the inbuilt GLM of the storage controller).

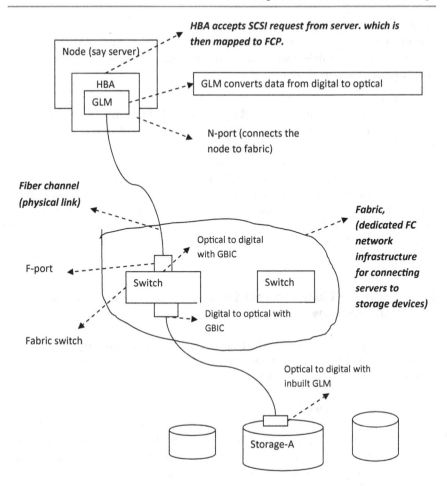

Fig. 5.22 Overview of how FC SAN works

5.5.6 Data Access Methods in a Storage Area Network

Disk storage devices are used to store data in the form in blocks of fixed size. Blocks are identified using an identifier that can be used to store and retrieve them. To store and retrieve data in the form of blocks from high-level applications it is essential to have a file system. In general, the application requests data from the file system (or operating system) by specifying the filename and location. The file system must be applied on top of the block-level storage device to map "files" onto a sequence of blocks. The file system consists of two components: user component and storage component. The user component of the file system performs such functions as naming a file, setting the hierarchy, and setting access control. The storage component maps files to a physical location on the storage device. The file system maps the file attributes to the logical block address (LBA) of the data and sends the request to the storage device. The storage device converts the LBA to a cylinder–head–sector (CHS) address and fetches the data.

There are three standard data access methods that can be performed in FC SAN:

- file-level access;
- block-level access; and
- object-level access.

File-Level Access

In file-level access the file system is created on a separate file server at the storage device end and the file-level request is sent over a network (as shown in Fig. 5.23).

Because data are accessed at the file level this method has a higher overhead than data accessed at the block level. File-based storage is usually accessed via a standard protocol like NFS or SMB/CIFS. Fixed file attributes, such as type, size, date created, and date modified, are stored in the file system. File-based storage is good for sharing files and sharing directories over a LAN or WAN.

Block-Level Access

In block-level access (as shown in Fig. 5.24) the file system is created on a client compute system, and data are accessed on a network at the block level. In this case raw disks or logical volumes are assigned to the compute system, which the client compute system can format to create its own file system. Access to block storage is

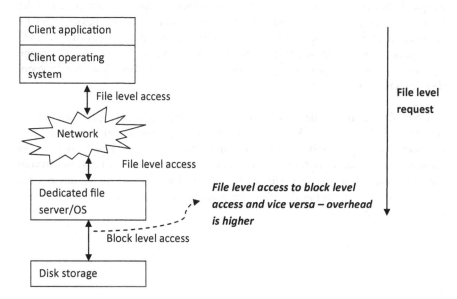

Fig. 5.23 File system access

Fig. 5.24 Block-level access

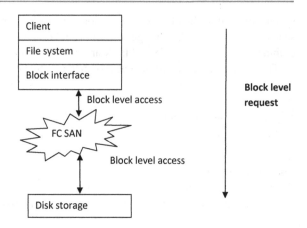

usually through a client on the operating system over the FC. Block storage is ideal for databases or VMs. The block-level access mechanism is the typical data access mechanism used in SAN. Data access in this mechanism is done in terms of blocks of fixed size. The typical block size in most scenarios is 512 bytes.

Object-Level Access

In object-level access (as shown in Fig. 5.25) data are accessed in terms of variable-sized chunks called objects. Each object gets a unique identifier called an object identifier (OID), which is calculated from the file content and the metadata. Applications access the object using this OID. The OID is generated with the help of a 128-bit random number generator, which helps to ensure that the OID is unique. Other details about the object, such as location and size, are stored in the form of metadata. Data that are stored in object-based storage devices can be accessed using web service APIs such as Representational State Transfer (REST) and Simple Object Access Protocol (SOAP). Some types of object-based storage devices also offer support for protocols such as Hyper Text Transfer Protocol (HTTP) and XML.

Object-based storage devices incur much less overhead when performing concurrent read/writes, file locks, and permissions. This significantly improves performance and gives massive scaling capabilities to object-based storage devices. In addition, the amount of rich metadata associated with each object helps in carrying out analytical operations very efficiently. Hence object-based storage devices are ideal candidates for storing data that are generated/used by high-performance big data applications.

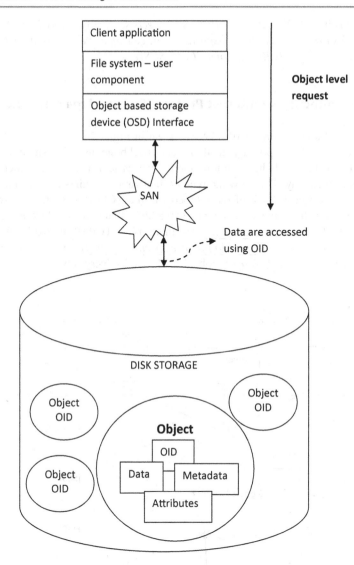

Fig. 5.25 Object-level data access

5.6   Internet Protocol Storage Area Network

FC SAN provides high performance and high scalability. However, these advantages of FC SAN bring with them the burden of the additional cost of buying FC components such as HBA, FC switches, and establishing the FC fabric. There is another type of SAN called IP SAN that has the aim of transporting storage traffic over the existing TCP/IP network. *IP SAN connects servers typically in a LAN to a pool of disk storage devices by transporting storage traffic over the existing TCP/IP network using protocols like internet SCSI (iSCSI).*

5.6.1 Architecture of Internet Protocol Storage Area Network

The high-level architecture of IP SAN is shown in Fig. 5.26.

The internet is the primary medium and backbone used to share massive amounts of all kinds of digital information, such as text, audio, and video, in a highly distributed way. The growing trend of digitization requires a huge amount of network storage space. Each of the protocols in the TCP/IP network are used for communication. The primary advantage of IP SAN is that networked storage can be made *available at any place wherever* there is a TCP/IP network. Another advantage is that there is *no need to procure special hardware* since the network is already existing. Hence the *cost* involved in IP SAN is very low.

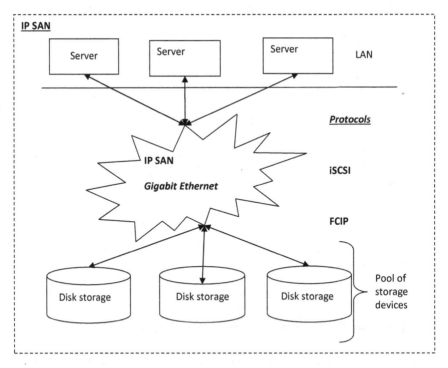

Fig. 5.26 Architecture of IP SAN

5.6.2   Storage Protocols for Internet Protocol Storage Area Network

5.6.2.1   Internet Small Computer System Interface (ISCSI)

Small Computer System Interface (SCSI) is one of the standard interfaces and command sets used to transfer data between computers and disk storage, whereas *internet SCSI* (iSCSI) uses the same SCSI command set to communicate between computing devices and storage devices via a TCP/IP network. iSCSI is a storage networking protocol stack that allows storage resources to be shared over an IP network. iSCSI is a mapping of the SCSI protocol over TCP/IP. The layered architecture of the iSCSI protocol is as shown in Fig. 5.27.

iSCSI is the most common protocol used in IP SAN. Using SCSI initiates an SCSI request that is mapped onto the internet by the iSCSI layer. At the physical layer, iSCSI supports a Gigabit Ethernet interface that enables systems supporting iSCSI interfaces to be directly connected to *standard Gigabit Ethernet switches and IP routers* (as shown in Fig. 5.27). The iSCSI protocol sits above the physical and data link layers and interfaces to the operating system's standard SCSI access method command set. IP SAN uses TCP as a transport mechanism for storage over Ethernet and iSCSI encapsulates SCSI commands into TCP packets (as shown in Fig. 5.28), thus enabling the transport of I/O block data over IP networks.

iSCSI can be supported over all physical media that support TCP/IP as a transport, but today's iSCSI implementations are on Gigabit Ethernet. The iSCSI protocol runs on the host initiator and on the receiving target device. iSCSI can run

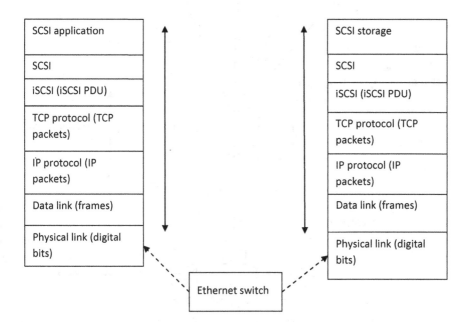

Fig. 5.27 iSCSI over the TCP/IP storage network

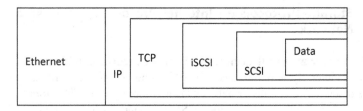

Fig. 5.28 Encapsulation of SCSI commands into TCP/IP

in software over a standard Gigabit Ethernet network interface card (NIC) or can be optimized in hardware on an iSCSI host bus adapter (HBA) for better performance. A typical deployment of IP SAN using iSCSI is shown in Fig. 5.29.

As Fig. 5.29 shows, there are *three key components for iSCSI communication* in IP SAN:

1. *iSCSI initiators (like an iSCSI HBA).*
2. *iSCSI targets (such as a storage system with an iSCSI port).*
3. *An IP-based network (such as a Gigabit Ethernet LAN).*

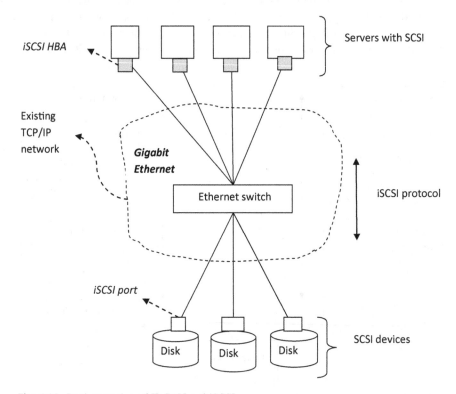

Fig. 5.29 Implementation of IP SAN and iSCSI

An iSCSI initiator sends commands and associated data to a target and the target returns data and responses to the initiator. IP SAN using iSCSI is composed of initiators and targets connected by an IP network in which the server acts as the initiator or iSCSI host and the iSCSI storage device acts as the target. iSCSI storage devices and iSCSI servers are connected using one of the following *four types of iSCSI interface*:

(i)   a standard NIC with a software iSCSI adapter;
(ii) a TCP offload engine (TOE) NIC with a software iSCSI adapter;
(iii) an iSCSI HBA; and
(iv) a converged network adapter (CNA).

- *Standard NIC using a software iSCSI adapter*: A software iSCSI adapter is an operating system (OS) or hypervisor kernel-resident software that uses an existing NIC of the compute system to emulate an iSCSI initiator. It is less expensive and easier to implement than most compute systems since it comes with at least one, and in many cases two, embedded NICs.
- *TOE NIC using a software iSCSI adapter*: A TOE NIC offloads TCP/IP processing from the CPU of a host and leaves just iSCSI functionality. The host passes the iSCSI information to the TOE NIC and then the TOE NIC sends the information to the destination using TCP/IP. Although this solution improves performance, iSCSI functionality is still handled by a software adapter that requires CPU cycles of the compute system.
- *iSCSI HBA*: An iSCSI HBA is a hardware adapter with built-in iSCSI functionality. It is capable of providing performance benefits over software iSCSI adapters by offloading all iSCSI and TCP/IP processing from the CPU of a compute system. This offloads all TCP and iSCSI processing from the host CPU to the processor on the host bus adapter (HBA). They also have optional ROM, which allows disk-less servers to be booted from an iSCSI SAN.
- *Converged network adapter*: A CNA offers everything an iSCSI HBA offers, such as reduced pressure on host CPU and booting options, but has the added versatility of being dynamically configurable for protocols other than iSCSI.

5.6.2.2   Fiber Channel Over TCP/IP (FCIP) Protocol

Fiber Channel over TCP/IP (FCIP) is used to interconnect different FC SANs over the TCP/IP network (as shown in Fig. 5.30). There are some situations when the **interconnection of FC SANs** may be required. In such situations, *instead if establishing dedicated FC fabric networking which is expensive, the existing TCP/IP network between the relevant FC SAN may be used with FCIP.*

While internetworking is used by FC SAN over the TCP/IP network, FCIP is adopted for communication.

The FCIP protocol stack is shown in Fig. 5.31. As shown in the figure, applications generate SCSI commands and data that are carried out as a *payload in the lower FCP layer.* **The FCIP layer encapsulates the FC frames as a payload for IP**

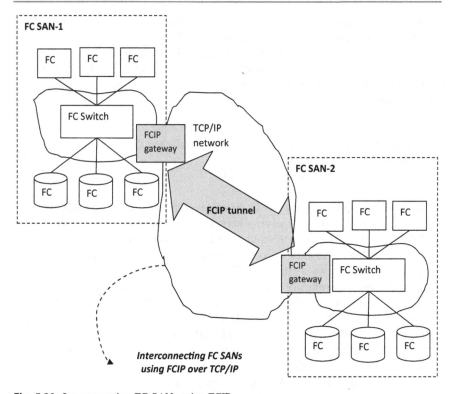

Fig. 5.30 Interconnecting FC SANs using FCIP

and passes them to the TCP layer for transportation. TCP and IP are used for transporting the encapsulated information across Ethernet, wireless, or other media that support the TCP/IP traffic.

The encapsulation of FC frames into IP packets is shown in Fig. 5.32.

The encapsulation of FC frames into an IP packet is performed using the FCIP gateway. Figure 5.30 shows there are two FCIP gateways. Consider that *FC SAN 1* is sending data to *FC SAN 2*. Now what happens is that the gateway connected to the fabric of *FC SAN 1* encapsulates the FC frames into an IP packet. At the receiving end (i.e., *FC SAN 2*) the IP wrapper is removed by the FCIP gateway connected to the fabric of *FC SAN 2* and all FC frames reach the receiving end. Actually, IP addresses are assigned to the *port on the FCIP gateway.* Once IP connectivity is established between the two FCIP gateways an FCIP tunnel is created via the TCP/IP network. Once the FCIP tunnel is created nodes can independently communicate with each other. Another important aspect is that multiple FCIP tunnels can be created to increase throughput. Moreover, FC SANs are unaware of being connected through the FCIP tunnel.

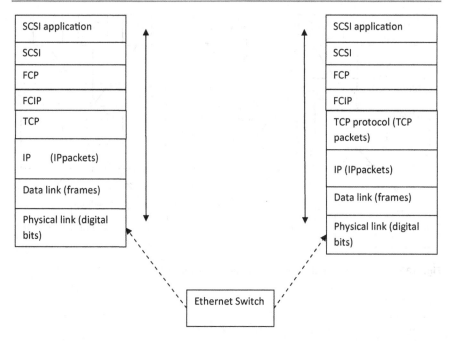

Fig. 5.31 FCIP protocol stack

Fig. 5.32 FC frames
encapsulated into IP packet

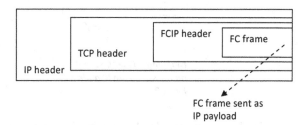

5.6.2.3   Internet Fiber Channel Protocol (IFCP)

internet Fiber Channel Protocol (iFCP) is used to interconnect FC devices, like a server, with HBAs, FC disks, FC switches, etc., over the existing TCP/IP network (as shown in Fig. 5.33).

As shown in Fig. 5.33 iFCP can also be used to combine the FC fabric and TCP/IP network. Another example in which an FC host and an FC disk are connected using an iFCP gateway via the existing TCP/IP network is shown in Fig. 5.34.

As shown in Fig. 5.34, an N-port attached to the iFCP gateway is served by a standard F-port interface on the gateway. This means the N-port not only provides the fabric services but also performs the change in address mapping from the FC fabric to the IP network. Thus the packets travel through the IP network. At the

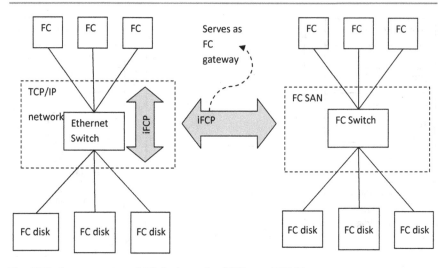

Fig. 5.33 Interconnection of FC devices using iFCP over TCP/IP

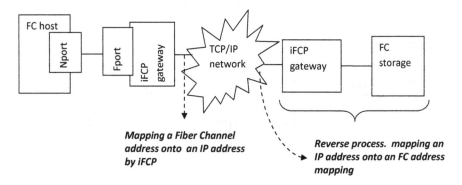

Fig. 5.34 Interconnection of FC devices using iFCP through the TCP/IP network

other end the iFCP gateway once again performs the reverse process of mapping the IP network to the fabric address conversion.

Advantages of IP storage area network

- IP SAN does not require a separate network to manage connections to storage systems. It uses the existing TCP/IP network to create the storage area network. Hence the cost of creating an IP SAN is much less than is the case with other networks.
- IP SAN does not have any distance limitation. Hence an enterprise can establish its data center at any location where its network is over a LAN, WAN, or the

internet. This allows IP SAN to be used flexibly and conveniently at any place to establish disaster recovery.

- IP SAN can co-exist with FC SAN. Hence an enterprise has the option of combining IP SAN with an already existing FC SAN to keep investments costs for storage to a minimum.
- IP SAN can use either a specialized HBA to connect servers to the SAN or just use standard NIC cards/Ethernet ports to do the same. This enables server I/O consolidation and reduces complexity/cost.
- Gigabit Server Adapters (NIC cards) can be used to connect to the network and thereby provide the Gigabit speeds so necessary today.
- Implementation and maintenance of IP SAN is easier than is the case with other networks.
- IP SAN is highly suitable when implementing a SAN in virtual server environments.

Disadvantages of IP storage area network

- IP SAN does not run on a separate network, but on the existing TCP/IP network. This means that the existing bandwidth is shared by both storage-related traffic and other IP traffic. This leads to network congestion and bandwidth constraints during peak hours. Hence the need to plan and design bandwidth requirements according to the needs of applications.
- Server CPUs may be burdened with iSCSI and TCP/IP stack processing if HBA/NIC cannot offload that function. Hence the performance of servers will be affected.
- Delivery of packets in IP SAN is based on the *best effort network* model. Hence packets may get dropped during network congestion, which means packet delivery in IP SAN is not reliable.

5.7 Converged Enhanced Ethernet

Basically, FC SAN networks provide highly reliable transmission of data but they are distance limited. The operating distance is only around 10 km. The existing TCP/IP network is used to transmit data, but it is slow. Enterprises are unwilling to invest in two lots of infrastructure (Ethernet infrastructure and Fiber Channel). Hence IT experts invented a hybrid network infrastructure that combines both Ethernet and Fiber Channel technologies called *Converged Enhanced Ethernet* (CEE). The concept underlying CEE is shown in Fig. 5.35.

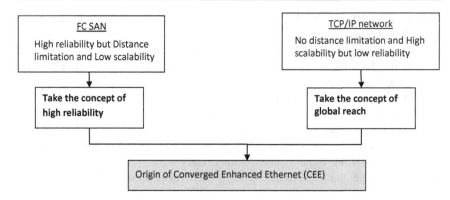

Fig. 5.35 Origin of CEE

The main goals of CEE are

- to reduce the number of network adapters in physical servers;
- to reduce the number of cables coming out of each physical server; and
- to reduce the number of switches in the infrastructure.

Instead of having one set of network adapters, cables, and switches dedicated to the Fiber Channel and another set of adapters, cables, and switches dedicated to the Ethernet, a CEE allows use of a single set of network adapters called converged network adapters (CNAs), which are capable of providing the function of both an NIC card and an HBA adapter. Converged Enhanced Ethernet (CEE) represents a new specification in the existing family of Ethernet standards. It eliminates the lossy nature of Ethernet and enables the convergence of various types of network traffic on a common Ethernet infrastructure. CEE eliminates the dropping of frames due to congestion and thereby ensures lossless transmission with the help of an FCoE (Fiber Channel over Ethernet) SAN. The concept underlying FCoE SAN is discussed in the subsequent section.

5.7.1 FCoE Storage Area Network

FCoE SAN is a Converged Enhanced Ethernet (CEE) network that is capable of transporting FC data along with regular Ethernet traffic at high speed (such as 10 Gbps or higher) over Ethernet. This is shown in Fig. 5.36.

FCoE provides FC services to FC servers and FC storage devices over Ethernet without using TCP/IP (as shown in Fig. 5.36). This means that FCoE technology allows encapsulation and transmission of Fiber Channel frames over the conventional Ethernet network without using the Ethernet default forwarding scheme with TCP and IP.

The FCoE protocol stack is compared with iSCSI in Fig. 5.37.

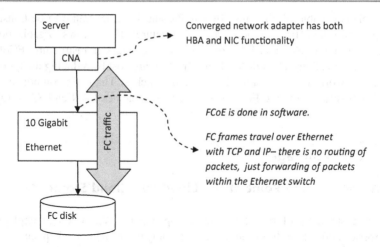

Fig. 5.36 Concept underlying FCoE SAN

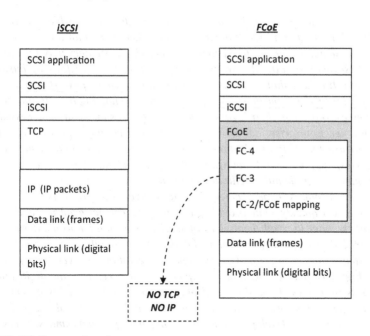

Fig. 5.37 FCoE protocol stack

The FCoE protocol specification replaces the FC-0 and FC-1 layers of the Fiber Channel stack with Ethernet. With FCoE, Fiber Channel becomes another network protocol running on Ethernet. FCoE operates directly above Ethernet in the network protocol stack, in contrast to iSCSI which runs on top of the TCP and IP. As a consequence FCoE is not routable at the IP layer, and will not work across routed IP networks.

FCoE is capable of allowing SAN traffic and Ethernet traffic to be transmitted using a common 10-Gbit network infrastructure. This allows organizations to consolidate their LAN and SAN over the same network infrastructure. FCoE also allows organizations to cut down their infrastructure cost by reducing the number of cables, network interface cards (NICs), and switches. The main component of the FCoE infrastructure is the FCoE switch, which separates LAN and SAN traffic.

5.8 Cloud Storage

5.8.1 What's the Point of the Cloud and Cloud Storage?

The core strengths of the cloud are recapped here. We go on to explain why enterprises depend on the cloud and cloud storage to provide backup support of all their data:

- *The present and <u>urgent need</u> is to collect as many data as possible, archive them, and run immediate and real-time analytics on them such that an enterprise can deliver a seamless service to customers (otherwise customers may turn to other enterprises that are already involved in digitization and transforming businesses digitally). It is here that the cloud serves as <u>an integrated, powerful solution and a driver for bringing business innovations.</u> Cloud computing has already enabled businesses to provide their legacy systems as services that can be accessed over the internet. Enterprises can now go to the next level and employ the cloud as a base to use for their digitization. They can store all the data, deploy all the processes, and move all the workloads to the cloud. The cloud computing environment significantly facilitates digitization.*
- *Today's customers expect enterprises to deliver the products and services required very quickly while providing a seamless customer experience. Basically, customers want to avail themselves of services via intuitive user interfaces that deliver 24/7 availability, real-time fulfillment, personalized treatment, global consistency, and zero errors (i.e., customer expectations are very high). To meet such high customer expectations companies must accelerate the __digitization__ of business processes. Here the cloud plays a major role. It helps by employing information technology to manage operations and drive digital customer experience, as well as developing and delivering new products and services on a platform-based methodology.*
- *In addition, enterprises are adopting a model of IT called hybrid IT in which on-premises computing and cloud-based solutions are mixed. Enterprises are shifting most of their applications and workloads to the cloud while keeping core sensitive applications within their enterprises. In a nutshell, modern enterprises mix the on-premises and cloud environment to meet their needs.*
- *Another area where businesses are focusing is __globalization__. The demands of customers know no boundary. Enterprises are compelled to prove their*

competitive edge by attracting customers and delivering services to them any-
where in the world.

- *Another big challenge facing enterprises is that customers compare their service*
  *providers when it comes to such critical factors as **quality, cost, and time**.*
  *Customers expect their products or services to be delivered with a **high-quality***
  ***service, reduced cost, and in less time** (i.e., since customers only use a limited*
  *number of service providers/businesses they **rationally** choose their needs). This*
  again compels businesses to digitize not only all their processes but also what-
  ever else they can.
- *The next level of expectation customers want from their business providers is they*
  want to work with providers very closely. For example, if they place an order for
  a product they need access to the website of the manufacturer to know the status
  of the order (i.e., businesses should be as transparent to customers as possible).
  The cloud is an appropriate base for bringing transparency. It allows business
  processes to connect with customers and let them know about prospective deals
  and the status of orders.

In the final analysis the cloud environment serves as a base for bringing in
digitalization, globalization, rationalization, and transparency in any enterprise.
Without these transformations it is really tough for enterprises to survive.

Critical needs underlie business decisions to push their data to cloud storage.
Data are fundamental to making the right business decisions. Cloud computing has
brought a revolutionary change in the way to develop and run programs in the cloud
infrastructure instead of running programs on individual desktops or laptops.
Similar to servers and platforms provided by the cloud, cloud storage provides
storage as a service. Cloud storage does not refer to any specific storage
device/technology, but to a service that can be accessed over the internet by cloud
users for storing their data. Thus *cloud storage is a service in which data are*
remotely maintained, managed, and backed up. The service is available to users
over a network, which is usually the internet. It allows the user to store files online
so that the user can access them from any location via *the internet*:

- Storage as a service provides a cheap solution for *backup, replication,* and *dis-*
  aster recovery.
- Users can avail themselves of the storage using an on-demand price, which
  reduces operational costs significantly.
- Cloud storage can offer literally any amount of storage.
- Providers are responsible for providing a redundancy plan and *maintenance* of
  hundreds or thousands of data servers to ensure that all customer data will
  be available at all times.
- Businesses often have an on-site backup system. However, that is not sufficient
  during a natural disaster. Hence cloud storage is the ideal choice for businesses
  wanting to maintain a *remote backup* system.

- A reputable cloud storage provider will have multiple copies of an enterprise's data for *redundancy*, often in different geographic locations. Hence it's highly unlikely that an enterprise will lose its data.
- For enterprises that have more stringent security requirements and compliance needs, cloud providers can offer *advanced encryption techniques* and other security mechanisms.
- Many cloud storage services include *collaboration tools* that can help your business operate more efficiently.

5.8.2   What Form Do Storage Devices Take Inside the Cloud? What Does the Architecture of Cloud Storage Look Like?

This section has been designed to provide food for thought for readers. So far in this chapter various kinds of storage devices have been discussed. Major storage devices are DAS, NAS, and SAN. Of these types DAS is distinct in that it cannot be shared. Obviously, enterprises need sharable storage devices. The two choices left are NAS and SAN. NAS almost only serves as a dedicated file server. DAS and NAS generally serve only small businesses with limited functionalities. Since SAN provides a dedicated network it is going to be the next trend in storage. In a nutshell, enterprises avail themselves of FC SAN for reliable storage traffic, IP SAN for scalable traffic, and FCoE SAN for both reliable and scalable storage traffic.

As can be seen from the above, cloud storage can have as its base a variety of means of storage, such as DAS, NAS, FC SAN, IP SAN, and FCoE SAN, distributed across different geographical locations. These storage devices are interlinked using a network, like leaf spine, that has been specifically developed for storage–server communication, software-defined networking, and network function virtualization.

So, heterogeneous storage systems form the physical storage infrastructure and are networked with one another and with servers using a number of different networking mechanisms. Of such virtualizations, storage service offering, security, and management remain the same. The following sections describe the generic architecture of cloud storage.

5.8.2.1   Architecture of Cloud Storage

The architecture of cloud storage (as shown in Fig. 5.38) consists of four layers:

(i)   access layer;
(ii) application interface layer;
(iii) infrastructure management layer; and
(iv) storage layer.

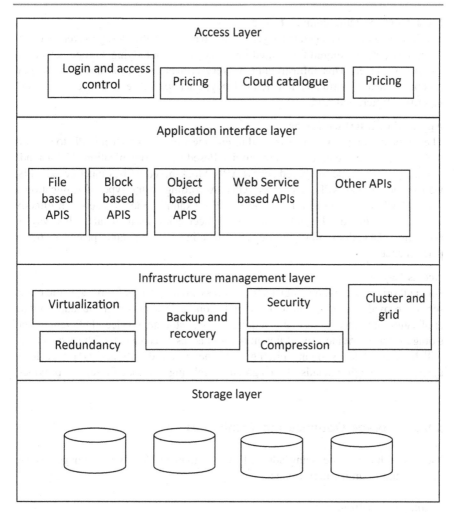

Fig. 5.38 High-level architecture of cloud storage system

Storage Layer

The storage layer consists of various types of storage devices:

- DAS storage devices like SCSI;
- IP storage devices such as NAS and iSCSI;
- Fiber Channel storage devices; and
- object-based storage devices.

Storage devices are typically distributed at different geographical locations. They are connected using different networks such as LAN and WAN.

Infrastructure Management Layer

The infrastructure management layer is the layer above the storage layer. It offers the infrastructure required for unified management of underlying storage devices in the storage layer. This infrastructure is very critical as it provides various vital functions such as virtualization, redundancy, backup and recovery, compression, security, cluster, and grid.

Application Interface Layer

The application interface layer is used to provide various interfaces/APIs to support the cloud storage use cases that are provided/used by the organization. Major kinds of data access include file-based access APIs, block-based APIs, object-based APIs, web service–based APIs, and other APIs. According to the type of application a suitable API will be used for data access. For example, mobile users can directly use an object-based API and retrieve the object using its metadata. This way of accessing data does not require an operating system and provides better performance.

Access Layer

Any authorized user who is registered to access cloud services from a specific cloud service provider can log into the cloud storage system via a standard public application interface to use the required cloud storage service. Different cloud storage service providers use different types of access mechanisms. The access layer will have a catalog showing pricing and other usage details and a service level agreement providing details of the agreement relating to a specific service provider.

5.8.3   Storage Optimization Techniques

Various techniques are being adopted in the cloud to effectively manage storage devices and optimize performance:

- storage virtualization
- thin provisioning
- storage tiering
- software-defined storage
- redundancy.

Storage Virtualization

Storage virtualization is a mechanism used to ensure that different heterogeneous types of storage devices are stored and managed as a single logical storage system. This in turn will enable unified storage management, easier deployment, and integrated monitoring of the entire storage infrastructure. Storage virtualization mainly involves splitting the available storage into virtual volumes. Virtual volumes can be created by combining different types of storage devices. These virtual volumes are then presented to the operating system as storage devices after abstracting the details of the storage devices present in that volume. Virtual volumes can be expanded, created, and deleted as per storage requirements without any downtime. There are various techniques used in the creation of virtual volumes.

Thin Provisioning

One of the major challenges faced by present-day organizations is most of the storage capacity allocated to various applications remains unused—an expensive affair for organizations. Most such situations arise due to over provisioning of storage needs. Thin provisioning refers to storage provisioning only as per actual need. In this technique logical storage is allocated to applications based on anticipated requirements. Actual storage allocated is much less than logical storage and is based on the current need of applications. Whenever the storage needs of an application increases, storage is allocated to it from a common pool of storage devices. In this manner thin provisioning provides efficient utilization of storage and reduces waste due to unused physical storage.

Storage Tiering

In general, different applications require different storage devices with different characteristics. An enterprise purchases storage devices according to the needs of applications and cost. For example, simple archival of data requires only low-cost, low-performance storage devices whereas real-time applications require quick access to data, which essentially needs high-performance storage devices. In short, organizations require techniques that enable them to store the right data in the right type of storage device so that they can be made available at the correct point in time to various applications. Storage tiering is a technique that provides this capability. It is a mechanism to establish a hierarchy (i.e., in various tiers) of storage devices and then store data in them based on the performance and availability requirements of applications (as shown in Fig. 5.39). Each storage tier has different levels of

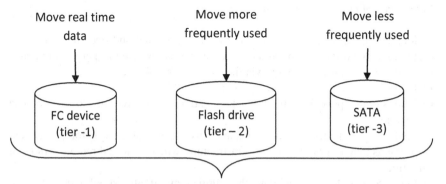

Allotting storages/segregating storages into logical tiers so as to meet the storage needs of applications effectively with high performance

Fig. 5.39 Storage tiering

protection, performance, data access frequency, cost, and other considerations. For example, moving the data storage of real-time applications to tier 1, moving active or frequently used data to flash (tier 2), and moving inactive or less frequent data to SATA devices (tier 3) will help in meeting the storage requirements of different applications effectively. Compression and deduplication are used to optimize storage:

- *Compression*: Compression reduces the size of data to be stored by eliminating blank spaces present in the data. A major drawback of compression is that it consumes computing cycles. Another concern is that decompression has to be carried out while users retrieve their data. Hence compression may only be applied to data that are not frequently used like backup data.
- *Deduplication*: Deduplication is a technique to ensure that data are not duplicated in the storage system or, in other words, to ensure that no duplicate copies of data are stored in the system. Deduplication will only be applied in the case of a normal application where availability and scalability is normal. Whenever high-availability or high-scalability data are typically duplicated in such applications, deduplication will not be adopted. In addition, fault-tolerant applications will essentially require data redundancy.

Deduplication works with the help of a method that generates hash values. Each time a new file reaches the storage system the deduplication software generates a hash value for the file and compares it with the existing set of hash values. Deduplication can be performed at two levels: *file level* and *block level*. File-level deduplication is carried out on files to ensure that only a single copy of each file exists in the system. In block-level deduplication the deduplication file is split into blocks and the software ensures that only a single copy of the file is stored in each block. Identical files or blocks are detected by comparing the hash value generated from a preexisting list of hash values for files or blocks.

Advantages of cloud data storage

- Cloud storage devices are cheap and avoid both capital and operational cost.
- Cloud storage offers unlimited data storage that can be used as per requirements.
- Cloud storage can be accessed via the internet or a WAN.
- Cloud storage does not require any maintenance cost.
- Cloud storage provides inbuilt backup and recovery systems to ensure data protection.
- Cloud storage devices do not consume any additional energy for power and cooling as they run on the cloud infrastructure, which is hosted remotely most of the time.
- Cloud storage devices facilitate the digitization of almost all industries and domains.
- Cloud storage devices facilitate big data storage and processing.

- Cloud storage devices provide data redundancy and hence prevent data loss.
- Cloud storage devices provide hardware maintenance and high availability.
- Cloud storage devices are the ideal choice for a remote data backup facility.
- Storage technologies, such as DAS, SANs, and NAS, provide high performance, availability, and accessibility using industry standard interfaces.

Disadvantages of traditional enterprise storage devices

- In general, enterprise storage devices are very costly.
- Enterprise storage devices have a limited life.
- Enterprise storage devices require backup and recovery systems to ensure data are fully protected.
- Enterprise storage devices may require dedicated hardware and software infrastructure.
- Storage infrastructure like FC SAN requires personnel with the necessary expertise to manage it.
- Enterprise storage devices consume a considerable amount of power, take up a lot of storage server room, and need mechanisms to keep them cool.
- Storage networks like FC SAN are distance limited, but enterprises need to establish storage networks at different geographical locations.
- Similarly, storage networks like IP SAN have reliability issues.
- Storage systems like NAS share the existing enterprise LAN with storage traffic, which typically leads to bandwidth issues.
- DAS devices cannot be shared among servers.
- Along with the above issues the concept of digitization has led to an enormous growth of data. Data are now growing exponentially and require huge storage. Enterprises are reluctant to establish storage systems of their own as the expenses involved are too great. Thus cloud storage is preferred to on-premises storage.

Examples of Cloud Storage

- Dropbox.com (https://www.dropbox.com): Dropbox.com is one of the most popular cloud storage services available. Dropbox uses encryption to help keep user data secure. Hence everything a user uploads becomes automatically private. Dropbox offers different plans for individuals and businesses but it starts off giving each individual 2 GB of free storage.
- *Google Drive* (https://www.google.com): Google Drive allows users to store their files. It gives users the opportunity to share their files, folders, or any data with certain email addresses, the public, or anyone who has a link to the file (e.g., if you email a link to your friends). It provides 15 GB of storage for free. Any user who has a Gmail address will automatically have access to Google Drive. Google Drive also allows users to collaborate and make changes to files at the same time.
- *Microsoft OneDrive* (*SkyDrive*) (https://onedrive.live.com): SkyDrive is an Internet-based storage platform offered for free by Microsoft to anyone with a

Microsoft account. *SkyDrive is now called OneDrive.* It allows users to store, synchronize, and access their files across Windows PC and Mac OS computers and laptops as well as mobile devices. OneDrive is closely linked to an individual's Microsoft account. A limited amount of free storage is included as part of each Microsoft account. Additional storage can be purchased for a fee, or users can get additional storage free when they purchase an Office 365 account. OneDrive is fully integrated with Microsoft's Office 365 subscription, which includes full program access (such as Word, Excel, PowerPoint, and Outlook) along with 1 TB of built-in OneDrive storage space. A variety of storage-only plans are also available depending on how much space you need, ranging from a free 15 GB plan, to a 50 GB plan, and up to a 1 TB plan.

- *Amazon Cloud Drive*: Amazon.com offers a cloud storage service that gives users 5 GB of free storage. If you have an Amazon.com account, you can log into the cloud storage service using your existing username and password.

5.9 Software-Defined Storage

Software-defined storage (SDS) is an approach to data storage in which the programming that controls storage-related tasks is decoupled from the physical storage hardware. Similar to SDN, the goal of software-defined storage is to provide administrators with flexible management capabilities through programming. A single software interface can be used to manage a shared storage pool that runs on commodity hardware. At a higher level SDS can be perceived as shown in Fig. 5.40. Whether storage is virtualized or not, SDS provides a simple managing interface that automates the tasks of managing storage. SDS is not related to virtualization. However, cloud providers employ storage virtualization for effective sharing of storage and to abstract the heterogeneity in storage types and vendors. The concept underlying SDS is shown in Fig. 5.40.

As shown in Fig. 5.40, SDS is a management API that provides a standard way of configuring software devices. This API hides the heterogeneity in devices, vendors, hardware, etc. This makes it easier for database administrators to configure devices automatically through software. There is no need to set the required parameters in hardware, and by so doing human error during configuration is prevented.

Characteristics of Software-Defined Storage

- *Abstraction*: In SDS architecture the software that manages storage decouples and abstracts the heterogeneity in hardware, vendors, etc.
- *Automation*: In SDS the configuration and management tasks of storage devices are automated using software configurations, scripts, etc.
- *Industry standards*: SDS solutions rely on industry standards and hence prevent vendor lock-in.

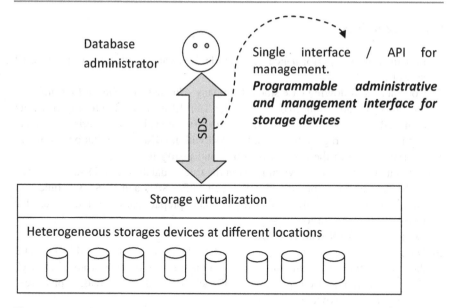

Fig. 5.40 Concept of software-defined storage

- *Scalability*: SDS supports the concept of virtualization and hence SDS makes it easier to add or remove storage devices.
- *Flexibility*: SDS allows users to choose hardware according to their needs and removes the constraint of having to deal with a specific vendor.
- *Virtualization*: SDS architecture pools together storage resources and manages them as a cohesive unit. It virtualizes storage devices in much the same way as server or network virtualization.

5.10 Summary

This chapter discussed the different kinds of storage devices in detail. The advantages and disadvantages of the different types were mentioned. The way in which disadvantages found in one type led to the invention of a successor type was discussed. Special emphasis was given to SAN. The way in which SAN supports conventional SCSI and the way in which the existing TCP/IP network can be exploited to implement SAN were presented. Different types of storage protocols, such as SCSI, FCP, iFCP, FCIP, and FCoE, were discussed in detail. The applicability of different types was mentioned. The need for cloud storage and its architecture were briefly discussed. Modern optimization techniques, such as deduplication, compression, security, storage tiering, and storage virtualization, were described. Finally, the concept of SDS was discussed.

5.11 Exercises

1. Explain how the performance of NAS devices can be affected in the TCP/IP network.
2. Consider the following case study. Company *ABC* has branches at four different locations that are connected through the TCP/IP network. Each branch has its own dedicated FC SAN. For the purpose of analysis a need arises to interconnect these storage networks at low cost with no distance limitation. Come up with a solution to the above case study and justify it.
3. When a 10 Gb Ethernet switch is given the role of database administrator, which of the various data storage networks, such as FC SAN and IP SAN, would you prefer when the necessity arose that you had to prepare backup servers to use for recovery during data loss.
4. Compare FC SAN with IP SAN.
5. Do a comparative study among SCSI, iSCSI, FCP, iFCP, FCIP, and FCOE. Did the comparative study enlighten you as to the purpose of each protocol clearly? Write an assignment on the purpose of each protocol and provide typical scenarios for its deployment.
6. Compare different data access models. Compile a list of the advantages of object-based data access.
7. What is the point of software-defined storage? Justify your reasoning with an example.

References

1. Shrivastava A, Somasundaram G (2009) Information storage and management: storing, managing, and protecting digital information. Wiley. ISBN: 9780470294215
2. Tate J, Rajani Kanth, Telles A Introduction to storage area networks. ibm.com/redbooks
3. http://www.sanog.org/resources/sanog8/sanog8-san-functional-overview-asimkhan.pdf
4. Spalding R (2003) Storage networks: the complete reference, 1st edn. Mc Graw Hill India
5. Jian-Hua Z, Nan Z (2011) Cloud computing-based data storage and disaster recovery. In: International conference on future computer science and education, pp 629–632. http://doi.ieeecomputersociety.org/10.1109/ICFCSE.2011.157

Cloud Security

6

Learning Objectives

Cloud solutions are third-party solutions available to any enterprise/user. Cloud users avail themselves of a number of different services deployed in the cloud provider's infrastructure. The initial reaction to this is one of security, which is of course a major concern. The objective of this chapter is to present security-related concepts in the cloud. The reader should get a thorough understanding of how security is provided in different service models such as IaaS, PaaS, and SaaS. By the end of this chapter the reader should also understand that putting security in place is a shared responsibility and that the cloud user is responsible for data security, compliance, and regulatory and privacy requirements. Security is a topic that attracts a lot of attention and users tend to ask the following motivational questions.

Motivational Questions

1. What are the generic security concepts that inform a conventional IT infrastructure? Are they the same for the cloud?
2. Will the security concepts in the cloud environment be the same as those in the IT infrastructure of a traditional enterprise? If they differ, in what way do they?
3. Will the security concepts be the same in all kinds of cloud deployment? Or do they differ in the private and public cloud?
4. Who is responsible for implementing security concepts in the cloud? Is it the cloud service providers? Or is it the cloud users? Or both?
5. Is the sharing of security responsibilities the same in all service models?
6. What are the impacts of virtualization and multi-tenancy on security?
7. How does the geographical distribution of resources affect security?
8. Who is responsible for data in the cloud?

© Springer Nature Switzerland AG 2019
S. Chellammal and C. Pethuru Raj, *Essentials of Cloud Computing*,
Texts in Computer Science, https://doi.org/10.1007/978-3-030-13134-0_6

Preface

In the previous chapters the reader should have learned the basics of cloud computing and of the two major core topics: cloud networking and cloud storage. Now is an appropriate time to discuss security. Since cloud services are considered third-party solutions by an enterprise, security is treated as a major and critical concern. Enterprises cannot simply disregard the security concept in the belief that —having moved their workloads to the cloud—cloud providers will take care of everything. Security is a shared responsibility in the cloud environment. This is the reason this chapter goes into great detail on the essentials of cloud security. The chapter begins with an overview of the basic security requirements of any IT infrastructure: authentication, authorization, access control, confidentiality, integrity, availability, accountability, and privacy. It describes the various security threats inherent in any IT infrastructure. The chapter gradually introduces the vulnerabilities brought about by virtualization and multi-tenancy. It discusses the way in which security implementation is significantly influenced by *virtualization, multi-tenancy, distribution of resources at different geographical locations, and the type of deployment*. In this way it categorizes the types of security threats such as data security threats, application-level threats, VM-level threats, and network or server-level threats. After introducing security concepts and attacks the chapter describes different isolation techniques and how security responsibilities are shared between cloud providers and cloud users in IaaS, PaaS, and SaaS.

6.1 Basic Security Requirements

The information technology infrastructure of any enterprise—be it traditional or cloud based—has to provide the following basic security requirements to ensure IT assets are secure:

• authentication
• authorization and access control
• confidentiality
• data integrity
• availability
• accountability
• privacy.

Authentication

Authentication is the process involved in verifying one's identity, genuineness, and credibility. In information systems users have to prove that they are authenticated users who have unique identity features. There are various methods of authentication such as *password-based authentication, biometrics-based authentication, token/dongle-based authentication, multifactor authentication*, and *out-of-band authentication*.

Password-based authentication

Authentication between a user and computer (or cloud service provider) is built around the exchange of unique authentication data such as *passwords, security secrets* or *tokens, digital signatures,* and *digital certificates.* When strong security measures are needed, security administrators recommend passwords should contain 12 characters made up of a combination of numbers, special characters, and both uppercase and lowercase letters. However, there are issues with password-based authentication:

- passwords can be easy to guess or find, especially if they are easy to remember;
- passwords can be stolen, if written down;
- users may share passwords; and
- passwords can be forgotten, especially if they are difficult to remember.

Biometrics-based authentication

Biometrics refers to the technique that uses the *unique physiological and behavioral traits of a user* to authenticate his or her identity. This is ideal since no two people share the exact same physical traits. Physiological biometrics is based on the use of fingerprints, facial recognition, iris scans, hand geometry, and retina scans. Behavioral biometrics is based on voice recognition, gaits, keystroke scans, and signature scans. Fingerprints and handprints are the most widely used biometric method in use today. Many laptops include fingerprint readers and they are even available on USB flash drives. The drawback with biometrics-based authentication is that it requires specialized hardware. With applications where more security is needed a combination of more than one biometrics-based authentication is used. DNA identification is another method used for biometrics-based authentication.

Token-based authentication

A token is a device, such as a dongle, card, or RFID chip, that is required to access secure systems. Token authentication makes it tough for a hacker to access a system since the hacker has to actually possess the device, which is more or less impossible for a hacker to obtain.

Multi-factor authentication

Multi-factor authentication (MFA) is an authentication technique that requires two or more independent ways of verifying an identity. For example, ATM access requires a person to insert a card (which is the physical device) and enter a personal identification number (PIN).

Out-of-band authentication

Out-of-band authentication employs two different channels to ensure it takes place. For example, an online banking transaction sends a one-time password to a mobile and receives a confirmation from the user before performing the transaction. Using two different channels makes it much more difficult for a hacker.

Authorization and Access Control

Authorization determines the permissions an authenticated user has to access different resources and controls the access a person has to resources according to those privileges. Typically, permissions are set by the owner of a resource. For example, an owner of a file can set different permissions, such as *read permission*, *write permission*, and *execute permission*, while the file is being created. Privileges use a number of techniques such as *access control lists (ACLs), access controls for URLs*, and *role-based access control (RBAC)*. Authentication, authorization, and access control are shown in Fig. 6.1.

Confidentiality

Confidentiality is a security mechanism that prevents data or information from being accessed by unauthorized persons. *It ensures that data or information are accessed only by the person or persons for whom the data are intended.* For example, if a message is sent to a receiver, only the intended receiver should be able to access it and no one else (as shown in Fig. 6.2). The generic method of achieving confidentiality is through *encryption*. The sender of the message encrypts a plain text message using encryption algorithms and a *secret key* (which is known only to the sender and receiver). At the receiving end the receiver decrypts the message using the secret key and obtains the original message. In this way the message is made confidential to the intended user.

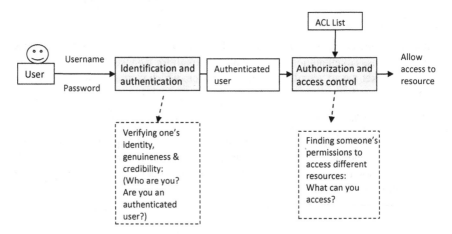

Fig. 6.1 Authentication and authorization

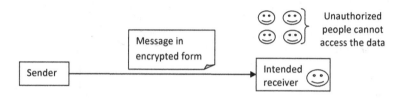

Fig. 6.2 Confidentiality

Data Integrity

Integrity ensures that data or information are not altered by any unauthorized persons. Data integrity is the maintenance of accuracy and consistency of data. Data integrity may be lost intentionally due to data security issues or may be lost due to hardware failure or human error. Data integrity and data security go hand in hand. Data integrity ensures that data have remained unaltered during transit from the moment of their creation throughout their entire lifetime. It is a measure of the validity of the data object. *Data integrity is implemented using data security mechanisms.*

As a function related to security a data integrity service maintains the data exactly how they were input and the service is auditable to affirm its reliability. Data integrity should ensure that data retain their integrity and accuracy during various operations such as capture, storage, retrieval, update, transfer, processing, and other decision-making tasks. Data integrity is also a performance measure during various operations based on the error rate detected. *Data must be kept free from corruption, modification, or unauthorized disclosure* to achieve business goals accurately. Inaccuracies can occur either accidentally (e.g., through programming errors), or maliciously (e.g., through breaches or hacks). Database security professionals employ a number of practices to assure data integrity:

- data encryption, which uses a cipher to lock data;
- data backup, which stores a copy of the data in an alternate location;
- access controls, such as the assignment of read/write privileges;
- input validation, to prevent incorrect data entry;
- data validation, to certify uncorrupted transmission; and
- database integrity constraints, to enforce business rules on data when entered into an application. (Business rules specify conditions and relationships that must always be true or must always be false. When a data integrity constraint is applied to a database table, all data in the table must conform to the corresponding rule.)

Another term related to integrity is message integrity during data transit. Message integrity can be achieved using irreversible mathematic hash functions (as shown in Fig. 6.3). The hash value of a message is obtained using fast but irreversible mathematical (one-way) hash functions. The hash value of a message is called a *message-authenticated code* (*MAC*). Both the *message and MAC* are sent to

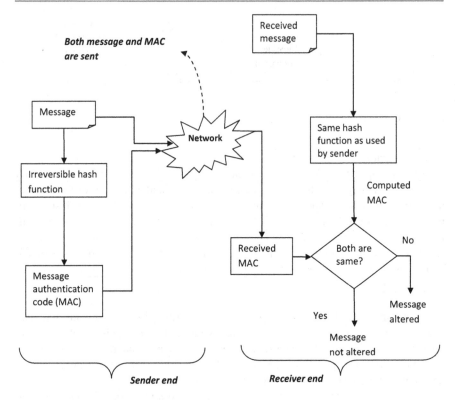

Fig. 6.3 Message integrity using hash function

the receiver through the network. At the receiver end the hash value of the received message is computed using the same hash function as that of sender to ensure message integrity. If the *computed MAC and received MAC are the same*, then *message integrity is preserved* and has not been altered by any unauthorized person.

Availability

Availability means that the data or resource should be available and accessible by authorized users *at all times*. There are two aspects to availability. Data may become unavailable to an authorized user due to *poor scalability* (server may be overloaded) or *hardware failure* (server may go down), or it may be due to security issues or intentional attack (i.e., hackers stop the authorized user from accessing the data, server, or resource as shown in Fig. 6.4).

To ensure the availability of resources a number of considerations should be kept in mind: hardware and other infrastructure should be maintained in a very good reliable condition; sufficient resources, such as load balancers, should be provided to ensure scalability and availability; and there should be a sufficient mechanism for fault tolerance and sufficient security mechanisms to prevent security attacks.

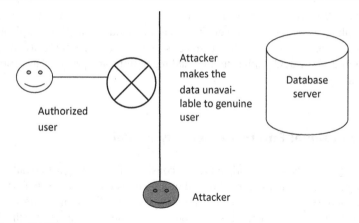

Fig. 6.4 Availability

Accountability

Accountability is the process that verifies whether authorized persons have performed actions in accordance with the rules and privileges set for them. This is done by tracing the activities of authentication, authorization, and control that are in place (as shown in Fig. 6.5). Accountability ensures whether proper control mechanisms are in place to prevent the abuse of any resource. Audit, a mechanism for inspecting and reviewing resources, can provide data for accountability. Various items, such as password policies, software licensing, and internet usage, can be audited. Logging mechanisms, such as software error logs, user logins and logouts, and monitoring hardware failures and resource accesses/tasks performed by various users, help in implementing accountability.

Privacy

Privacy [1] refers to the rights of individuals to safeguard their information from any other parties. It involves protecting individuals' data from being freely disseminated over the internet or sold to third parties. Any IT infrastructure has to guarantee data privacy for its users. Data privacy decides which, if any, data of an

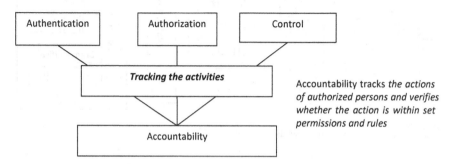

Fig. 6.5 Accountability

individual or enterprise can be shared with third parties. This is done by setting laws and compliance regulations. When it comes to cloud computing, implementing compliance regulations is difficult since systems are geographically dispersed throughout the world. Compliance rules and regulations and privacy laws vary from country to country.

6.2 Traditional Enterprise Security Model

A traditional enterprise network typically consists of an external firewall, demilitarized zone (DMZ), and internal firewall to protect its corporate assets from public networks and external users (as shown in Fig. 6.6). Traffic from an untrusted network, such as the internet, passes through the external firewall to the DMZ. The DMZ exposes the services of an enterprise to public access. It involves a single host or a network of security services that sit between an untrusted public network and the corporate network. It isolates any direct access to corporate assets by a public network. The traffic from the DMZ has to cross another internal firewall to access corporate assets. In a traditional enterprise system, information systems are by and large *centralized* and hence there will be a single point of entry or access from an external untrusted network. In a traditional enterprise, *it is the enterprise that fully controls the security of the infrastructure. Security control and management is centralized. Enterprises define their security policies and assess the enforcement of such policies periodically*.

As business processes become more Agile and requirements more dynamic, enterprises have adapted the cloud computing paradigm to implement business processes that reduce capital and operational costs and satisfy short time to market. In cloud computing, dynamically scalable and virtual resources are offered as

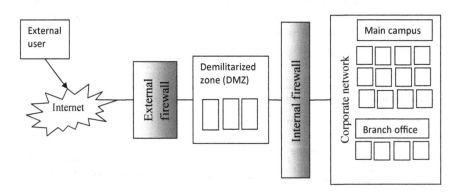

Fig. 6.6 Traditional enterprise security model

utilities over the internet. *Hence there has been a shift from the centralized enterprise model to the cloud-based enterprise model.* In cloud computing servers are distributed across wide geographic regions.

6.3 Aspects/Factors that Influence Security in Cloud

In cloud-based business models cloud users typically avail themselves of more and more services offered by cloud service providers. In general, cloud service providers offer three major kinds of services: Infrastructure as a Service (IaaS), Platform as a Service (PaaS), and Software as a Service (SaaS). For example, Amazon EC2 is an IaaS service provider whereas Microsoft Azure is a PaaS provider and Salesforce.com is an SaaS provider. In addition to the different types of services offered in the cloud, cloud providers deploy their services using different deployment models such as public and private. Different service types and deployment types are shown in Fig. 6.7. When it comes to security *there are three major aspects to be considered regarding service types and deployment models*:

- *Sharing of responsibility*: Depending on the types of services chosen by the cloud consumer security responsibilities will be shared between providers and

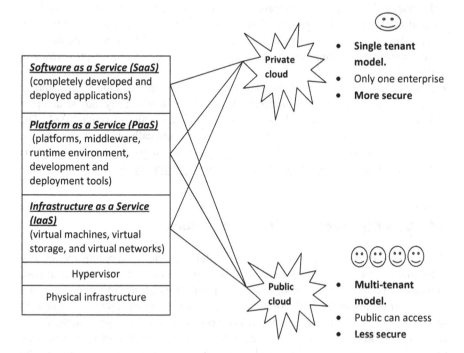

Fig. 6.7 Service types and deployment models in cloud

consumers. The sharing of responsibility over different security aspects needs to be agreed by both the provider and consumer and should be mentioned as part of the SLA. In a normal enterprise-based model control lies fully with the enterprise. Administration, control, and management are centralized. However, in cloud computing enterprises move their workloads to the cloud provider's site/infrastructure. Cloud users should not assume that the cloud will take care of everything simply because they have moved their workloads to cloud, as this is quite simply not true. Security in cloud computing is a shared responsibility. Responsibilities should be equally shared by both cloud providers and cloud users. A more important point to remember is that *data security* **is fully under the control of cloud users**.

• *Type of cloud deployment*: In public cloud deployment cloud service providers share and offer the available resources to multiple tenants by means of virtualization. Since the *available resources are shared among multiple tenants public cloud providers should ensure* that each tenant is *logically isolated from other tenants*. It is the responsibility of service providers to provide security for their resources. **Virtualization and multi-tenancy** *bring no benefit to cloud consumers*, but they are crucial techniques for cloud providers in implementing an effective way of sharing resources among multiple users. Private cloud deployment supports just a single tenant. This involves the relevant enterprise adopting the cloud for its infrastructure. A private cloud is set up within an organization's internal data center. It is easy to establish security compliance and regulatory policies. It is the responsibility of the enterprise to provide security in its very own private cloud deployment. If a private cloud is deployed in a third-party facility, then depending on the service model (i.e., whether the model is IaaS, PaaS, or SaaS) the security responsibilities will be shared between cloud service providers and cloud users.

• *Dynamic provisioning and location of resources*: In the cloud environment resources provisioned for a user may change dynamically. They may scale up or down. Based on the availability of resources they will be provisioned. The location and distribution of resources also dynamically change as per the demands of users. *Changes in location will have an impact on security aspects as the security and privacy policies of different countries/regions vary*.

6.4 Security Threats in Cloud Computing

Compared with the traditional enterprise model the cloud computing model provides many advantages such as reduced or no capital cost, reduced operational cost, dynamic scale-up or scale-out of resources, rapid provisioning of resources, and a pay-as-you-go pricing model. Another point is that the cloud provides a range of services that users can avail themselves of according to their requirements. Cloud computing is driven by many technological drivers the most important of which are virtualization, grid and utility-based computing, microservices architecture, and

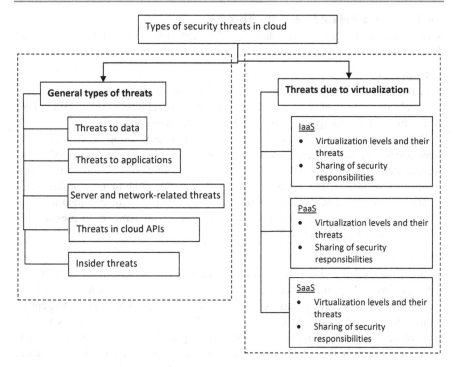

Fig. 6.8 Types of security threats in cloud

advances in hardware technology like multicore processors. Resources in the cloud environment are physically distributed at different locations. Cloud computing supports *access to the cloud using mobile devices*. This means users can move from place to place and still access the cloud. In addition, the cloud supports *bring your own device (BYOD), a means of getting connectivity to the cloud. All the above aspects and features of cloud computing differ drastically from a conventional enterprise infrastructure.* The Cloud Security Alliance (CSA) has identified many threats [2] when using the cloud such as *data breaches, data loss, account hacks, compromised interfaces and APIs, insider threats, malware code, virtualization attacks, overlapping trust boundaries,* and *SQL injection* (see Fig. 6.8 for possible threats when cloud computing).

6.4.1   General Types of Threats

As shown in Fig. 6.8 the general types of threat include data-related security threats, application threats, server and network-related threats, threats in cloud APIs, and insider threats.

6.4.1.1 Data-Related Security Threats

Security threats to data include data breaches, data loss, data/vendor lock-in, and data remanence.

Data Breach

Data breach is a situation or incident in which the confidentiality of someone's personal information, such as a health record or financial information, or the client information of an enterprise is disclosed to unauthorized persons.

Data in motion and at rest can be encrypted, thus preventing being viewed by unauthorized persons. Enterprises can use cloud access security brokers (CASBs) to prevent data breaches. CASBs are APIs that examine network traffic to ensure that a company's security policies remain intact. These APIs continuously monitor and control or prevent downloading of information and sharing of confidential data. They detect and proactively raise alerts to network administrators to prevent any security breach and protect data.

Data Loss

Data loss can occur at any time for various reasons such as natural disaster, server failure, human error, and network failure. Hence, data recovery should be supported by systems that efficiently and periodically backup data. Recovery management should be integrated into a data backup facility so that cloud services can be brought back to normal operation as quickly as possible. Disaster recovery management duplicates the complete cloud computing environment including data, services, servers, and networks and ensures almost zero downtime for users. However, complete recovery management is expensive. Recent data recovery tools have a number of different features:

- automatic backup at different geographic locations;
- deletion control in which deleted items are stored in a protected area and can be restored in case of need;
- version control in which multiple backup points are provided with respect to time so that data recovery can be selected from a specific time; and
- proactive reporting in which tools proactively monitor the status related to data loss and raise alerts thereby protecting data against loss.

Data/Vendor Lock-In

Data lock-in refers to the situation cloud users find themselves in with a particular cloud provider when they are unable to switch to another provider due to proprietary technologies, interfaces, and other legal contracts. In such a situation cloud users are not sure about what will happen to their data when they migrate from one service provider to another. Data may get altered for the sake of compatibility and hence data integrity will become an issue. Data lock-in can be overcome by choosing a vendor who provides standardized open interfaces and technologies.

Data Remanence

Data need to be protected not just against attacks and loss but also against deletion. *Data remanence refers to data that remain even after deletion.* For example, deleted data may be marked with some kind of flag instead of actual deletion. Residual data that are not deleted may lead to both advertent and inadvertent disclosure of sensitive information to others.

6.4.1.2 Application-Related Security Issues

Threats to applications include *malware injection, backdoor and debug options, hidden field manipulation,* and *misconfiguration of applications.*

Malware Injection

Malware injection refers to an attacker injecting malicious software into an application by exploiting the vulnerabilities in applications. Once the application is executed the code injected will get executed and an unwanted attack will occur. Moreover, an attacker can even inject a malicious virtual machine or a malicious service into a cloud system. When this malicious VM or code gets activated an attack will occur.

One way of preventing this kind of attack is to do an integrity check on VMs and service instances. Another is to use anti-malware software to detect malicious software and to take protective measures.

Backdoor and Debug Options

Backdoor and debug options are common development practices used by developers. Backdoor code has been specifically designed for debugging purposes. If that code is accidentally left in the application, then not only will the application get deployed but also the backdoor code. Hackers may exploit backdoor code as entry points for security threats.

A solution is to use robust network monitoring of open-source applications.

Hidden Fields in Web Forms

Hidden fields refer to hidden form fields in HTML. These fields usually contain state variables, like passwords, and can become visible by using the *view source* option of a web page. This makes it easy for hackers to modify the content of hidden fields.

Solutions include encrypting the contents or using session variables, which are more secure than hidden fields. Hence session variables should be used.

Misconfiguration of Application

When applications are configured with less secure settings, security threats become a distinct possibility. For example, a web server may be deliberately configured with an insecure setting to allow any user to navigate and access the directories, data, and resources of the system.

6.4.1.3 Server and Network-Related Threats

Server and network-related threats include both passive and active attacks:

- traffic eavesdropping;
- replay attack;
- man-in-the-middle attack;
- malware injection attack;
- session-hijacking attack; and
- denial of service attacks.

Traffic Eavesdropping

When data are sent from a cloud user to a cloud service provider they can be passively intercepted by an attacker (as shown in Fig. 6.9). Data confidentiality is lost in the figure because data have been disclosed to an unauthenticated and unauthorized attacker. Eavesdropping can be prevented by encrypting.

Replay Attack

A replay attack or playback attack is an attack where an attacker may sniff a message and replay the same message to recipient who assumes that the message is sent from the original sender (as shown in Fig. 6.10). Replay attacks can be avoided by combining or attaching the message with a random session identity.

Man-in-the-Middle Attack

In a man-in-the-middle attack an attacker positions himself between an authenticated cloud user and a cloud service provider. The attacker may passively eavesdrop and gain access to information or may impersonate the authenticated user and perform active attacks. In the second case, communication between the authenticated user and the cloud is broken. The user is unaware of the "man in the middle" and communicates with the attacker in the belief that he is communicating with the cloud service provider (as shown in Fig. 6.11).

The man-in-the-middle attack can be avoided using authentication and a message integrity check with a digital signature.

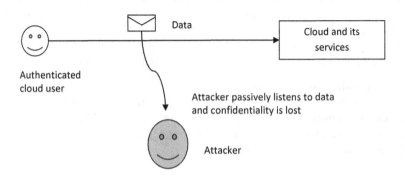

Fig. 6.9 An attacker passively listens (eavesdrops) to the data sent to cloud

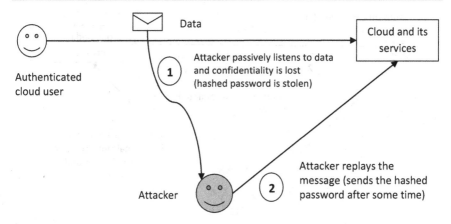

Fig. 6.10 Replay attack

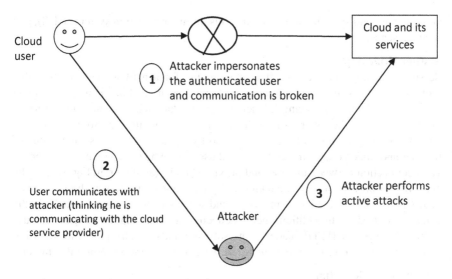

Fig. 6.11 Man-in-the-middle attack

Malware Injection Attack

A malware injection attack involves an attacker inserting a malicious service or malicious code in services offered by cloud service providers by exploiting vulnerabilities in the cloud software (as shown in Fig. 6.12). Malware can be any kind of code or script that has active content such as a virus or worm. Growth in the number of mobile devices being used and in social network media has increased malware creation. Different types of malware deliberately target different resources in the cloud infrastructure.

Malware injection can target such hardware as servers, data storage devices, networks, browsers, and application interfaces. It can be prevented by using

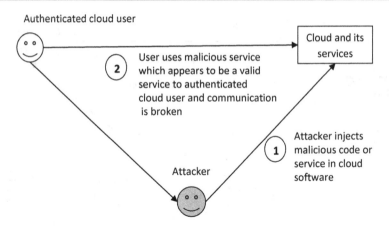

Fig. 6.12 Malware injection attack

anti-malware and spyware software, firewalls, intruder detection systems (IDS), and security scans.

Session Hijacking
Session hijacking involves an attacker searching for a network with high traffic, looking for users using less secure protocols, such as File Transfer Protocol (FTP) and Telnet, and placing himself between a targeted user and cloud service provider. With the help of different network-monitoring tools, such as packet-sniffing software and port-scanning software, he steals the session identity of the user and impersonates the authenticated user. Once he impersonates the user the valid connection between the user and provider breaks (as shown in Fig. 6.13). The best way to prevent session hijacking is by enabling protection at the cloud user end. Cloud users should use anti-virus and anti-malware software and keep the software up to date. In addition, there is effective software that cloud users can use to track changes in HTTP headers. The software adds penalty points to a session and if they exceed a *preset or configured penalty value*, the session will time out.

Denial of Service Attack
A denial of service (DoS) attack in cloud computing refers to an attack that stops any cloud server from providing services to legitimate users for a period of time or even indefinitely. The different types of DoS attacks are shown in Fig. 6.14.

Attackers try to consume the available network bandwidth and attack servers by flooding them with bogus data or bogus requests so that servers and their resources will be overwhelmed. The knock-on effect of this is that servers will deny legitimate users who will be unable to avail themselves of services. In a simple DoS attack the attacker uses one system to attack the victim server, whereas in a distributed DoS (DDoS) attack the attacker uses a network of hosts to attack the target server.

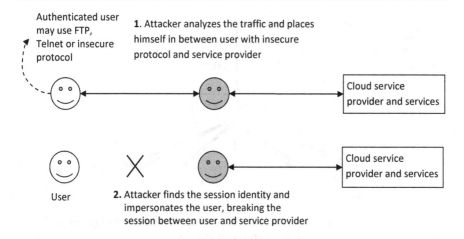

Fig. 6.13 Session hijacking attack

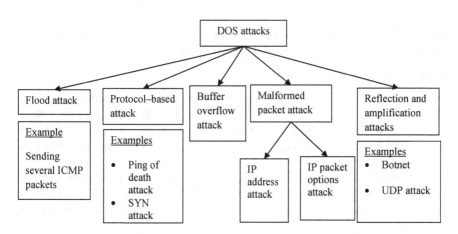

Fig. 6.14 Different types of DoS attack

Flooding attack

A flooding attack (as shown in Fig. 6.15) involves an attacker impersonating an authenticated user and gaining access to the cloud as an authorized user. Once the attacker becomes an authorized user he creates huge bogus Internet Control Message Protocol (ICMP) requests and sends them to service providers. The load balancer dispatches the requests to configured servers. The servers will be engaged with validating the authenticity of bogus requests rather than serving legitimate users. An ICMP flood attack overwhelms the server targeted rendering it unable to respond to the huge number of requests. In addition, the attacker overloads the network connection with bogus traffic. DoS attacks can be prevented by blocking

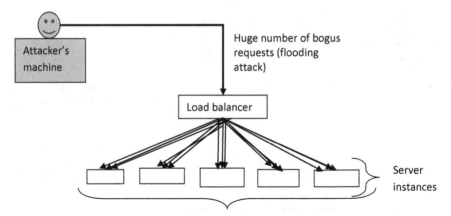

**Server instances focusing on authentication of bogus requests
rather than offering real services**

Fig. 6.15 Flooding attack

the originating IP address at the firewall level and killing the bogus requests. There
are security tools that can detect and prevent flood attacks.

Ping of death attack

The ping command is a utility used to test the reach of a network resource.
According to the Internet Protocol the size of a ping (IP) packet along with its
payload is 65,535 bytes. Most operating systems do not know how to handle
oversized IP packets resulting in them crashing or rebooting (as shown in
Fig. 6.16).

System reboot or system crash can be avoided by introducing some alternate
mechanisms so that during packet recombination the system will not reach the
maximum packet size constraint. Another way is to allot extra buffer to load the
oversized packet.

SYN flood attack

A SYN flood attack involves an attacker intentionally sending several SYN requests
with fake source addresses. It does so by exploiting the three-way handshaking
process of TCP (as shown in Fig. 6.17).

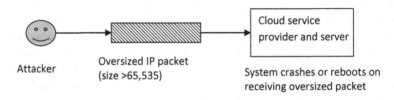

Fig. 6.16 Ping of death attack

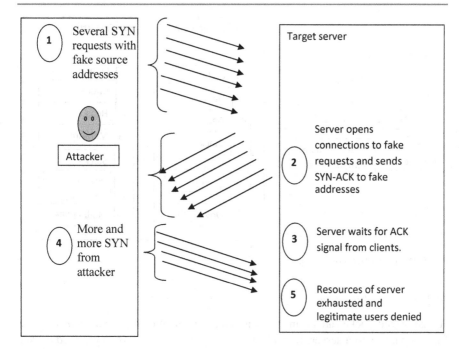

Fig. 6.17 SYN attack

When a TCP connection is established between a client and server, three-way handshaking is carried out between the client and server according to the TCP design. The handshaking process can be described in three steps:

Step 1—Client sends a SYN request to establish TCP connection with server.

Step 2—Server accepts and acknowledges the SYN request with a SYN-ACK signal.

Step 3—Client sends an ACK to acknowledge the server's SYN-ACK.

A SYN flood attack involves an attacker intentionally sending several SYN requests with fake source addresses. This obliges the server to acknowledge each and every SYN. In addition, it opens connections to fake source addresses. It sends a SYN-ACK to the client and waits for an ACK from the client. *But the client never sends an ACK to the server. Hence the server has several open connections to fake addresses* and, at a certain point in time, the TCP queue of all ports of the server will be engaged with fake addresses, rendering it unable to work with real clients.

Buffer overflow attack

A buffer overflow attack (as shown in Fig. 6.18) involves an attacker trying to send fake data whose size is larger than the existing buffer size. Hence the extra data overflow into the adjacent buffer, corrupting the actual data.

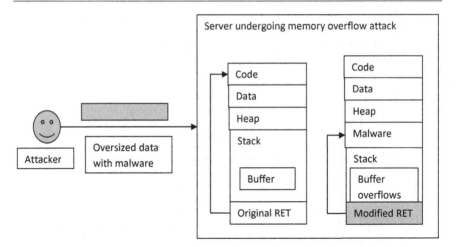

Fig. 6.18 Buffer overflow attack

Malformed packet attack

A malformed packet attack involves an attacker intentionally sending incorrectly formed packets to a server. IP packets are prone to two types of malformed packet attacks: IP address attack and IP packet option attack. In an IP address attack the attacker uses the same source and destination addresses. The server targeted does not know how to handle the malformed packet and it may crash. An IP packet option attack involves an attacker intentionally filling up all the options in the packet. It takes the server a long time to process this kind of packet. The server spends time in processing fake packets rather than serving legitimate users, resulting in the resources of the server being exploited for no good reason.

Reflection and amplification-based attack

Reflection and amplification-based attacks are typically DDoS attacks. This kind of attack (as shown in Fig. 6.19) involves an attacker using several intermediate systems to attack the victim server (with the aim of remaining undetected by security systems). The attacker designs a network of compromised systems called a *botnet*. This *botnet* is configured to reflect or forward bogus requests to the server targeted. When the attacker gives botnet the command, botnet initiates the DoS attack. In addition, the attacker may use a diverse range of IP addresses for botnet such that it too remains undetected. DDoS attacks are difficult to prevent. Nevertheless, there are techniques that can be used to prevent DDoS: service providers can make use of excess bandwidth; they can prevent vulnerabilities in system resources; and they can use firewalls, IDS, and other security products.

An amplification-based attack is similar to a reflection-based attack, but more overwhelming. It involves the attacker using protocols like Network Time Protocol (NTP), which consists of queries known to have very long responses. For example, the command MON_GETLIST queries addresses a server has communicated with.

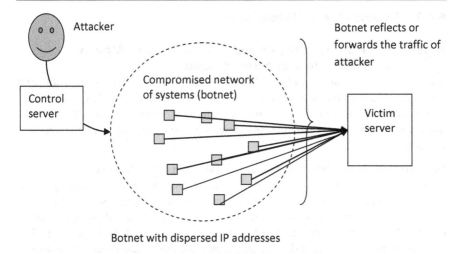

Botnet with dispersed IP addresses

Fig. 6.19 Distributed DoS attack with botnet as reflector network

The response to the above command is very long since it is allowed to return the addresses of up to 600 machines. Attackers intent on wasting the resources of the cloud send such commands to servers in the knowledge that responses of such a length will simply overwhelm servers.

6.4.1.4   Vulnerabilities in Cloud Application Programming Interfaces
When cloud service providers offer their services to customers they include a set of APIs. APIs are front-end interfaces used to configure, monitor, control, and manage resources. These APIs are used by external users and end users. Any vulnerabilities in these APIs can easily be exploited and the security of resources compromised. Hence it is important that APIs are designed to support encryption and to have adequate authentication and access control methods.

6.4.1.5   Insider Threats
Insider threat is defined as the threat posed by an authorized person (i.e., someone who has access rights to an information system) who misuses his privileges. Insider threat is more serious because the insider has much more access than an outside cyber attacker. In the cloud computing environment an insider may be working for the cloud service provider or for the enterprise using services provided by the cloud. There are insider detection models to predict the behavior of insiders and provide timely prediction. Cloud service providers can use a range of preventive measures against insider threat such as separation of duties, logging of activities, auditing, and redundant data centers.

6.4.2 Threats Due to Virtualization

6.4.2.1 Virtualization Threats and Related Security Aspects in Infrastructure as a Service Cloud

This subsection is made up of five further subsections that discuss, first, different levels of virtualization; second, isolation and multi-tenancy; third, threats due to virtualization in IaaS cloud; fourth, mechanisms to avoid virtualization threats; and, fifth, how security responsibilities are shared between cloud service providers and cloud users.

Different Levels of Virtualization in Infrastructure as a Service

There are two techniques of cloud computing that are key to bringing about effective resource sharing, dynamic scaling, and provisioning of resources for users: virtualization and multi-tenancy. As shown in Fig. 6.20 the underlying hardware of the cloud is abstracted by means of a software layer called the hypervisor. The concept of hiding hardware details, geographic locations, and other details and of making distributed and heterogeneous hardware into a single unified resource is called virtualization. The hypervisor hides the internal workings of physical hardware and consolidates them into a single logical resource. In general, virtualization is applied to servers, storage devices, and network devices. Physical servers, physical storage devices, and physical network devices are consolidated into a single logical server, a single logical storage device, and a single logical network,

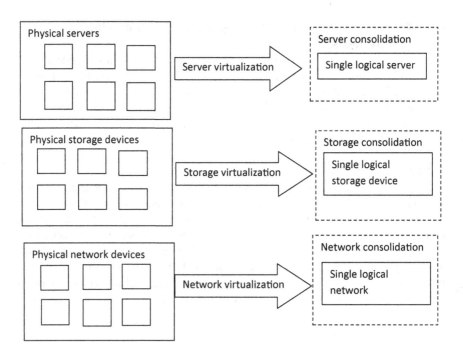

Fig. 6.20 Virtualization and hardware consolidation

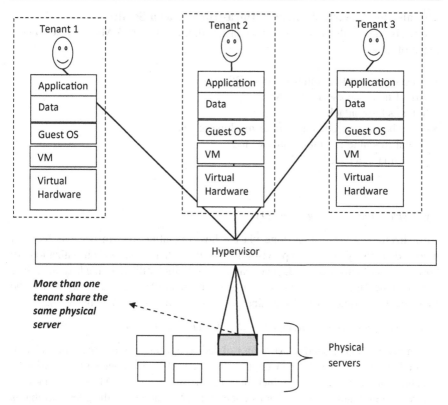

Fig. 6.21 Hardware-level isolation

respectively (as shown in Fig. 6.20). Although virtualization helps in effectively sharing resources, the security of the hypervisor and of virtual resources become very important. Hypervisor and virtualized resources should also be protected against security attacks similar to the way in which physical resources are protected. Virtualized environments are more vulnerable to security attacks.

Isolation and Multi-tenancy in Infrastructure as a Service

As mentioned above physical servers are consolidated into a logical server that is shared among multiple tenants. *Multi-tenancy refers to the configuration of virtual machines for two or more tenants on the same physical server* (as shown in Fig. 6.21). Further, more than one physical server may be configured to the same client. Clients can deploy virtual machines on the top of virtualized hardware. Guest operating systems and applications can be installed in VMs as per the client's needs.

From a security point of view it is essential to isolate the virtual hardware and virtual machines of one user from those of other users. The hypervisor is responsible for ensuring this.

Threats Due to Virtualization in Infrastructure as a Service

Vulnerabilities in the virtualization layer [3–5], guest OS, or VMs can lead to new kinds of attacks:

- hypervisor attack through the host OS;
- virtual machine escape attack;
- hyperjacking attack;
- cache-based side channel virtual machine attack;
- virtual machine migration attack; and
- guest image attack.

Hypervisor attack through host OS

Virtualization is very often done via the host operating system because the cost involved in using a host hypervisor is less than that of native virtualization. In host-based virtualization an attacker can exploit vulnerabilities in the host operating system. Once the attacker gains control of the host OS, he can easily attack the hypervisor and other virtual machines on top of it (as shown in Fig. 6.22).

Virtual machine escape attack (a kind of hypervisor attack)

In general, a VM is a sandbox (i.e., an isolated computing environment) provided to a cloud user such that he can deploy his guest OS and other software without affecting the environment in which they run. However, in a VM escape attack an attacker intentionally runs malicious code on a VM that allows the guest OS that is running within the VM to exploit any vulnerability in the VM and to break out of the sandbox environment and interact with the underlying hypervisor or with other VMs that share the same hardware (as shown in Fig. 6.23).

Hyperjacking attack

Hyperjacking involves an attacker leasing a virtual machine with the intention of installing a malicious guest operating system (as shown in Fig. 6.24). This malicious guest OS exploits any vulnerabilities in the underlying hypervisor. It may

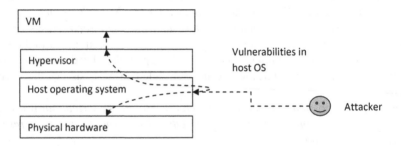

Fig. 6.22 Attacking the hypervisor through host operating system

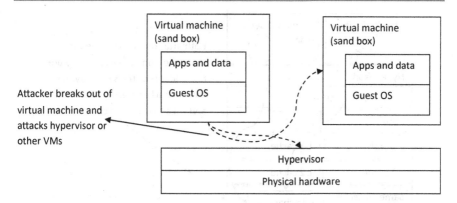

Fig. 6.23 VM escape attack

change the source code of the hypervisor to gain control over memory and the data of other VMs. Using a malicious guest OS to gain control over the underlying hypervisor is called hyperjacking.

Cache-based side channel virtual machine attack

Each core in multi-core hardware architecture has separate cache memory only for two levels: L1 and L2. However, L3 cache is common and shared by more than one core (as shown in Fig. 6.25).

   Attackers will exploit the fact that L3 cache can be shared by more than one core. When an attacker has his VM co-located with the target VM (i.e., the VM the attacker aims to attack), data and information may leak out due to *inadequate logical isolation in L3 cache*. Data leaking through L3 cache is typical of a side channel cache attack (see Fig. 6.25).

Fig. 6.24 Hyperjacking (attacking the hypervisor via virtual machine and malicious guest OS)

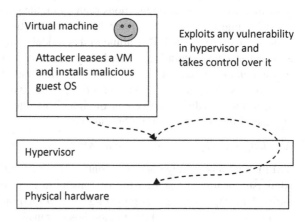

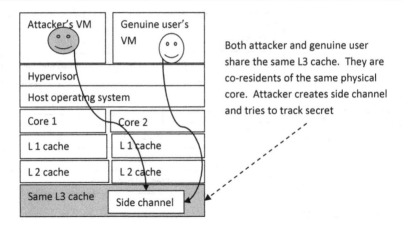

Fig. 6.25 L3 cache side channel attack

VM migration attack

A virtual machine is simply a set of files stored on a host computer. It can consume different resources: CPU, disk, memory, and network. *Virtual machine migration refers to the process of moving a virtual machine and the states of its resources from one physical server to another.* Virtual migration is necessary to meet different objectives such as load balancing, availability, reliability, power management, maintenance, and recovery from host failure. The process of migration involves transferring VM files from the source host to destination host and then transferring the states of the CPU, memory, and network. The migration of VM as well as the states of its resources is done with the help of a module called the *VM migration module.* The migration process is shown in Fig. 6.26.

VM migration can be carried out in two ways: cold migration and live migration. Cold migration involves applications running on the guest OS *being stopped* before the VM migrates from the source host to destination host. After migration the applications are restarted. Downtime in this model is high. Live migration involves a virtual machine migrating to the destination host without *disturbing the running of applications.* Users will never know that their underlying operating system and applications are migrating. From a security perspective there are three areas that are prone to attack: administrative console interfaces, the contents or data of the VM, and the virtual machine migration module.

Attacking the administrative console interfaces during virtual machine migration

VM migration is usually under the control of the system administrator. The system administrator uses the administrative console to carry out a number of operations during VM migration such as preparing for VM migration, setting up the necessary resources in the source and destination hosts, transferring the states of process and memory, creating a new VM, activating the new VM, and deleting the VM at source.

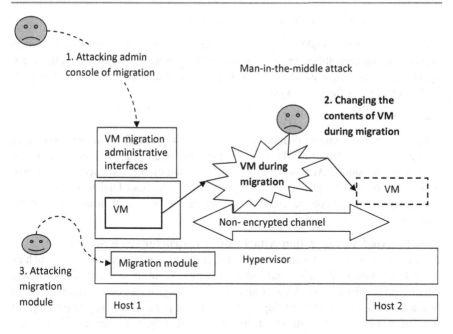

Fig. 6.26 VM migration attack

Any security vulnerabilities in the administrative console are prone to a number of attacks:

- unnecessary VM migration (initiated by an attacker);
- denial of service attack (an attacker may create many VMs and overload the host OS with as many VMs as possible making it impossible for the host OS to accept any migrated VM); and
- an attacker can migrate a VM to a target host of his own choosing.

Attacking the states of virtual machine during migration

Attackers have been known to carry out passive and active attacks on the states of a CPU, memory, and network while a VM is being migrated from the source host to destination host over a non-encrypted channel:

- passively gaining information such as application data, messages, passwords, and security tokens; and
- actively modifying the states of applications, processes, and memory.

Attacking the virtual machine migration module

The VM migration module is part of the hypervisor. Attackers have been known to exploit the vulnerabilities present in the VM migration module and attack the hypervisor. Having gained access to the hypervisor an attacker takes control over all VMs and disturbs the entire system.

Guest image attack

Creating too many guest OS images and storing them on disk not only consumes storage resources but runs the risk of attackers accessing data or code in an unauthorized manner. Attackers can gain information on the VM checkpoint, which is a snapshot of VM physical memory contents. This can lead to disclosure of confidential data. Hence the creation of unnecessary guest OS images should be avoided.

How to Avoid Virtualization Attacks in Infrastructure as a Service

A hypervisor is software that distributes the computing resources available, such as the CPU, storage devices, and network devices, to many virtual machines. Although virtualization facilitates multi-tenancy many attacks occur simply because physical isolation is absent. Multiple tenants are simply logically separated. Logical separation alone is not sufficient to ensure the required security. Hence the hypervisor and virtual components should be subject to appropriate security solutions to prevent attacks. There are a number of methods that can be used to avoid virtualization attacks:

- The physical cloud infrastructure should be kept safe from insider attacks. Cloud service providers should ensure that server rooms, computers, storage devices, network devices, and other physical infrastructure are secure. Cloud service providers should consider the behavior of insiders because social engineering is one of the preferred attacking mechanisms employed by hackers.
- Setting strict hypervisor console access privileges will reduce attacks.
- The code integrity of the hypervisor should be maintained with the help of tools such as HyperSafe.
- The hypervisor should be hardened (i.e., the process of stripping unnecessary software from the hypervisor to reduce potential vulnerabilities).
- Communication between the hypervisor and the virtual machine should be properly configured.
- The hypervisor should be updated with patches against the latest threats.
- Since network intrusions affect hypervisor security it is important to install cutting-edge firewalls and intrusion prevention systems.
- The cloud infrastructure should be protected by proper firewalls, intrusion detection systems, network-monitoring tools, etc. The guest OS and VMs should be updated with anti-malware and protective tools. The guest OS and VM and other system-level software should be hardened against all possible vulnerabilities. Any kind of unnecessary code should be stripped.

- Guest OS image files must be scanned to detect viruses, worms, spyware, and any other malware and protect against potential attacks. When VMs are migrated from one machine to another cloud service providers should ensure that all the data are completely removed from the previous disk. When the VM is stored for backup it should be encrypted. Similarly, when a VM is deleted its backup must also be deleted completely from the system. Unnecessary images should not be kept.

Shared Security Responsibilities in Infrastructure as a Service

Security responsibilities in IaaS are shared between the cloud service provider and cloud user (as shown in Fig. 6.27). The shaded area denotes the responsibilities of the cloud user and the white or blank area denotes the responsibilities of the cloud service provider.

As Fig. 6.27 shows, IaaS cloud service providers provide security facilities for servers, data centers, network interfaces, storage devices, other physical infrastructure, and the hypervisor. The cloud consumer is responsible for the virtual network, virtual machines, operating systems, middleware, applications, interfaces, and data. In a nutshell, cloud service providers are only responsible for providing security for the physical infrastructure they offer and everything else is left to the user. Hence the user has more responsibility. The cloud user is responsible for implementing sufficient security mechanisms for all layers that remain on top of the hypervisor.

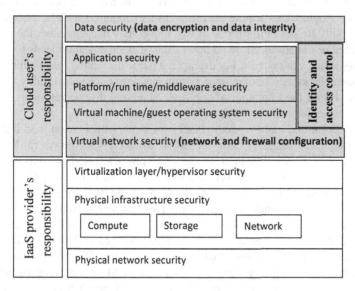

Fig. 6.27 Shared security model in IaaS

6.4.2.2 Virtualization Threats and Related Security Aspects in Platform as a Service Cloud

Platform as a Service cloud offers additional services on top of its physical infrastructure. Virtualized physical resources, virtualized infrastructure, virtualized middleware platforms, runtime environments, development and deployment tools, and other platform services are consumed as services in PaaS cloud. Hence PaaS cloud service providers must acknowledge there are additional constraints and possibly more potential security threats caused by various services and components. Not only must virtual machines be protected against malicious attacks, maintaining the integrity of the development and deployment environment and applications is another important concern. The most common examples of PaaS cloud service providers are Google Apps and Microsoft Windows Azure.

Common security threats in Platform as a Service

- *Heterogeneous resources and misconfiguration of applications*: PaaS cloud consists of heterogeneous hardware and software resources distributed across different locations. This heterogeneity causes problems *in configuring security settings* as the settings are different for different types of resources. If an application developer mistakenly configures an application with poor or less secure settings, then the configuration itself will become vulnerable.
- *Migration of applications and lack of standardization in resource access APIs*: To achieve efficient resource provisioning and performance, availability, scalability, etc., user applications are migrated among operating systems and hosts. Since resources are heterogeneous and diverse in nature, access to them is not uniform. Applications acquire the resources they require via APIs. Since resource access APIs are not uniform one of two things may happen: either the resources are halted or underutilized. In addition, lack of standardization leads to improper security settings in systems. For example, a particular setting may be more secure in a particular system but the same setting may introduce vulnerability to another system. Hence the migration of applications among diverse resources opens up new avenues for security threats.
- *Virtualization and multi-tenancy*: PaaS uses more virtualization than IaaS. PaaS very frequently employs two levels of isolation (as shown in Fig. 6.28): hypervisor-level isolation to share the same physical resources with more than one tenant and application-level isolation to share the same guest OS with more than one application. As shown in Fig. 6.28, in the hypervisor layer more than one virtual machine may share the same physical server. Similarly, at the guest OS level the same guest OS may be shared by more than one application. This means that more than one application may be deployed in the same OS. PaaS not only deploys more than one application on the same OS, but also deploys an application in multiple systems at the same time. More and more virtualization tend to bring in more and more vulnerabilities. Hence it become essential for PaaS provider to introduce more security mechanisms.

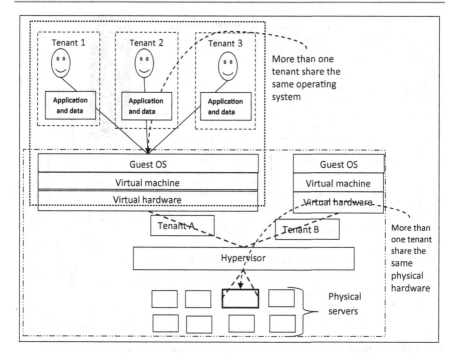

Fig. 6.28 Application-level isolation

- *Vulnerabilities in user applications*: Vulnerabilities in a user's applications, such as *backdoor code* and *hidden form fields*, can create security threats from other users and hackers. Applications and data should be protected against attacks by putting in place secure coding and security mechanisms to reduce attacks.
- *Vulnerabilities in functional layers of PaaS and shared security responsibilities*: Not only does PaaS cloud have different functional layers (as shown in Fig. 6.29), it also provides different services: load balancing, orchestrations, integration, connectivity, and caching. In addition to services, PaaS cloud has a core management layer and security layer. The management layer is responsible for resource provisioning, monitoring, and management tasks. The security layer is responsible for managing security threats and attacks and should protect all PaaS layers against guest OS-level attacks, virtualization attacks, DoS attacks, man-in-the-middle attacks, API attacks, third-party development and deployment tool attacks, database attacks, application framework attacks, and middleware attacks. When moving from bottom to top in the PaaS architecture there are increasing numbers of components and functional layers, which inevitably leads to more vulnerability and more threats. At the hypervisor level at the bottom guest OS-level threats occur, whereas at the top threats occur in development and deployment tools, APIs, databases, etc. Network-level and application-level attacks are prone to occur.

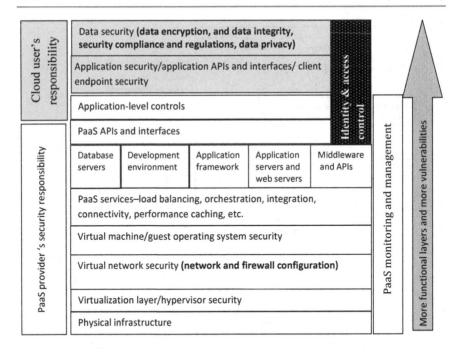

Fig. 6.29 Functional layers and shared security responsibilities of PaaS

How security responsibilities are shared in Platform as a Service

The sharing of security responsibilities between a PaaS cloud provider and user is illustrated in Fig. 6.29. *PaaS cloud providers are responsible for providing security up to the development and deployment layer.* In a nutshell, PaaS cloud implicitly offers infrastructure, platforms, and common services to users. Hence **providers** are responsible for providing security for infrastructure and all layers (such as hypervisor, guest OS, middleware, and database servers) up to platforms.

  Cloud users are responsible for providing security for applications and data. In addition, security for application-level controls and identify and access controls is shared by both the provider and user. Cloud users are not only responsible for controlling passwords, role-based access, and privileged users to secure the deployment of applications, they are also *responsible for security compliance and regulatory and privacy policies.*

Common Security Mechanisms in Platform as a Service

- PaaS cloud providers should offer *standardized means of accessing resources.* This will reduce interoperability issues and related security issues.
- Encryption, strict authentication, authorization, and traceability should be implemented.
- Platforms, tools, frameworks, and APIs should be hardened.

- Events and activities that have occurred should be continuously tracked and event records audited.
- All VMs and software tools should be protected with anti-spyware, anti-virus, and anti-malware.
- All tools should be protected with the latest patches.
- All perimeter and end point security should be tight such that cloud surface-level attacks are kept to a minimum.

6.4.2.3 Virtualization Threats and Related Security Aspects in Software as a Service Cloud

Software as a Service is a cloud service model in which applications are hosted by cloud service providers and made available to end users over the internet on demand using a pay-as-you-go pricing model. Cloud service providers implicitly employ virtualization at different levels:

- SaaS providers may use hypervisor-level isolation so that the same physical infrastructure can be shared with multiple tenants.
- They may use application-level isolation so that the same guest OS can be shared with more than one application.
- They may use data-level isolation so that the same application instance can be shared with more than one data set.
- They may also employ application-level isolation so that the same data set can be shared (i.e., more than one application can access the same data).
- Very frequently they may deploy the same application instance in multiple VM instances according to availability, scalability, and performance requirements (see Application A in Fig. 6.30).

These situations are captured and shown in Fig. 6.30.

SaaS extensively employs virtualization and multi-tenancy, which implies it has to meet many security-related challenges. SaaS providers own the applications and users are allowed to use them according to the service level agreement (SLA) signed between the parties. SaaS applications can interact with other applications and data. They are accessed using browsers and web service interfaces. Hence they are prone to browser attacks, XML attacks, and web service attacks.

Web Services (WS) security, Extendable Markup Language (XML) encryption, and the Secure Sockets Layer (SSL) protocol can be used to implement security.

The way in which security responsibilities are shared between the SaaS provider and cloud user is shown in Fig. 6.31.

As shown in Fig. 6.31 the cloud service provider is responsible for providing security to all layers except data security. Moreover, identity access management and client end security are shared between cloud users and cloud service providers. Cloud users are responsible for providing security mechanisms to safeguard their own data.

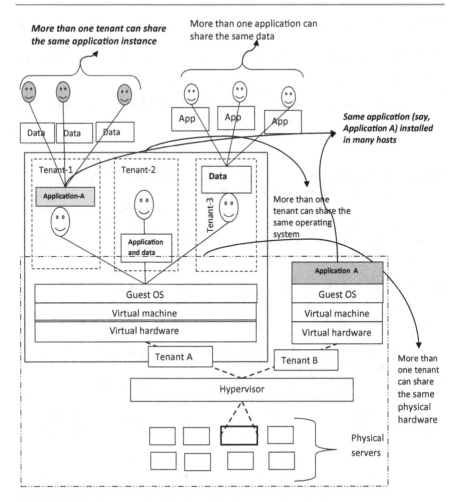

Fig. 6.30 Virtualization and multi-tenancy at different levels in SaaS

Typical threats related to data in Software as a Service

- *Unpredictability and instability*: Although SaaS provides high-quality and proven solutions and applications, there is always the question: *What happens if the SaaS provider goes out of business or, more specifically, what happens to the data?* Currently the situation is unpredictable, but an answer needs to be found.
- *Lack of transparency*: SaaS providers are often not very forthcoming despite assuring their clients that they are better at keeping client data safe than any other provider. This raises concerns regarding the provider's lack of transparency on how their entire security protocol is being handled.
- *Uncertainty in data location*: Most SaaS providers do not disclose where their data centers are. Hence customers are not aware of where their data are actually

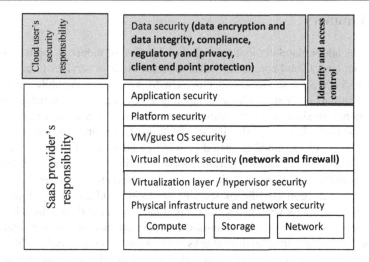

Fig. 6.31 Shared security responsibilities in SaaS

stored. Cloud users need to be aware of the Federal Information Security Management Act (FISMA) which states that customers need to keep sensitive data within the country. However, SaaS providers, like Symantec, offer their services across many countries. Where the data are stored could then be a major concern for cloud users.

- *No direct control of user's data*: In SaaS users move their data to the SaaS provider's location. Users are often only given indirect control over their data. It all depends on the level of *customizability the provider offers*, which again may be limited. Although data are stored at the provider's site, appropriate data security has to be provided by the user (the critical point to remember here is that ***identity and access management*** *should be implemented as a shared responsibility*).
- *SaaS services may not keep up with modern security standards*: Although most SaaS providers employ security standards, they are not always up to date. Another point to note is that SaaS providers typically persuade users to sign a *long-term agreement for service access*. Since security standards are not always up to date and users go for long-term agreements, it is likely that today's data may not be secure, although it may be with respect to old standards. There is no surety about data security after a year or two as protocols, standards, and policies are continuously changing.

Ultimately, it is the responsibility of users to plan and use SaaS applications as effectively as possible.

6.5 Summary

Enterprises adopt cloud computing with the objective of reducing capital cost and operational cost. Cloud computing offers different kinds of services to users: IaaS, PaaS, and SaaS. Such services are deployed in different ways via public, private and hybrid deployment models. Cloud computing extensively uses virtualization and multi-tenancy to share available resources efficiently, which significantly impacts security aspects. Basically, the implementation of security mechanisms across different layers of the cloud is shared between cloud service providers and cloud users. The chapter began by describing basic security requirements and how the cloud computing infrastructure differs from the conventional enterprise security model. It then categorized different security attacks in cloud computing. It presented an overview of data-level attacks, application attacks, network attacks (like traffic eavesdropping), active attacks, man-in-the-middle attacks, and replay attacks. It described different virtualization attacks such as hypervisor attack, VM escape attack, hyperjacking attack, and cache side channel attack. After presenting basic security aspects and different attacks the chapter described security aspects in IaaS, PaaS, and SaaS. In addition, it described in detail how security responsibilities are shared between user and provider in the above models.

6.6 Exercises

1. Company A is offering its business solution, say, for logistic management, which is its core competency. Company A wants to offer the solution quickly to its customers so it is looking to deploy its applications immediately. Company B is providing the infrastructure and platform to Company A. Draw a schematic to highlight how security will be shared between the two companies using the above inputs.
2. Assume you are health service provider with patient data. You are about to use a healthcare application offered by, say, Company K. Explain how you prepare your security requirements. Prepare a matrix to show how security responsibilities are shared.
3. Compare the security aspects in IaaS, PaaS, and SaaS.
4. Since multi-tenancy brings much vulnerability why do we need it? Justify your answer. Who benefits from multi-tenancy?
5. Data locality is a major issue with the cloud? Nevertheless, enterprises prefer to use the cloud despite of possible data breaches. Why is this?

References

1. Mather T, Kumaraswamy S, Latif S (2009) Cloud security and privacy—an enterprise perspective on risk and compliance. O' Reilly Publishers
2. Ahmed M, Hossain MA (2014) Cloud computing and security issues in the cloud. Int J Netw Secur Appl (IJNSA) 6(1)

3. Rittinghouse JW, Ransome JF (2010) Cloud Computing implementation, management and security. CRC Press
4. Krutz RL, Vines RD (2010) Cloud security a comprehensive guide to secure cloud computing. Wiley Publishing Inc
5. Akinola Kayode E, Odumosu Adesola A (2015) Threat handling and security issue in cloud computing. Int J Sci Eng Res 6(11)

Cloud Migration

7

Learning Objectives

Having dealt with security it is now time to introduce a decision-related concept: cloud migration. The objective of this chapter is to introduce the fundamentals of cloud migration. By the end of the chapter the reader should understand the migration process, different migration strategies, and the taxonomy of applications, such as cloud-enabled, cloud-optimized, and cloud-native applications, according to the migration strategies.

Motivational Questions

1. What is cloud migration?
2. Since there are different service offerings in the cloud environment and many ways to deploy, which cloud should I migrate to?
3. What about the cost involved in migration? Will it be expensive?
4. What can I migrate? Is it just applications or just data or everything?
5. What is the best way to migrate? Will it be the same for applications?
6. Is it safe to migrate my applications?
7. Is any risk involved in migration?
8. Will the data be safe?
9. What are cloud-ready, cloud-optimized, and cloud-native applications?

Preface

Right from the first chapter the reader has been gradually guided through the various concepts underlying the cloud, especially core technologies such as virtualization, networking, and storage. More importantly, the reader should now have a

© Springer Nature Switzerland AG 2019
S. Chellammal and C. Pethuru Raj, *Essentials of Cloud Computing*,
Texts in Computer Science, https://doi.org/10.1007/978-3-030-13134-0_7

deeper understanding of the various security threats in the cloud environment. Moreover, the reader should now understand that it is the user who has to implement appropriate security mechanisms (especially regarding his own data) and has sole responsibility to protect the privacy and compliance of security policies. Having learned the core technologies and security concepts it is now time for the reader to be introduced to another management-related theme: cloud migration. *Cloud migration is the movement of applications, data, or services or any IT system from an organization to the cloud.* This chapter describes the migration process and different migration strategies. It also looks at the reasons enterprises opt for migration as well as the different types of migration. One of the reasons is, of course, that cloud migration brings modernization to applications. According to business drivers, technical drivers, and the level of complexity, applications are migrated with different migration strategies. According to the migration strategy employed, migrated applications will turn out to be one of three types of applications: cloud ready, cloud optimized, or cloud native.

7.1 Motivations for Cloud Migration

The term migration refers to movement. Cloud migration refers to the migration or movement of applications, data, services, or any proprietary facility from an organization's onsite computing facility to the cloud, which provides a cost-effective, reliable, versatile, interoperable, flexible, and manageable environment. An *enterprise should prepare a business case* outlining the advantages of cloud migration. *It should analyze the business from the technical, security, and privacy viewpoint to ascertain whether migration is justified.* If deemed justifiable, the enterprise has *to analyze the benefits and risks* of cloud migration, cost involved in migration, and complexity involved in migration. Only when the pros outweigh the cons should the enterprise adopt cloud migration.

Cloud migration is a systematic process [1] that includes many phases. Moreover, no single migration strategy or method is common to all applications. The method chosen depends on the nature or type of application. After migration the services are available to enterprise users over the internet. To avoid failure it is important for any enterprise to carefully analyze its motivations for migration from a business, technical, and security and privacy viewpoint (as shown in Fig. 7.1).

Business Motivations
Most enterprises generally opt for cloud migration for the following reasons:

- *Reduced capital and operational costs*: Cloud computing offers different classes of services from infrastructure to platform to software applications *in short time* and according to the *demands of users*. The cloud offers services at *low cost through pay-as-you-go models*. Hence *the capital and operational expenditure involved in the IT infrastructure of an enterprise is significantly reduced.*

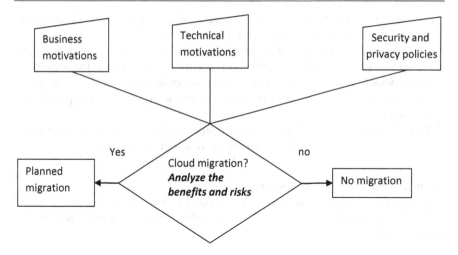

Fig. 7.1 Decision making for cloud migration

- *Fast time to market*: Since services in cloud computing are rapidly provisioned (within minutes to hours) enterprises can focus on core application development rather than on infrastructure and other platforms. This helps companies deliver their <u>core services very quickly</u>.
- *Mobility options*: Cloud users can access cloud services through their internet connection even if they are mobile. Hence an employees of an organization <u>can work</u> with applications <u>even</u> when they are on the <u>move</u> over a secure connection provided by cloud service providers.

Technical Motivations
In addition to business drivers there are many technical factors that drive cloud migration:

- *Reduced maintenance*: Cloud service providers manage the resources they offer to users. According to the type of service the user chooses, responsibilities are shared by both provider and consumer. In addition, cloud computing extensively uses virtualization at various levels such as hardware and operating system. This <u>reduces hardware resources significantly</u> and hence management becomes easier.
- *Dynamic scale-up and scale-out facility*: If an enterprise in an on-premises environment plans to meet spikes in load or peak loads, then it is essential to invest heavily to procure and establish the required resources to meet peak load conditions. <u>Resources would only be used during peak loads and remain underutilized most of the time</u>. Although an enterprise may be able to meet peak loads, to do so may well involve huge capital cost or investment. However, in the cloud computing environment cloud service providers dynamically provide not only horizontal (scale-up) and vertical (scale-out) resource provisioning but also a

scale-down option. Since services are paid for using a pay-as-you-go model the enterprise will only need to pay for the resources used.

- *Application development and modernization*: A conventional on-premises environment may not readily support the modern services needed for application development. However, the cloud computing environment with its integrated approach easily adopts modern services for application development and deployment.
- *Flexible storage options*: Cloud storage offers vast amounts of data storage at low cost. Cloud users can easily expand and shrink their storage needs.

Security and Privacy Motivations

Although there are many business and technical factors motivating enterprises to opt for cloud migration, security and privacy policies play a vital role when making the decision:

- First of all, an enterprise should be very clear that its workloads are being migrated to a third-party computing facility. This inherently implies that the enterprise trusts the cloud service provider it has chosen. The enterprise should be aware that, just because it has decided to migrate its workloads to the cloud, it cannot put the entire burden of security on cloud service providers. The enterprise should understand that *the maintenance of privacy and security policies is primarily its own responsibility and not the cloud provider's*. Security responsibilities are shared between cloud providers and users. Hence an enterprise needs to assess the effect migrating into the cloud might have on its security and privacy policies. Although the cloud offers many services, data protection is the responsibility of cloud users.
- Cloud users or enterprises should be aware that their data will be geographically located across different locations and each location or country may have its own privacy laws and regulations. It is imperative for an enterprise to make a clear decision in this regard because sensitive data, such as health care information, financial information, and other personal information of customers, should never be disclosed to anyone, not even unintentionally.
- The enterprise has to analyze, in addition to privacy policies, all the fundamental security mechanisms such as service availability, reliability, authentication, authorization, access control, confidentiality, integrity, and auditing. *Enterprises should understand there is always the possibility of data loss as a result of natural disasters or security breaches.*
- Enterprises *should be aware that they will be working in a multi-tenancy environment when they migrate to the public cloud.*
- Enterprises should *scrutinize backup facilities* and other data protection mechanisms offered by cloud service providers.
- Enterprises should understand that they *do not have direct control over their data.*
- Enterprises should be aware of the *data lock-in problem*. On migration data are naturally locked in with a provider and enterprises have no idea where their data

reside. Enterprises may have difficulty in migrating their data from one service provider to another as most vendors have their own proprietary interfaces. Hence compatibility issues may arise.

• Data stored in the cloud may suffer from the data remanence issue, which means that data may still be present (but flagged for deletion) in physical storage even after being deleted.

In a nutshell, an enterprise has to analyze the pros and cons associated with each and every management, technical, security, and privacy aspect prior to migration.

Typical Examples Where Cloud Computing Provides Benefits

• applications experiencing huge traffic;
• applications experiencing uncertain loads;
• applications that need quick and continuous development and deployment;
• applications that have growing storage demands;
• applications experiencing peak loads as a result of seasonal traffic;
• applications that have no sensitive data;
• enterprises needing to distribute an application across different locations;
• enterprises needing to undergo frequent software upgrades, regular database backup, and periodic maintenance;
• applications that do not have stateful information; and
• applications with only internal users.

Enterprises should be wary when migrating workloads to the cloud as there are risks. It is important to determine whether migrating an application to the cloud is risky or not. According to Yusuf Rangwala, technical architect with Syntel's cloud labs, there are a number of typical migration issues [2]:

• It is difficult to migrate mission-critical applications to the cloud. Hence such applications should not be considered for migration or should be given low priority for migration.
• If an application makes use of stateful data during its operation, then there may be a risk of losing such information due to hardware failure in the cloud network.
• If the application uses third-party tools or software, license issues may arise during migration.
• If an application has external users, then it is likely to have security risks as a result of being deployed in the public cloud.
• Applications that experience unpredictable loads will benefit from migration, whereas applications that experience predictable or consistent loads are best handled by the enterprise itself. For example, the peak loads of a financial application are likely to be certain, whereas those of a retail application are likely to be uncertain. Human resource management applications have consistent peak loads. Applications that experience certain or consistent loads are best managed by the company itself.

- In addition to the cases pointed out by Yusuf Rangwala, applications that have sensitive data may suffer from unintentional or intentional disclosure of data if they are migrated to cloud.
- Similarly, high-performance applications are not suitable for migration.

At the same time as an enterprise analyzes the business, technical, and security/privacy aspects, it has to consider another important aspect of the cloud computing environment: type of cloud service and type of cloud deployment. These two factors affect the type of cloud migration an enterprise decides on. Consider an enterprise that holds health-related data. It wants to migrate to the cloud computing environment. The cloud deployment it decides on is a major decision. In this case private cloud deployment is better. Were it to adopt public cloud, it would face security threats since public cloud supports multiple tenants and data might get disclosed to others in violation of security and privacy policies.

7.1.1 Types of Migration

Different types of migration have appeared as a consequence of the different service classes and deployment models of cloud computing (migration types are shown in Fig. 7.2).

Migration to Infrastructure as a Service Cloud
IaaS cloud service providers (like Amazon) provide cloud consumers with the basic infrastructure: servers, storage devices, network devices, and other physical infrastructure. Administrative, hardware, and configuration services are also

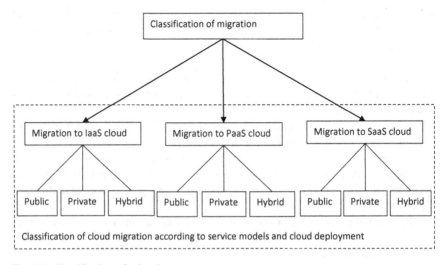

Fig. 7.2 Classification of migration

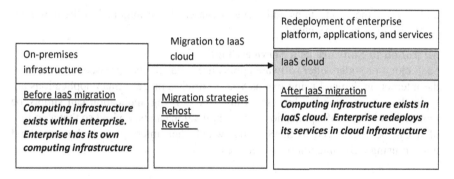

Fig. 7.3 Migration to IaaS cloud

provided. Any enterprise choosing IaaS cloud hosts its computing environment (platform, tools, applications, and data) on top of the IaaS cloud infrastructure [3].

In a nutshell, platforms and applications are deployed on virtual machines offered by the provider (as shown in Fig. 7.3). Enterprises typically migrate resource-intensive applications to the cloud to meet dynamic resource requirements and data storage needs. While migrating to IaaS cloud, virtual machines should be properly configured and guest operating systems rightly chosen such that the applications and other workloads can very easily be redeployed in the new cloud infrastructure.

Migration to Platform as a Service Cloud
PaaS cloud providers (such as Microsoft Azure) provide both the infrastructure and platform for cloud users. If an enterprise chooses migration to PaaS cloud, it has to tailor its applications and services and then redeploy them on top of the platform provided by the cloud (as shown in Fig. 7.4). The platform, middleware, databases, and development and deployment tools in this migration are provided by providers. Hence it is essential to acquire suitable platform, middleware, databases, and other

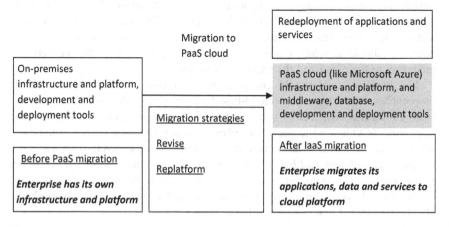

Fig. 7.4 Migration to PaaS cloud

tools so that the applications and services can easily be migrated to the new platform provided by PaaS cloud.

Migration to Software as a Service Cloud
SaaS cloud providers offer software applications that can be accessed by users over the internet on demand using pay-as-you-go pricing models. SaaS applications are typically accessed using a browser. Either the existing application can simply be replaced with the SaaS application or the application can be revised so that a portion of it can be outsourced to SaaS cloud, which then interacts with the non-cloud portion using SOA integration techniques.

7.2   Migration Process

According to Stephen Orban, Global Head of Enterprise Strategy at Amazon Web Services, cloud migration is a process that consists of five phases [3] (as shown in Fig. 7.5):

(i)   opportunity evaluation
(ii)   portfolio discovery and planning
(iii) application design
(iv)   migration and validation
(v)   operate.

(i) Opportunity evaluation

The opportunity evaluation phase analyzes the events and factors that drive migration to the cloud.

It is important to note that, although the cloud provides reduced capital and operational costs, scalability, rapid provision of resources, etc., *these benefits are only generic.* Any company wanting to migrate to the cloud *should clearly define its specific motivating factors* and reasons for migration. These are the business values and driving factors that will justify *the scope of critical migration* decisions. The company should *develop a business case* that clearly defines the **reasons** for migrating to the cloud and the expected **benefits**.

The business case should compare the total cost of ownership (TCO) of on-premises IT solutions and cloud-based IT solutions. The comparison should consider various cost factors such as those involved in cloud infrastructure and migration. TCO is used to decide whether a cloud-based solution is viable or not. For example, analysis of the business case will lead to concrete findings like *a company's developers will be 50% more productive in cloud-based IT than they are in on-premises IT.* Along with this analysis the budget and time constraints, customer demands, market pressures, business competitors, etc. of the company should also be considered before making the decision.

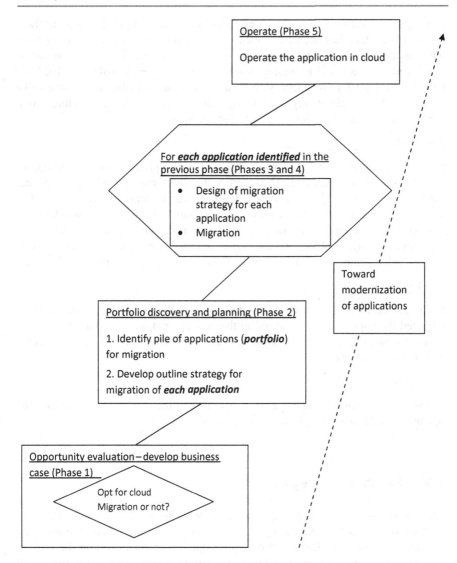

Fig. 7.5 Different phases of migration process

(ii) *Portfolio discovery and planning*

In the portfolio discovery and planning phase, portfolio refers to the pile of applications (all applications) of the company. The applications of the company may be interrelated or independent. Hence it is necessary to find the interdependencies among applications and the migration of applications should be accordingly planned. In addition, each application has its own software architecture. Every application would have been developed using a specific set of tools. Tools have different license policies. Hence the *complexity involved in migrating an application varies from application to application*; for example, a company might have two applications one of which has been developed using the latest microservices architecture whereas the other is a legacy application. A legacy application is an application developed using any old technology such as PowerBuilder, COBOL, CORBA, or CGI. It is difficult to move a legacy application to a new computing environment like the cloud. The complexity involved in migrating a microservices architecture–based application is easier than that of a legacy application.

(iii) Application design

Since applications are heterogeneous in nature each application has to be appropriately designed for migration. The nature of the application has to be identified and the feasibility of migrating it has to be determined. An appropriate strategy should be adopted for that application according to its nature and type. Seven standard migration strategies have been defined by Stephen Orban: (i) rehost, (ii) replatform/revise, (iii) replace/purchase, (iv) refactor/rearchitect, (v) reengineer, (vi) retire/decommission, and (vii) retain. These strategies are discussed in Sect. 7.3.

(iv) Migration and validation

Each application is migrated to the cloud as per its design and strategy. Once migrated the application is validated in the new environment in all aspects. As an aside, the two phases *application design* and *migration and validation* are often called a *migration factory*.

(v) Operate

In the operate phase the application is operated in the new environment and the operation model of the application is enhanced.

7.3 Migration Strategies

While performing the opportunity evaluation phase for cloud migration (Phase 1) an enterprise decides whether to opt for the cloud or not based on an analysis of the relevant business case. Before an enterprise opts for cloud migration the type of each application is identified and the application thoroughly analyzed to see how it can be migrated to the cloud environment (the different migration strategies [2, 4] are shown in Fig. 7.6). After identification and assessment of each application an appropriate migration strategy is chosen for it.

Rehost
Rehost strategy is also called as *lift and shift* method. In this method an application is lifted from on-premises servers and hosted in a cloud server (as shown in Fig. 7.7).

   Enterprises that are looking to migrate quickly without disturbing existing applications will choose rehost strategy. Rehost removes the need for on-premises

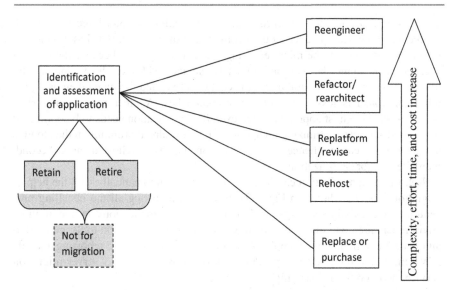

Fig. 7.6 Different migration strategies

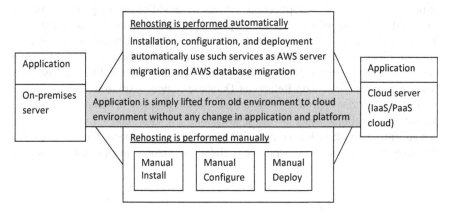

Fig. 7.7 Rehost an application in cloud server

servers, large network and internet connection, and manpower to manage the servers. When an enterprise wants to migrate quickly at minimal cost the rehost approach is the ideal choice. Large-scale legacy systems are typically migrated using this approach. For example, General Electric Oil & Gas has around 45,000 employees working across 11 different regions of the world and around 9000 applications. Approximately one-tenth of these applications (i.e., 900 applications) are accessed by around 100 users. General Electric Oil & Gas has migrated 311 applications to Amazon cloud. It took 18 months to do and cost $14.2 M. As a consequence it managed to reduce its TCO by 52%.

In the rehost approach enterprises move applications by and large unchanged. Moreover, if the enterprise has bought commercial off-the-shelf (COTS) products or solutions, they have to be migrated using the rehost approach because the code of such products cannot be modified. Other advantages with the rehost approach are that the risks involved are minimal, it is cost effective, and the time taken using the rehost approach is less than with other approaches. Another reason enterprises prefer to use the rehost approach is that even if an application needs to be optimized with cloud services, optimizing an application that is already running in the cloud is comparatively easier; hence the application is, first, rehosted and, second, rearchitected for optimization.

Rehosting an application can be done manually or automatically with the help of migration tools (as shown in Fig. 7.7). In manual rehosting all the installing procedures, configuration settings, and deployment of applications in the runtime environment are done manually. In automated rehosting migration tools are used to automate migration. For example, Amazon migration tools for rehosting include AWS migration hub, AWS application discovery service, AWS server migration service, and AWS database migration service.

Replatform

The replatform approach is also called the *lift-tinker-and-shift* approach. In this approach codebase of an application will not be modified but its platform may be modified a little to reduce cost and improve performance (as shown in Fig. 7.8). These modifications do not affect the functioning of an application. Consider a company that is maintaining records and data manually. However, modifications are introduced so that database management will be handled by Database as a Service cloud like Amazon Relational Database Service (Amazon RDS).

The replatform approach only makes minor changes without affecting the architecture or functioning of the application. The time taken to carry out the replatform approach is longer than that of the rehost approach. Consider another example for the replatform approach. Before migration an application may be

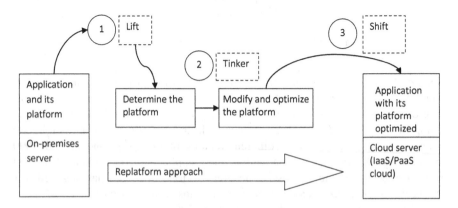

Fig. 7.8 Replatform or revise approach

running in a server like WebLogic whose license cost is very high, whereas Apache Tomcat is license free. Hence the platform is modified and the application is migrated.

Refactor or Rearchitect

Legacy applications are generally not easy to maintain or showcase using modern approaches or platforms like mobile platforms. Refactoring involves legacy code being converted into fully maintainable code. The application is restructured to improve its performance, portability (without changing core functions), and external behavior. The critical or core application is preserved (as shown in Fig. 7.9). Refactoring can be employed at the code level or architecture level so that the application can utilize cloud services. For example, a monolithic architecture-based application can be converted using a microservices architecture–based solution. Refactoring is chosen when there is a need to extend the usability and life cycle of a legacy application or when there is a need to port the application to multiple mobile platforms. Refactoring involves code being changed to simple, independent, flexible, and easily manageable modules.

Reengineering

In the reengineering approach an application is completely redesigned, rearchitected, and redeveloped using modern tools in a loosely coupled and modular fashion (as shown in Fig. 7.10). This enables the application to avail itself of all the services provided by the cloud. The cloud can yield Agile features such as quick and continuous deployment, high scalability, high performance, improved portability, increased usability, and easy maintainability.

For example, consider a legacy application that has been completely redesigned and redeveloped using advanced language, framework, platform, and other technologies so that it covers a wide range of users of web and mobile platforms.

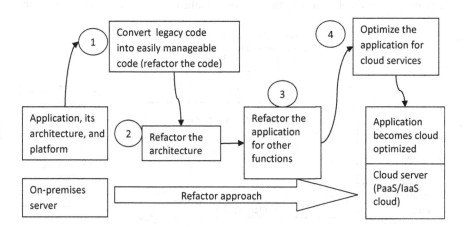

Fig. 7.9 Refactor or rearchitect approach

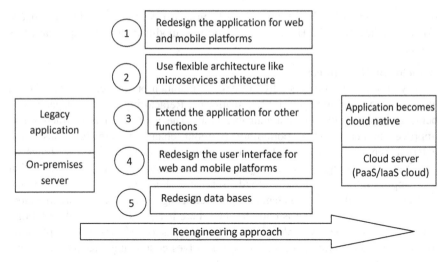

Fig. 7.10 Reengineering approach

Replace or Purchase

In the replace or purchase approach (as shown in Fig. 7.11) the existing application is replaced with some commercial software, like COTS software, or with an application provided by the SaaS cloud provider.

Software applications are offered in SaaS cloud. The applications are fully managed by SaaS cloud and data are maintained by users. If needed, an enterprise can migrate data to cloud-based storage.

Retain

If an application is found to be unsuitable for migration, it will have to be retained in the old environment. For example, an application that has many interdependencies is unsuitable for migration. Such applications are best retained in the

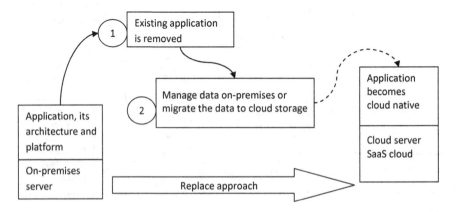

Fig. 7.11 Replace approach

on-premises setup and revisited later. They may be taken for decommissioning at a later time.

Retire/Decommission
If an application is found not to be required during the discovery phase, then it should be chosen for the retire strategy. In some cases the application may not be required but will still be running and consuming resources. Hence such applications should be considered for the retire option.

7.4 Cloud-Ready, Cloud-Optimized, and Cloud-Native Applications

When an application is migrated from an on-premises environment to the cloud, it falls under one of three main categories according to the level at which it can accept or avail itself of cloud services:

- cloud-ready/cloud-enabled applications;
- cloud-optimized applications; and
- cloud-native applications.

Cloud-Ready Applications
Cloud-ready applications were originally developed for traditional on-premises infrastructure like a single server. However, these applications become cloud ready when they are migrated to the cloud using rehost or replatform migration strategies. In these strategies the code base of applications is not modified. Hence these applications cannot utilize all the services offered by the cloud. Nevertheless, they run in the cloud environment and deliver the expected execution at low cost when compared with that of on-premises applications. These applications are also called cloud-enabled applications.

Cloud-Optimized Applications
When applications are migrated from a traditional on-premises infrastructure to the cloud, their codebase and architecture are modified so that they can utilize cloud services. They can avail themselves of almost all cloud services such as elasticity, performance, scalability, software-defined security, and software-defined storage or cloud data storage. The refactor strategy is typically used to convert traditional on-premises applications into cloud-optimized applications [5] by refactoring the application, database, architecture, etc. In addition to the refactor approach, reengineering an application makes it fully optimized for the cloud. Reengineering involves an application being redesigned as simple and independent modules mostly by using microservices architecture. Data are decoupled from applications. Communication methods among components of applications are optimized. Scalability and performance of applications are optimized with cloud services. Usability

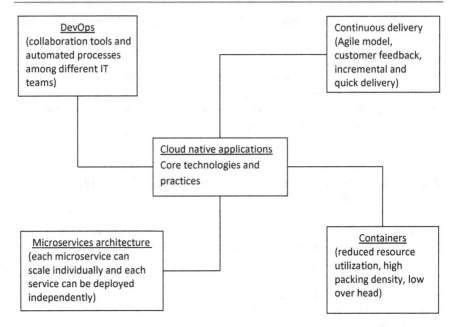

Fig. 7.12 Core technologies for developing cloud-native applications

is enhanced. Refactoring only modifies the internal structure without disturbing the external behavior of an application, whereas reengineering recreates an existing application as a new application with extended functional and non-functional features. The application is significantly modernized for the cloud.

Cloud-Native Applications
Cloud-native applications are applications that are designed, developed, and deployed to primarily exploit all the advantages of cloud computing such as multi-tenancy, elasticity, rapid deployment, Agile software development, dynamic requirements in application, shorter time to market, increased usability (e.g., support for mobile users), scalability, high performance, reliability, flexibility, and easy maintenance. Cloud-native applications are typically built using the following techniques (as shown in Fig. 7.12):

- DevOps
- continuous delivery
- microservices architecture
- containers.

DevOps

Development Operations (DevOps) is a set of practices and tools that automates the processes used by software development teams and other IT teams such as the testing team and deployment and delivery team. Traditionally, IT teams worked in data silos. DevOps aims to get different teams to collaborate so that software releases can be performed quickly. Moreover, DevOps helps critical issues to be fixed quickly; it facilitates Agile model continuous delivery; and increases trust and facilitates systems management. Ultimately, it creates a culture, a philosophy, and environment in which the building, testing, and releasing of software occurs rapidly, frequently, and more reliably. DevOps has a strong effect on organizational structure. It emphasizes that the hierarchical structure of an organization should be based on the skill set of its people so that the teams formed are assigned with appropriate tasks to promote Agile development.

Continuous delivery

Continuous delivery is one of the key attributes of the Agile model. It mandates release of an application as soon as a change is made rather than waiting for other changes to be made. Continuous delivery facilitates reliable software release with almost no failure, allowing organizations to roll out software releases frequently and at less risk. Continuous delivery helps in getting feedback from users and suggestions by users incorporated in further releases. Hence customer satisfaction improves significantly.

Microservices architecture

Microservices architecture promotes the design and development of applications as simple, independent, interoperable, autonomous, self-contained micro services that can be individually deployed in the cloud. Microservices have a number of features:

(i)   A microservice can be deployed and redeployed independently without affecting the integrity of an application.
(ii)   A microservice can independently scale in response to demand without consuming unnecessary resources.
(iii) A microservice can be individually versioned and maintained.
(iv)   A microservice can communicate with another service using standard communication protocols and well-defined interfaces.
(v)   Since each module is independent and interoperable it is not necessary that all the microservices of an application have to be developed using the same language. Each microservice can be developed using different languages.
(vi)   When microservices architecture is used an application is simply the sum of its constituent but composable components. Since each service runs as a unique process it usually manages its own database. This provides development teams with a decentralized approach to building software.

Containers

Containers use operating system–level virtualization in which an operating system is dynamically divided into one or more isolated containers. Containers have been found to be a better choice for the deployment of microservices for a number of reasons:

(i)   Containers do not require a full operating system like a virtual machine.
(ii) The overhead associated with the creation and destruction of containers is low.
(iii) Multiple containers can be packed with a single host OS. More than one microservice can be deployed in a single container. The packing density of containers is high.
(iv) Containers prevent vendor lock-in issues.
(v)   Containers are portable among different cloud service providers.

These features make containers an ideal choice for deploying individual microservices.

7.5 Pros and Cons of Different Migration Strategies

The pros and cons of different migration approaches are compared in Table 7.1.

7.6 Summary

The chapter began with an overview of the motivations that persuaded enterprises to opt for cloud migration. The different phases of the cloud migration process were discussed. A major phase in the migration process is identifying the individual applications of an enterprise and determining the appropriate migration strategy for each application. Different migration strategies were described with this in mind. According to the migration strategy adopted an application is categorized as cloud ready, cloud optimized, or cloud native. A brief description of cloud-ready, cloud-optimized, and cloud-native applications was given. The chapter ended by pointing out the pros and cons of different migration strategies.

Table 7.1 Pros and cons of different migration strategies

Migration strategy	Pros	Cons
Rehost	• Cost effective • Provides immediate benefits of cloud computing • In general, complexity is less and minimal effort is required • Low risk and can be automated	• It may be difficult to migrate some applications with the as-is strategy • Stateful applications are not scalable • The application cannot be optimized as it can only use very limited cloud services
Replatform	• It receives more benefits from the cloud than the rehost approach • Cost effective and fast • Reduced operational overhead, fully managed solutions • Choice of open platform, removing the risk of vendor lock-in	• The application may not be able to fully utilize the services offered by the cloud • It is not fully optimized
Refactor/Rewrite	• It receives more benefits from the cloud than the rehost and replatform approaches and is optimized • Applications offer high performance • Highly scalable and resilient solution • Agile and quick time to market in future	• Takes a long time to migrate • Much higher cost since the method involves several changes
Reengineer	• Highly scalable • Provides quick deployment • Easily manageable • Flexible • high performance	• Very expensive as the application is completely redesigned and redeveloped from scratch • Takes a very long time and more effort to migrate
Replace	• Less administrative overhead • Mobile, better features, flexibility, and support. • Good value, cost-effective, and cloud-native applications	• Customization is limited • Might need to change the business process in line with the application

7.7 Exercises

1. What essential factors should an enterprise be aware of before migrating to a cloud computing platform?
2. Consider an oil and gas organization that is supposed to collect data from its branches once, say, every half an hour. The organization has no IT support. In such a situation what do you, as a cloud architect, think? Would you suggest cloud migration? If so what type of migration would you suggest? Justify your suggestion.

3. Consider a company that has three core applications: Application 1 was developed using COBOL, Application 2 was developed using Python, and Application 3 was developed using Java. Compile a list of the migration strategies you would choose for the above applications. In case you need to optimize them all what strategies would you suggest?
4. Compile a list of differences between SOA and MSA (write an assignment).
5. In what way do MSA and DevOps facilitate an Agile software model? Explain your ideas with a case study.

References

1. Musale AD, Khot PG (2016) A roadmap towards cloud migration. IOSR national conference on recent trends in computer science and information technology, J Comput Eng 30–33. e-ISSN: 2278-0661, p-ISSN: 2278-8727
2. https://www.computerweekly.com/tip/Application-migration-to-the-cloud-Selecting-the-right-apps
3. https://s3-ap-southeast-1.amazonaws.com/mktg-apac/Cloud+Migration+to+AWS+Campaign/AWS+ebook+Migrating+to+AWS.pdf
4. Jamshidi P, Ahmad A, Pahl C (2014) Cloud migration research: a systematic review. IEEE Trans Cloud Comput 1:142–157. https://doi.org/10.1109/TCC.2013.10
5. Abdelmaboud A, Jawawi DNA, Ghani I, Elsafi A (2015) A comparative evaluation of cloud migration optimization approaches: a systematic literature review. J Theor Appl Inf Technol 79 (3):395–414

Cloud Monitoring

8

Learning Objectives

The objective of this chapter is to highlight the basic concepts that underlie cloud monitoring. By the end of the chapter the reader should fully understand the role monitoring plays in bringing about the fundamentals of cloud computing and optimizing the cloud.

Motivational Questions
1. Why do we monitor the cloud?
2. What is the need for cloud monitoring?
3. What should be monitored in the cloud?
4. How do we monitor?
5. What are the benefits of cloud monitoring?
6. What tools, if any, are available for monitoring the cloud?
7. What are the challenges in cloud monitoring?

Preface
Previous chapters introduced the core technical concepts of cloud computing. The reader should now have a good understanding of the basics of cloud computing, key technological foundations of cloud computing, cloud networking, cloud storage, cloud security and cloud migration. The reader is now ready for an insight into cloud monitoring. Hence this chapter looks at the need for cloud monitoring and the degree to which and how cloud monitoring is being performed. It also provides an overview of what tools are currently available for cloud monitoring as well as the challenges involved in cloud monitoring.

© Springer Nature Switzerland AG 2019
S. Chellammal and C. Pethuru Raj, *Essentials of Cloud Computing*,
Texts in Computer Science, https://doi.org/10.1007/978-3-030-13134-0_8

8.1 Need for Monitoring Cloud

Cloud computing provides many benefits to enterprises. Small and medium-sized enterprises choose the cloud for infrastructure and storage services, while large enterprises depend on the cloud for modernization of applications, operational efficiency, and flexibility. Cloud computing offers enterprises the opportunity to increase the levels of service they provide to their customers as well as reduced cost of ownership. Since there are physical and virtual resources that are distributed at different geographical locations in the cloud, without proper monitoring of cloud resources and services enterprises may fail to achieve the performance they set for themselves and benefits provided by the cloud. They run the risk of failing to achieve the return on investment targeted.

Cloud monitoring is the process of monitoring, evaluating, and managing cloud-based services, applications, and infrastructure [1]. Continuous monitoring of cloud resources and services using many types of probes as well as monitoring platforms is crucial for a number of reasons (as shown in Fig. 8.1).

Cloud monitoring is fundamental to

- *capacity planning* (e.g., imagine a service is utilizing excess CPU—unless it is monitored, adjusting resource allocation and planning cloud capacity become impossible);
- *calculating the usage of resources* and providing *billing* to consumers;
- identifying and addressing *potential issues* and providing *troubleshooting*;
- delivering services according to the *service level agreement*;

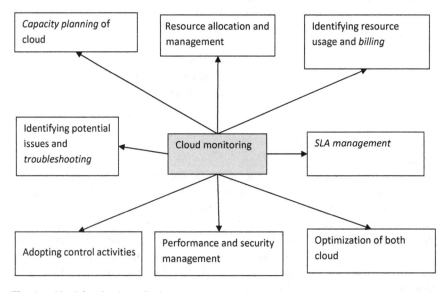

Fig. 8.1 Need for cloud monitoring

- providing detailed reports, in-depth graphs, and different metrics for _performance management_;
- _optimizing_ cloud solutions and services;
- determining the status of resources hosted in the cloud;
- adopting control activities and performing various core activities of the cloud such as resource allocation;
- migrating without data loss;
- managing _security_; and
- finally, achieving those characteristics that are unique to the cloud: scalability, elasticity, and resource provisioning.

8.2 Characteristics of Cloud Monitoring Systems

- _Scalability_: A cloud monitoring system should be scalable as the cloud environment is massive consisting of thousands of servers distributed across different geographical locations. Any monitoring system needs to be scalable to monitor cloud resources.
- _Portability_: A cloud monitoring system should provide portability as resources in the cloud are highly heterogeneous, consisting of hardware and software from various platforms and vendors. Any monitoring tool needs to be portable to allow it to be used on different platforms.
- _Non-intrusiveness_: A monitoring system should not impede the resource being monitored, nor should it consume more than the least resources possible.
- _Accuracy_: A monitoring system should give accurate information.
- _Autonomicity_ or self-manageability: A monitoring system should be able to self-configure according to dynamic changes in the cloud.
- _Comprehensiveness_: A monitoring system should be able to monitor different types of resources such as physical and virtual resources and resources used by multiple tenants.
- _Timeliness_: A monitoring system should report the metrics and data monitored within the stipulated time for their intended use.
- _Resilience, reliability, and availability_: A monitoring system should be able to function even if any component fails or if there is a system fault. It should deliver its findings within a stipulated time.

8.3 What to Monitor?

The architecture of the cloud consists of different layers: physical infrastructure, network, virtualization, IaaS layer, PaaS layer, SaaS layer, and user interfaces (as shown in Fig. 8.2). The physical infrastructure layer consists of several servers, storage devices, and networks. These resources are geographically distributed

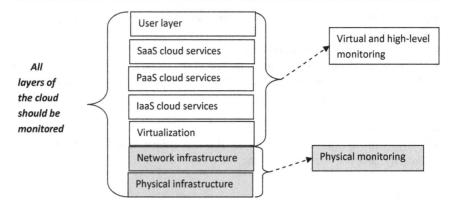

Fig. 8.2 Layers of cloud to be monitored

across different locations. The virtualization layer sits on top of the physical layer and abstracts heterogeneity from physical resources. It provides a unified logical view of physical resources. When it comes to monitoring, physical resources can be monitored using low-level computation-based tests and network-based tests. However, the virtual layer is more difficult to monitor. It requires high-level monitoring. On top of the virtualization layer different service offerings, such as IaaS, PaaS, or SaaS, are deployed.

8.4 Who Should Monitor and Levels of Monitoring?

Two groups of people perform cloud monitoring: cloud service providers and cloud users or consumers. Cloud service providers are more important in that they continuously perform cloud monitoring to ensure that objectives, such as capacity planning, resource management, performance management, SLA management, security management, and billing, are achieved. The cloud monitoring performed by cloud service providers is usually extensive and includes all layers of the cloud architecture: physical infrastructure, networks, virtualized resources, virtual machines, platforms, applications, etc. This is done using a wide range of monitoring probes, monitoring platforms, and tools. Low-level and high-level monitoring are performed so as to achieve complete control over and optimization of the cloud. Physical servers and resources can be monitored using *low-level, traditional distributed monitoring systems*. However, monitoring virtualized resources requires *high-level, advanced software-based monitoring* techniques, code instrumentations, etc. Cloud service providers perform two major kinds of monitoring: physical monitoring and virtual monitoring.

Physical Monitoring

Physical monitoring, of course, involves monitoring the physical infrastructure of the cloud. It deals with the internal status of cloud resources. From the cloud point of view it refers to the server level. Physical system monitoring is the basis for cloud system management as it is related to the physical computing infrastructure on which the cloud itself is built. It is here that conventional monitoring techniques, such as *computation-based tests* and *network-based tests*, are carried out. Computation-based tests are based on classical statistical measures such as mean, median, mode and temporal characteristics.

Metrics measured by computation-based tests

• CPU utilization, CPU latency, CPU speed, CPU-related errors
• memory utilization, memory page exchanges per second, memory latency, memory-related errors
• operating system metrics like system load.

Metrics measured by network-based tests

• network latency, network utilization, network traffic, load patterns, network capacity
• bandwidth, throughput, response time, round trip delay, jitter, packet/data loss
• available bandwidth, capacity, traffic volume.

Virtual Monitoring

Virtual system monitoring provides information about the virtual system characteristics of cloud services:

• In IaaS cloud the system manager can monitor the status of every VM instance in the cloud and its internal resources.
• In PaaS cloud the system manager can monitor the use of platform resources such as hosting space used and simultaneous network connections.
• In SaaS cloud the system manager can monitor application usage patterns, resources shared among applications, etc.

Virtual monitoring is the main means of controlling quality of service metrics and ensuring service delivery according to the values mentioned in SLAs. Service providers use the metrics obtained from virtual system monitoring to calculate service costs and billing. Successful cloud business models almost always stem from virtual monitoring.

Cloud users perform high-level monitoring to determine how many resources they have consumed so that they can check their bills. In addition, such high-level

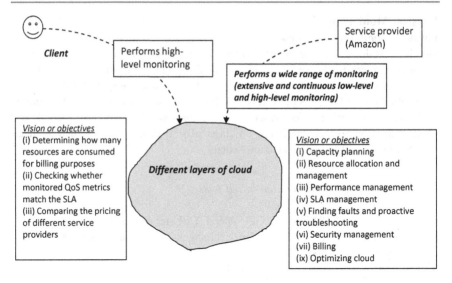

Fig. 8.3   Vision and levels of cloud monitoring

monitoring makes it easy for consumers to compare the pricing of different cloud service providers. The objectives (or vision) of monitoring and levels of monitoring for cloud service providers and cloud users are shown in Fig. 8.3.

8.5   Stages of Cloud Monitoring

Cloud monitoring is a process that comprises three stages (as shown in Fig. 8.4): collection of data related to the status of different resources and services in the cloud, analysis of the collected data, and reporting and decision making.

Collection
Data collection is carried out using a monitoring server or a network of monitoring servers managed by a _human cloud administrator_ or a scalable monitoring system using tree or decentralized architectures depending on the size of cloud deployment.

In _small cloud deployment_ the states of different resources are typically collected using a single monitoring server. The monitoring server polls different resources such as compute servers, storage servers, and network servers. In addition, different servers push their current state and status information to the monitoring server. The server archives the data and takes decisions according the state of resources. The cloud administrator is given inputs for him to take decisions and, if necessary, he reconfigures the cloud based on the data monitored. For example, the administrator may turn off a virtual machine that is found to be in a state of failure and take it for repair.

In *medium deployments* a single monitoring server is not sufficient. Typically, more than one monitoring *agents/child servers* are here tightly coupled with the centralized server, which forms the so-called *centralized monitoring station*. A monitoring station typically follows the server–agent model. It is a master–slave model. Monitoring agents are tied to the resources to be monitored and collect data from the relevant resource (as shown in Fig. 8.5).

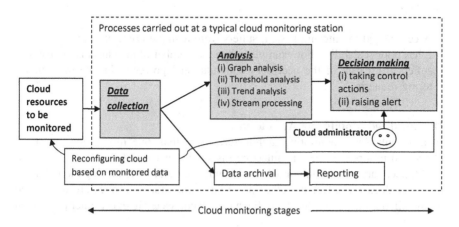

Fig. 8.4 Stages of cloud monitoring

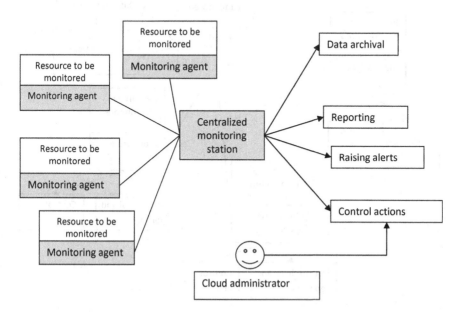

Fig. 8.5 Centralized cloud monitoring

The system collects states from different resources via polling and pushing. Polling involves the server asking the agent and getting the data. Pushing involves the agent or child server sending the data to the server, which archives the data collected. After analyzing the data the server carries out three tasks: reporting, pointing out errors or issues by raising an alert, and taking control (the latter task undertaken by skilled personnel or the cloud administrator).

Limitations

- A centralized monitoring system suffers from a single point of failure.
- It has poor scalability. For example, when the number of resources is increased it suffers from lack of the necessary computational power to handle huge monitoring requests.

Decentralized Monitoring Architecture

In a decentralized monitoring architecture more than one monitoring system is connected in a peer-to-peer architecture (as shown in Fig. 8.6).

All peers are equally important. In decentralized cloud monitoring the failure of one peer does not affect the other peers since monitoring probes are distributed across different layers of the cloud. Each peer is connected to every other peer. Such

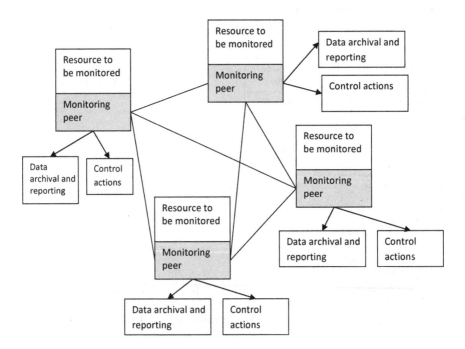

Fig. 8.6 Decentralized cloud monitoring

monitoring systems make use of distributed hash tables, epidemic-style communication, and various P2P overlays to discover and collect data from machines. Decentralized systems have inherent scalability improvements over centralized systems. Having archived the data the systems generate reports that are sent to the web-based front end, take appropriate control actions, or raise alerts.

Analysis
In this stage the data collected are analyzed using monitoring tools. Monitoring tools employ different techniques for analysis such as simple graphing, threshold analysis, trend analysis, and stream processing.

Simple Graphing
Graphing provides a holistic view of collected data to infer system-wide resource usage. The graphing tool also allows a user to obtain specific resource usage, if necessary, and to detect resource spikes, failures, etc.

Threshold Analysis
Threshold analysis is commonly used for analysis. It involves the values of collected data being continually checked against predefined conditions. If the values violate normal conditions, an alert is raised or other control actions are taken. Such a strategy is used to check the health of the system as well as failure detection. Although threshold analysis detects error conditions it is not sufficient to detect unexpected error conditions.

Trend Analysis and Stream Processing
Trend analysis and real-time stream processing can be used to provide rich data analysis about hundreds of millions of events per hour. Moreover, such advanced techniques for analysis contain bespoke code (i.e., tailor-made software), which even executes outside the monitoring environment and interacts with APIs to get more metrics. Many abnormal error conditions are detected by data collected in this way.

Decision Making
Depending on the analysis, decisions are made as to whether actions need to be taken such as reporting or raising an alert in case of error. Skilled personnel will supervise and take appropriate actions in case of complex situations.

8.6   Cloud Monitoring Platforms and Tools

Current cloud monitoring platforms and tools can be broadly divided into two categories: *commercial tools* and *open-source tools* (as shown in Fig. 8.7). Since there are so many cloud monitoring tools the *cloud administrator has to plan* when to use commercial tools and when to use open-source tools. *The cloud administrator keeps the following key points or guidelines in mind when choosing the tools.*

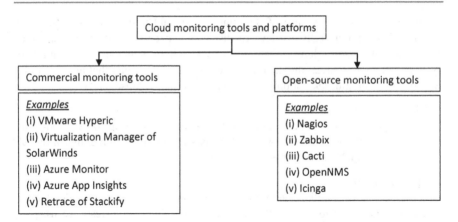

Fig. 8.7 Examples of commercial and open-source cloud monitoring tools

The cloud administrator is located at a relatively higher level in the cloud environment when looking at the layers of the cloud architecture. Since cloud administrators are working at a higher level it makes sense to choose cloud monitoring tools that are capable of interacting with the administrator when it comes to

- *setting up rules and policies*;
- *reconfiguring* resources;
- carrying out *automated corrective actions*;
- providing the capability of automatically provisioning more virtual resources, like virtual storage, when a database is running out of space (or) automatically provisioning a virtual machine when there is a need for high performance;
- providing support so that *monitoring tools can be integrated* making it easier for the administrator to obtain a global view with more details; and
- integrating cloud and on-premises monitoring tools, especially as enterprises are increasingly adopting hybrid cloud deployments.

Open-source tools are free and hence easy to download, install, test, and deploy. Open-source tools are typically based on community-driven projects. However, open-source tools are not as mature and stable as commercial tools. For example, it takes a long time to fix bugs in open-source tools because the providers of such tools lack the profit motive. Hence there is a significant delay in fixing bugs in open-source tools.

Commercial tools, in contrast, are stable and mature. Since the companies that release commercial tools do so for profit they realize the importance of delivering technical support services and maintenance services. Open-source tools lack such support. Cloud administrators end up using a mixture of commercial and open-source tools so that monitoring is as efficient as possible.

Another difficulty in choosing monitoring tools is that many lack the necessary attributes. Although there are many important features, such as scalability, portability, interoperability, reliability, availability, resilience, accuracy, timeliness, comprehensiveness, autonomicity, and non-intrusiveness, *no single monitoring tool possesses all the desired attributes*. *Many tools typically do not have such basic features as scalability, portability, and interoperability.*

Note also that cloud server providers have devised their own sets of tools to monitor their services and offerings. For example, Azure Monitor has devised its own set of tools, but the trouble is they remain abstract to the user. Such tools are tied to the platform; hence *the difficulty of integrating different tools*. After taking everything into consideration the cloud administrator then selects the most appropriate tools. Greater insight into currently available tools is given in the following subsections.

Commercial Tools

- *VMware Hyperic*: VMware Hyperic was developed by VMware, which is owned by Dell. VMware Hyperic monitors physical and virtual infrastructure as well as OS, middleware, and web applications. Its dashboards and reporting features help to ensure that a cloud provider stays SLA compliant.
- *Virtualization Manager*: SolarWinds has a tool called Virtualization Manager that makes predictive recommendations to improve the performance of the virtual environment. It also helps in capacity planning and raising alerts to indicate error conditions.
- *Azure Monitor*: The Azure Monitor blade consolidates activity logs and diagnostics logs across various events and resource types using various filtering options. Predefined metrics can be viewed against resource types such as virtual machines or storage accounts. This tool can be extended using any of the third-party monitoring and management solutions that are available in the Azure marketplace.
- *App(lication) Insights*: App(lication) Insights not only monitors but also manages application performance. It works with live web applications that are developed using .Net, Java, and Node.js and can be deployed on-premises or in the cloud. Application monitoring can be enabled during deployment or at runtime, although the latter limits the telemetry data. AppInsights presents the data on customizable dashboards and APIs can be leveraged to collect custom telemetry data.
- *Retrace*: Retrace from Stackify is an application performance monitoring (APM) tool for applications built in .Net and Java. It combines application performance metrics, errors, logs, and monitoring into one tool. Retrace is perfect for developers who want code-level insight into how their applications are performing. Its affordable price makes it accessible to small and medium-sized businesses.

Open-Source Tools

- *Nagios*: Nagios is capable of monitoring almost all types of components such as network protocols, operating systems, system metrics, applications, services, web servers, websites, and middleware. Nagios provides high performance by consuming fewer server resources. It can be integrated with any third-party tools. It has a number of unique features: it provides a centralized view of monitored data; it automatically restarts failed applications; it supports multi-user access; and it has an extendable architecture.
- *Zabbix*: Zabbix is enterprise-level software designed to monitor everything from performance to availability of servers, network equipment to web applications and databases. It has a number of unique features: it supports SNMP and provides better reporting; automation can be done by scripts in various languages such as Ruby, Python, Perl, PHP, Java or shell; and it provides support when integrating with other system management tools such as Puppet, cfengine, and Chef.
- *Cacti*: Cacti is a complete network graphing solution designed to tie the power of RRDTool (Round Robin Database tool) with data storage and graphing functionality. It has a number of unique features: fast, advanced graph templating, multiple data acquisition methods, and user management features. All these features are wrapped in an intuitive, easy-to-use interface that is suitable for LAN-sized installations up to complex networks with thousands of devices.
- *OpenNMS*: OpenNMS is a network-monitoring solution that collects system metrics using JMX, WMI, SNMP, NRPE, XML, HTTP, JDBC, XML, JSON, etc. OpenNMS makes it possible to discover layer-2 network topologies in a network. It is built on an event-driven architecture. It provides support for Grafana. OpenNMS has a built-in reporting facility and dashboard. It provides a great user interface. It has a number of unique features: it is specially designed for Linux, but Windows, Solaris, and OSX are also supported; it provides support for IPv4 and IPv6; and events can generate notifications via email, SMS, XMPP, and various other methods.
- *Icinga*: The Icinga monitoring framework allows all available systems in a network to be monitored, which alerts the user to errors and provides a database for SLA reporting. It has a number of unique features: monitoring of network services, host services, and server components; it provides support for event handlers and notifications; it provides cross-platform support for various operating systems; and it provides a great user interface for template-based reporting.

8.7 Challenges in Cloud Monitoring

Many businesses adopt cloud computing because the cloud offers dynamic scalability, reduced capital and operational cost, and rapid provisioning of required resources. Many enterprises are migrating their workloads to the cloud and in so doing demonstrate their confidence to fully rely on cloud service providers. Despite the cloud effectively offering the services required, *cloud outages are becoming more common. Cloud outages turn into business outages accompanied by great economic cost and running the risk of harming customer relations.* Many monitoring tools are used to continuously monitor and manage the cloud. However, ***there are challenges in cloud monitoring***:

- *Lack of holistic, actionable insights into cloud services and processes*: Most currently available tools are only capable of providing monitoring metrics. For example, a tool may report that CPU utilization is 60% without giving much detail about which process is responsible for consuming it. This results in very narrow visibility.
- *Limited insights into migration life cycles*: As organizations move applications and workloads to the cloud they need to be sure this is done reliably. However, existing monitoring tools provide only limited insights into migration. Hence it is likely many companies are not receiving optimum service levels and maximum benefits from the cloud.
- *Increased complexity due to heterogeneity of multiple monitoring tools*: As cloud adoption grows a number of monitoring tools are being used to monitor and manage cloud services and resources. As a result of tools being so diverse in nature the complexity involved in monitoring the cloud accordingly increases as cloud administrators have to spend more time and effort in analyzing the metrics produced by the various tools.
- *Virtualized resourcing*: Virtualization poses a new challenge to monitoring because it creates a dynamic capacity pool of resources that differs significantly from traditional tools.
- *Multi-tenancy*: Multi-tenancy introduces new challenges to monitoring as it is not sufficient just to monitor the status of any application or resource. Instead, it is more important to monitor the QoS parameters specific to a particular tenant. Monitoring tools find it difficult to detect the key performance indicators (KPIs) specific to a particular tenant.
- *Web-scale load testing*: As cloud resources and users are widespread throughout the globe as a result of the internet, load testing over the Web is tougher than in an enterprise, which is always bounded and predictable.
- *Profiling end-user response time*: As end users of cloud applications are distributed throughout the globe it becomes difficult to monitor the end-user response time metric. Response time varies according to the locations of users and ascertaining the cause for differences in response time is time consuming.

8.8 Summary

The fundamentals of cloud monitoring were presented in this chapter. The chapter began by explaining the need for cloud monitoring, describing the characteristics monitoring tools should have, and investigating the different levels of monitoring. The chapter went on to describe different architectures of cloud monitoring tools. The chapter ended by providing an overview of existing cloud monitoring tools and the challenges associated with cloud monitoring.

8.9 Exercises

1. Imagine you are a cloud administrator in a small IT firm. Your firm is running its own private cloud deployment. During peak loads the firm depends on Amazon EC2 for infrastructure. As cloud administrator, compile a list of the tools needed to monitor hybrid cloud.
2. Make a table comparing the desirable features of existing open-source tools. The table should cover all desirable features. Allot the stub column of the table to existing open-source cloud monitoring tools and the other columns to desirable features. Make a survey by filling up all cells (hint: use the following table as a guide). Include as many tools as possible.

Tool	Portability	Scalability	Accuracy	Interoperability	Availability	Reliability	...
Nagios							
Zabbix							
...							

References

1. Montes J, Sanchez A, Memishi B, Perez MS, Antoniu G (2013) GMonE: a complete approach to cloud monitoring. Preprint submitted to Elsevier, 15 Feb 2013

Basics of Cloud Management

9

Learning Objectives

Having mastered the technological, migration, and monitoring aspects of cloud computing the reader is now in a position to look at how the cloud computing environment is managed. The objective of this chapter is to introduce the basics of cloud management. By the end of the chapter the reader should have the necessary insights into cloud management functionalities and how they are managed by Cloud Management Platform (CMP) tools.

Motivational Questions
1. Why is cloud management necessary?
2. Who or what is managing the cloud? Is it done manually or using tools?
3. What tasks are involved in cloud management?
4. What are the currently available tools for cloud management and how effective are they?

Preface
In the previous chapter the reader was exposed to the concept of monitoring. Cloud monitoring is actually the basis of and a prerequisite for cloud management. In this chapter the reader will be taught the basics of cloud management.

© Springer Nature Switzerland AG 2019
255
S. Chellammal and C. Pethuru Raj, *Essentials of Cloud Computing*,
Texts in Computer Science, https://doi.org/10.1007/978-3-030-13134-0_9

9.1 Need for Cloud Management

Cloud environments are stuffed full of bare metal servers, virtual machines, and containers. Hence the number of moving parts within any cloud environment is growing steadily and the challenge of managing cloud environments accordingly increases. Cloud management refers to the technologies and software that have been designed for operating and monitoring applications, data, and services that reside in the cloud. The purpose of existing cloud management tools and platforms is to make sure that a company's cloud resources are working properly and kept under control, thus allowing administrators to focus on supporting other core business processes. Another noteworthy point is that cloud applications are increasingly microservices centric. Enterprise applications are constructed from hundreds of interacting microservices. There are several instances of each particular microservice to ensure high availability. In a nutshell, management is becoming increasingly complex in line with the consistent increase in the number of applications. These extremely complex environments present IT operations and DevOps teams with new types of management challenges:

(i)   Traditional IT management strategies and tools were designed for stateful applications that were tightly coupled to the underlying infrastructure. However, virtualized and containerized cloud environments no longer maintain such stable relationships with applications. Virtualization and containerization add an additional layer of abstraction and hence applications are not tightly coupled to the underlying infrastructure. *Virtual machines and containers inside a host are dynamic in the sense that they can be provisioned and decommissioned frequently.* This kind of dynamic and virtual environment is difficult to monitor and manage.

(ii) Businesses invariably expect to get more out of IT. This means *all the non-functional requirements/quality-of-service attributes of cloud systems and services need to be fulfilled with ease of scalability and on demand.* Fulfilling any dynamic non-functional requirement rapidly is certainly based on efficient management. This is obviously a challenge.

(iii) The way the cloud offers its services with ease and flexibility mandates operation teams to be able to proactively monitor infrastructural components, resources, and applications by using unified and automated tools. The data collected by monitoring tools have to be subjected to a variety of investigations to extricate actionable insights in time to ponder the next course of corrective actions.

(iv) The performance, scalability, security, availability, and other aspects of cloud systems should be measured and managed in time.

Enterprises that have technical expertise, mature processes, and centralized governance are the most successful in making and managing cloud deployments.

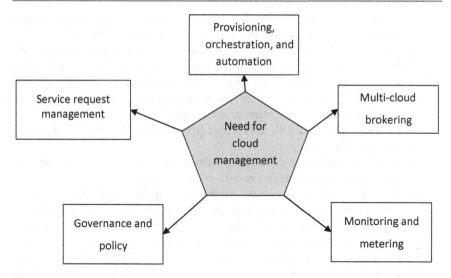

Fig. 9.1 Need for cloud management

9.1.1 Requirements of Cloud Management

As per the Gartner report, cloud management should be able to handle the following five requirements (as shown in Fig. 9.1):

- service request management;
- provisioning, orchestration, and automation;
- governance and policy;
- monitoring and metering; and
- multi-cloud brokering.

9.1.2 Need for Cloud Management Platform Tools

Cloud is such a complex computing environment that it cannot be managed manually. Most enterprises today use cloud services offered by different cloud service providers. *CMP is a suite of integrated software tools that an enterprise can use to monitor and control its cloud computing resources* [1]. CMPs can be used to manage exclusive private or public clouds, hybrid clouds, and multi-clouds. Almost every cloud management tool offers the basic requirements mentioned in the previous section. Along with core management functions *tools provide a number of benefits*:

(i) CMPs have the inherent ability to compare, collaborate, and correlate with multiple cloud services to arrive at deft decisions that enable the tactical and strategical requirements of cloud subscribers.

(ii) CMPs are stuffed full of policy-aware management capabilities to reduce any kind of human intervention, instruction, and interpretation.

(iii) CMPs provide depth and breadth of automation, monitoring, and analytics. Nowadays enterprises work with many vendors, services, application architectures, and middleware. Hence effective cloud management tools are required to ingest data from many sources, integrate and orchestrate workflows, and provide clear actionable insight.

(iv) CMPs are provided with reporting engines, visualization, query languages, and correlation analysis.

(v) CMPs offer robust discovery, dependency awareness, predictive analytics, and role-based insights in complex cloud environments.

(vi) By scaling infrastructure and applications rapidly, deploying new functionality as soon as it is ready, and keeping up with changing business requirements, CMPs can directly impact a company's ability to generate revenue and successfully engage with customers.

(vii) The use of more standardized and consistent configuration and automation leads to high productivity of IT staff. In addition, automation reduces manual labor and facilitates proactive/predictive monitoring.

(viii) Real-time analytics help in detecting emerging performance issues before they impact end users and help more rapidly identify and remediate the root cause of performance problems.

The following list provides examples of CMP tools and other popular tools:

- vRealize Suite
- IBM Cloud Orchestrator
- Cisco CloudCenter
- RightScale
- Scalr
- Red Hat CloudForms
- HPE OneSphere
- BMC Cloud Lifecycle Management
- Embotics vCommander
- CloudCheckr
- CloudBolt
- Morpheus.

9.2   Core Functions of Cloud Management Platforms

Service Request Management
This is a self-service interface provided by CMPs through which various cloud services are easily consumed by consumers. Cloud service providers offer service catalogs with SLAs and cost details. Based on the published information the CMP

chooses the appropriate provider and services. Service requests can be routed through this interface to the CMP solution to automate most activities. Some users expect a service interface that serves as a pass-through to native capabilities within a public cloud service. The service portal or marketplace is continuously updated with fresh features, functionalities, and facilities to gain an edge or retain the edge gained. There are service and support management systems and other automation tools that readily fulfill varying requests from users. There are operational team members employed by cloud service providers or third-party teams that team up together to fulfill service requests quickly.

Provisioning, Orchestration, and Automation

Provisioning, orchestration, and automation are the core capabilities of any CMP product. There is an arsenal of tools intrinsically enabling these vital features. There are plenty of cloud orchestration, provisioning, and configuration tools that are made available these days. There are industry strength standards for service and cloud infrastructure orchestration. Similarly, there are automation tools for job/task scheduling, load balancing, auto-scaling, resource allocation, etc. There are resource configuration management systems. Software deployment and delivery tools are also hitting the market. In a nutshell, cloud operations are being meticulously automated in an end-to-end fashion.

Monitoring and Metering

Monitoring, measurement, management, and metering are the basic requirements of any IT hardware and software packages. Service usage and resource consumption need to be accurately measured and metered. There are a bunch of tools for accomplishing these.

Multi-cloud Brokering

Brokerage solutions and services are very important at a time dominated by connected and federated clouds. Interconnectivity, intermediation, and other enrichment and enablement capabilities are being performed through cloud service brokers. There are connectors, adapters, drivers, and other solutions that establish a seamless linkage between public and private clouds. There are bridge solutions to establish direct connectivity between public clouds. Thus as a result of multiple clouds and services with different SLAs the role and responsibility of cloud brokers are bound to increase in the days ahead. Advanced CMPs are being fitted with brokerage tools and engines.

Security and Identity

Concern over security is, of course, widespread among cloud users who rightly insist on security requirements in the cloud environment. As customer-facing applications and data (corporate, customer, and confidential) are being held in the cloud environment, especially in public cloud, security is paramount. User identification, authentication, authorization, and other accountability and auditability are being pronounced as the most critical and crucial for continued spread of the cloud. The security and privacy of data while in transit, persistence, and usage are paramount for the intended success of the cloud idea. Key-based encryption and decryption, key management, etc. are getting a lot of attention these days. Single sign-on (SSO) is indispensable to multi-cloud applications. United threat and vulnerability management solutions are becoming highly popular in the cloud environment.

Service-Level Management
Ensuring service-level and operation-level contracts agreed between cloud consumer and server are complied with is an important facet of the cloud arena. Non-functional requirements (NFRs)/quality of service (QoS) attributes stand out as the key differentiators among all participating service providers. Scalability, availability, fault tolerance, security, and dependability are often repeated needs. Service resilience, application reliability, and infrastructure versatility are given utmost importance for boosting user confidence in the cloud "mystery." There is a stunning array of toolsets that can be used to facilitate these complex capabilities.

Cloud Migration and Disaster Recovery
Personal and professional applications that were built several years ago in monolithic and legacy forms and still in the reckoning are being consciously modernized and migrated to cloud environments to reap all the originally envisaged cloud benefits. Cloud migration may not be a straightforward task as this involves determining cloud readiness as well as discovering, lifting, and shifting workloads between and/or among on-premises and off-premises cloud environments. Use cases involve workloads being permanently migrated from one environment to another and workloads repositioned during disaster recovery (DR) testing or during an actual disaster. Thus applications being moved to cloud environments ought to be seamlessly managed by CMP solutions. There are tools that facilitate risk-free automation of application modernization and migration to multiple cloud environments. To ensure disaster and data recovery as well as business continuity (BC) secondary cloud centers are being set up. CMP products are expected to work with primary and secondary cloud centers.

Dynamic Capacity Planning and Resource Allocation
Dynamic capacity planning and resource allocation allow efficient operational usage of the infrastructure footprint. They are often tied to orchestration and automation functionality and are also increasingly being combined with cost transparency and optimization.

Cost Transparency and Optimization
Cost transparency and optimization are used to enable tracking, budgeting, and optimization of cloud expenses.

Customer Delight
CMPs provide robust automation to standardize and streamline application and infrastructure provisioning, resulting in more rapid availability of end-user services and more flexible scaling of resources as needed by changing business requirements. Proactive monitoring and predictive analytics allow IT teams to detect and remediate problems before they impact customers, which means service levels are more consistent and end-user satisfaction is higher.

Faster Time to Market
CMPs can be used to monitor on-premises and public cloud resource consumption and proactively predict when additional resources are required. Automated onboarding and application deployment as well as support for continuous DevOps integration and delivery combine to speed up the process of getting new services and applications to market. This can have a significant impact on time to revenue particularly for organizations that derive significant income from online services and mobile applications.

Enhanced Resource Utilization
Digital transformation, DevOps, and the cloud all drive more frequent and complex changes across corporate IT environments. Traditional manual processes are too slow and error prone to support the rapid rate of change seen today. CMP automation, self-service engines, orchestration technologies, and blueprint design systems enable IT organizations to focus limited staff on getting the template design correct the first time and then rely on automation to manage deployments and changes consistently. Similarly, more sophisticated monitoring and analytics allow limited staff to find and remediate problems much more quickly than they could with traditional approaches, freeing staff to focus on more strategic initiatives. With higher application and infrastructure availability developers and end users can focus on their jobs rather than waiting for resources.

Greater Business Flexibility and Extensibility
CMPs can monitor and detect changes in resource utilization and can pinpoint the best location for specific workloads based on cost, security, and performance. When paired with automated provisioning and migration capabilities, this type of analysis allows organizations to scale resources, react to rapid business changes, and maintain optimal cost and performance levels.

Affordability
With improved visibility into cloud infrastructure costs, performance, and availability, IT organizations are in a better position to use and reclaim resources as needed, migrate workloads to the optimal resource, and focus staff on highest impact problems and end-user requests. The resulting improvements in staff productivity and reductions in the cost of infrastructure can be substantial for many organizations.

9.3 Architecture of Cloud Management Platforms

To get an insight into the architecture of CMPs let us consider *vRealize Suite*, a popular CMP. *vRealize Suite is a product of VMware*.

vRealize Suite is a CMP that helps IT enable developers to quickly build applications in any cloud with secure and consistent operations. It provides developer-friendly infrastructure (supporting VMs and containers) and a common approach to hybrid and multi-cloud, supporting major public clouds such as Amazon Web Services, Azure, and Google Cloud Platform.

9.3.1   VMware Validated Design for Software-Defined Data Center

To emphasize the significance of management functions in the cloud the overall architecture of VMware Validated Design for a software-defined data center [2] is shown in Fig. 9.2.

Figure 9.2 shows that *except for the physical layer, pool of resources, and hypervisor all other parts of the architecture are related to management functions and control.*

VMware Validated Design architecture is based on a number of layers and modules that allow interchangeable components to be part of the end solution or outcome like an Software-Defined Data Centre (SDDC).

Physical Layer
The physical layer consists of physical x86-based servers, storage devices, and networks.

Virtual Infrastructure Layer
The virtual infrastructure layer consists of the hypervisor, which creates a pool of virtualized resources on top of the physical layer that is under the control of cloud management.

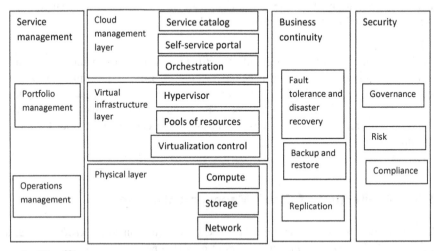

See https://docs.vmware.com

Fig. 9.2 VMware validated design for software-defined data center

Cloud Management Layer

• The cloud management portal is where cloud users interact with the cloud via APIs. Users can get details of services from the service catalog and consume the service they require using the self-service portal that is under the control of cloud management.
• The cloud management layer facilitates service consumption by making use of the *vRealize Automation* toolset, which includes *VMware Identity Manager*. *Vmware Identity Manager* manages security aspects while users consume services.
• *vRealize Automation* is used to author, administer, and consume VM templates and blueprints. *vRealize Orchestrator* calls for resources and then orchestrates the actions of the lower layers to achieve the request.

Figure 9.2 identifies the ***primary management functional blocks***:

• virtualization control (as mentioned above, the hypervisor performs virtualization under the control of cloud management);
• service management;
• business continuity; and
• security.

Service Management

• The service management area of this architecture mainly focuses on operations management (in particular, monitoring, alerting, and log management).
• *vRealize Operations Manager* tracks and analyzes the operation of multiple data sources within the SDDC.
• *vRealize Log Insight* provides real-time log management and log analysis using machine learning-based intelligent grouping, high-performance searching, and troubleshooting across physical, virtual, and cloud environments.

Business Continuity

• Business continuity ensures the business is always ready. It involves replication, backup and restore, and disaster recovery.
• *vRealize Business* manages overall business continuity.
• *vSphere Data Protection* provides functions related to data protection. Such functions include backup and restore virtual machines, organization of virtual machines into groups by VMware products, store data according to company retention policies, and inform administrators about backup and restore activities by issuing reports.
• *VMware Site Recovery Manager* provides disaster recovery.
• *vSphere Replication* manages the replication process.

Security

All systems need by design to be inherently secure. This is to reduce risk and increase compliance while still providing a governance structure. The security area outlines what is needed to ensure the entire SDDC is resilient to both internal and external threats.

9.3.2 Cloud Management Platforms: Consolidated View and Architecture

Section 9.3.1, "VMware Validated Design for software-defined data center," should have given the reader a fair understanding of various management-related functions. A consolidated view of CMPs can be had by using tools from the *vRealize Suite* given in Table 9.1 and from the conceptual architecture of CMPs given in Fig. 9.3.

Table 9.1 Description of tools in the *vRealize Suite*

Tool name	Functional description
vRealize Automation	Offers multi-vendor and multi-cloud support; allows IT infrastructure for personalization, resource provisioning, and configuration; and automates application delivery and container management
VRealize Orchestrator	A workflow engine that integrates with *vRealize Suite* and *vCloud Suite*
vRealize Operations	Provides operations management across physical, virtual, and cloud environments
vRealize Log Insight	Provides customizable dashboards that allow IT administrators to manage and analyze system log data, troubleshoot issues with vSphere, and perform security auditing and compliance testing
vSphere Data Protection	Manages data protection (backup and restore)
vSphere Replication	Manages replication
VMware Site Recovery Manager	Provides disaster recovery
vRealize Business	Provides business continuity services such as private and public cloud cost tracking and cost comparison
Vmware Identity Manager	Manages security aspects
vRealize Code Stream	Automates the delivery of new applications and updates
VRealize Infrastructure Navigator	Provides a comprehensive view of the application environment

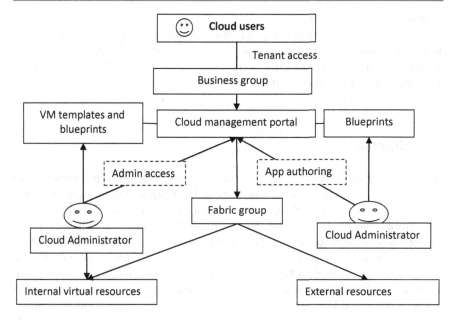

Fig. 9.3 Cloud management platform

A CMP consists of four primary entities:

(i) users;
(ii) tools and supporting infrastructure;
(iii) provisioning infrastructure; and
(iv) a cloud management portal.

Users
There are two types of users: cloud administrators and cloud users. Cloud administrators include a range of administrative staff such as tenant, group, fabric, infrastructure, service, and other administrators as defined by business policies and organizational structure. Cloud users are cloud tenants.

Tools and Supporting Infrastructure
VM templates and blueprints are the building blocks of the cloud. They are used to author the blueprints that tenants (end users) use to provision their cloud workloads.

Provisioning Infrastructure
Provisioning infrastructure includes internal and external resources.

Cloud Management Portal

A cloud management portal is a portal that provides users with self-service capabilities to administer, provision, and manage workloads. Cloud administrators interact with a cloud management portal using admin access. Cloud users interact with the cloud management portal using tenant access.

9.4 Summary

In this chapter the basics of cloud management were described. The chapter began by describing the need for cloud management. It emphasized the complexity of the cloud environment and explained why cloud management cannot be done manually. Since enterprises used to use more than one cloud solution as well as their own on-premises solution to meet business challenges management of the cloud now mandates the use of a set of integrated tools called *Cloud Management Platforms*. The chapter then turned to the benefits of cloud management tools and the core functions of cloud management. The chapter ended by providing the architecture of VMware Validated Design used for software-defined data centers and by showing how the Cloud Management Platform carries out its management role using different tools.

9.5 Exercises

1. Why do we need tools to manage the cloud?
2. Compile a list of the issues in handling a multi-cloud environment.
3. Give a holistic view of the Cloud Management Platform.

References

1. Ismaeel S, Miri A, Chourishi D, Dibaj SMR (2015) Open source cloud management platforms: a review. https://doi.org/10.1109/CSCloud.2015.84
2. https://docs.vmware.com/en/VMware-Validated-Design/4.0/com.vmware.vvd.sddc-design. doc/GUID-423FC133-DB4C-4AA2-BDBF-05DD4F8C67EA.html

Cloud Service Brokerage

10

Learning Objectives

The objective of this chapter is to introduce the reader to the basics of cloud service brokerage (CSB). By the end of this chapter the reader should have a fair understanding of CSB, the reasons enterprises need CSB, its typical capabilities, and architecture.

Motivational Questions

1. What is cloud service brokerage?
2. What is hybrid IT?
3. Do enterprises really need CSB?
4. Are there different types of CSB? If so, what are they?
5. What benefits do enterprises get from CSB?
6. What services are provided by CSB?
7. Are there currently available tools for CSB? If so, what are they?

Preface

Previous chapters have guided the reader through many aspects of cloud computing: its basics, service models, deployment models, networking, storage, security, monitoring, and management. This chapter will introduce the reader to an advanced concept: *cloud brokerage* from the perspective of hybrid IT. Enterprises using not only their own on-premises services but also cloud-based services from different public and private cloud service providers are finding hybrid IT attractive. Although this IT trend has brought business innovation, it suffers from lack of a unified way to handle different services from different providers. This led to the concept of

© Springer Nature Switzerland AG 2019   267
S. Chellammal and C. Pethuru Raj, *Essentials of Cloud Computing*,
Texts in Computer Science, https://doi.org/10.1007/978-3-030-13134-0_10

cloud brokerage. *Cloud brokerage solution sits between different cloud service providers and cloud users and serves as an intermediary.* It helps to get a consolidated and unified view of the service offerings of different providers and helps users to choose the best offering and helps in integrating different service offerings. It also helps by providing consolidated usage reports along with pricing.

This chapter discusses the modern business trend toward hybrid IT, the need for CSB, benefits of CSB, generic architecture of CSB, capabilities of CSB, and existing CSB tools.

10.1 Need for Cloud Service Brokerage

Cloud service brokerage serves as an intermediary between cloud providers and cloud consumers. It assists companies in choosing services and offerings that best suit their needs. They may also assist in the deployment and integration of applications across multiple clouds or provide options and possible cost savings by providing a catalog that compares competing services.

Urgent Need for Hybrid IT and its Associated Complexity

Cloud technology is increasingly playing a major part in bringing about digital business. An increasing number of enterprises are realizing the benefits of utilizing *multiple cloud infrastructures* and platforms to support employee productivity, collaboration, and business innovation.

As Fig. 10.1 demonstrates, modern enterprises need to work in the hybrid IT environment when they use on-premises computing and cloud-based services even from more than one provider. The rapid adoption of cloud services from multiple cloud service providers (CSPs) and communication service providers creates a unique set of challenges for IT, specifically because enterprise IT teams must now orchestrate onboarding, managing, and delivering IT and business services from multiple portals and vendors. *Such multiplicity makes it tough to ensure consistent performance, security, and control within the multi-cloud ecosystem and is the reason cloud brokerage platform solutions are becoming popular.* These could help to select the best cloud services for an organization's needs, support line-of-business requirements, and meet IT demands across disparate clouds without jeopardizing performance or security.

The availability of different (and even same) service offerings from different and distributed cloud environments poses a few challenges for institutions, innovators, and individuals in finding and leveraging an increasing number of cloud services with different SLAs and costs. *Hence choosing the right vendor, right services, and co-coordinating with multi-cloud service providers mandates brokerage solutions.*

The demand for immediate availability and unlimited scalability pushes enterprises toward multiple private and public clouds. If enterprises opt to manage services from multiple clouds without brokerage, they will have to face two issues:

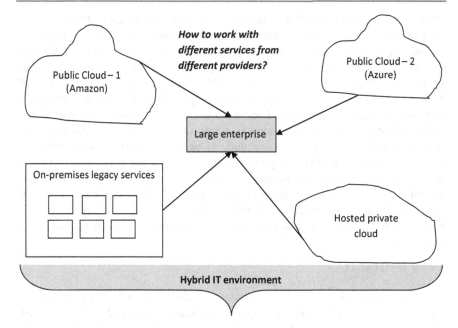

Fig. 10.1 Enterprises working in Hybrid IT environment

the task of managing a multi-cloud environment is not only tough but *time consuming* too, and the risk of failing to manage properly when costs can spiral out of control.

In short, cloud brokerage solutions are essential to handling multi-cloud environments. *Cloud brokers have emerged as master orchestrators who can manage the complexity of multiple cloud ecosystems and transform businesses into digital enterprises.*

10.2   Types of Cloud Brokers

Cloud brokers are classified into three categories according to *the major function* or *role* they play in enterprises: cloud aggregator, cloud integrator, and cloud customizer.

Cloud Aggregator

A cloud aggregator is a broker who packages and aggregates multiple service catalogs into a single user interface. The client then selects as many or as few services that fit their specific business needs but will only pay a single bill to the broker. The cloud aggregator model is generally seen as a more cost-effective and efficient approach for the client than purchasing each service individually. As part of their function as resellers, aggregators play a critical role in managing cloud provider relationships and services. The broker may also offer additional services on top of the cloud including security and governance. Overall, one of the main goals of the aggregator is to curate an actual catalog of services that includes all business and IT services, thus empowering agility and portability while saving time and money. Aggregation in cloud service brokerage creates a virtual service provider, offering normalized data models across cloud services and enabling data portability and security across a multitude of services. Cloud service aggregators should empower flexibility and portability between providers. Arbitrage in cloud service brokerage is a complementary function of aggregation, in which flexibility to move between cloud services and a single point of access enables end users to select the best choice based on metrics. Offering a choice of services is only beneficial if portability is available to take advantage of performance and cost savings.

Cloud Integrators

Cloud integrators add value by automating workflows across hybrid environments through a single orchestration to improve performance and reduce business risk. Once migration is complete the integrator can continue to provide support to the organization on an ongoing basis as needed. Integration is a function that maintains data fidelity for organizations using multiple on-demand B2B software services, SaaS, PaaS, IaaS, and the resulting silos they create. Cloud service integration can be complex and requires effort not only from cloud brokers but B2B vendors and infrastructure providers alike.

Cloud Customizers

As the name suggests, customization involves modifying existing cloud services to meet business needs. In some cases the broker may even develop additional features to run in the cloud as required by the organization. This function is critical to building a fully configured cloud with improved visibility, compliance, and integration of key IT processes. Intermediation cloud service brokerage provides specific value-added services to enhance the capabilities of existing cloud services. Examples might include identity or access management to multi-cloud services.

10.3   Benefits of Cloud Brokerage Solutions

Cloud service brokers serve to reduce the barriers in adopting, managing, and customizing services for the cloud because they fill in gaps in knowledge and skills [1]. Brokerage service providers and their consultancy team members are often hired to evaluate services from different vendors and provide the customer with information about how to use cloud services to power digital innovation. Once the research is complete the broker presents the customer with a list of recommended vendors along with a comparison of service features, cost breakdowns, SLAs, and other criteria. *In this way the broker's toolkit and expertise fosters objective, accurate, and informed decision making.*

Cloud brokers may sometimes be given the right to negotiate contracts with cloud service providers on behalf of the client. In such cases the broker is given the authority to contract services across several vendors, which can be an excellent strategy to keep costs low. In addition, CSBs typically have preexisting relationships with a number of vendors, and in some cases even have predetermined contracts, which helps to speed up the vendor acquisition process. This benefit is usually most common in the case of cloud aggregators.

Cloud service brokerage (CSB) providers can help eliminate redundancies, optimize resource utilization, and allow the IT organization to gain control of cloud consumption costs. Furthermore, having a real-time unified view of on-premises and public cloud resources also helps the organization to cut down òn errors relating to managing multiple cloud platforms across the organization.

As a result of faster and wider adoption of cloud services the IT spending of a company often occurs without the knowledge or approval of a centralized IT department (i.e., shadow IT is growing steadily). However, since cloud service brokers provide a unified cloud strategy they can help to align *lines of business with IT capabilities and improve the responsiveness of IT to operational demands of the organization.* IT can then transition from providing reactive support to delivering proactive solutions.

Cloud brokers could reduce the risk of migrating security services to the cloud by vetting vendors to ensure they meet robust security standards. This is especially critical in highly regulated industries, such as healthcare and financial services, where data protection is paramount. Here the broker automates cloud governance and compliance along with a single view to manage risk across the enterprise environment.

In short, CSBs enable the secure migration of data, applications, and infrastructure components between public and private clouds. Traditional IT environments can also benefit from using cloud brokers to participate in the growing cloud space.

10.4 Generic Architecture of Cloud Service Broker

At the highest level any CSB (as shown in Fig. 10.2) will contain a number of core processes:

  (i)   service catalog;
 (ii)   integration;
(iii)   provisioning;
 (iv)   security;

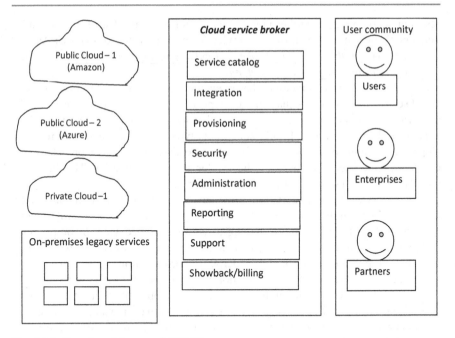

Fig. 10.2 Generic architecture of CSB [2]

   (v)   administration;
  (vi) reporting;
 (vii) support; and
(viii) billing.

- *Service catalog*: A service catalog aggregates content from external vendors or suppliers. Such aggregated content is presented in a simplified format that makes it easier for the customer to search, compare, and finalize required services.
- *Integration*: All external cloud services should be integrated into the CSB platform to make it easier for customers to request a service that combines multiple providers.
- *Provisioning*: CSB provides a central console for controlling services and user provisioning along with policy-based automated provisioning.
- *Security*: CSB provides authentication, authorization, and a single sign-on facility to access all services using a single password. It provides role-based authorization and granular control of cloud services access based on user role, user privileges, and uniform password policy enforcement.
- *Administration*: CSB administration provides user management and administration functions such as registration of new users, management of existing users, and deletion and updating of user details.

- *Reporting*: CSB reporting entails unified reporting and notification as well as usage statistics. Customers can access all these details from the management console of their account.
- *Support*: CSB support entails general helpdesk activities including submission of tickets, FAQs, knowledge bases, notifications, and alerts. Additionally, the customer receives first-level support directly from the service provider.
- *Billing*: CSB billing supports *pay-per-usage*, the unique pricing model of the cloud, which allows customers to check all details regarding service usage, cost, and usage reports. The billing calculation can be viewed on the management console of their account. Payment and settlement services are also integrated into billing.

10.5 Cloud Service Brokerage Tools

- *Jamcracker*: The Jamcracker Platform, from the company of the same name in Santa Clara, California, is a cloud brokerage service.
- *Odin Service Automation*: Odin Service Automation is a cloud brokerage service provided by Odin in Renton, Washington.
- *IBM Cloud Brokerage*: IBM Cloud Brokerage is a cloud brokerage service provided by IBM.
- *ComputeNext*: ComputeNext is a cloud brokerage service from the IT company of the same name in Bellevue, Washington.
- *Gravitant cloudMatrix*: Gravitant cloudMatrix is a cloud brokerage service acquired and now supported by IBM (November 2015).

A detailed description of Jamcracker and IBM Cloud Brokerage are given in the following subsections, which should provide the reader with much greater insight into CSB.

10.5.1 Jamcracker

Jamcracker is a comprehensive CSB, cloud management, and governance platform that includes risk and policy compliance, spend, and operations management. Jamcracker enables organizations to create, deliver, and manage multi-cloud services and to implement a cloud-enabled business model for offering, delivering, supporting, and billing of cloud services. Jamcracker ensures global flexibility and scalability by using a multi-tiered, multi-tenant architecture, RESTful (representational state transfer) APIs, and integration frameworks while supporting multiple currencies and languages. Jamcracker allows service providers, technology providers, system integrators, IT distributors, and enterprise/government IT organizations to unify delivery and management of private and public cloud applications/services and distribute them to customers, partners, and employees through a customer-facing self-service app store.

Jamcracker provides full support for Infrastructure as a Service (IaaS) Cloud Management Platform (CMP) functionality for multi-cloud and hybrid cloud service environments. Hence Jamcracker unifies cloud service management needs for SaaS, PaaS, and now IaaS is offering a holistic cloud service enablement solution across all flavors of cloud services.

Capabilities/Features of Jamcracker

Since the Jamcracker Platform has been built according to industry standards and technologies it has the following capabilities/features:

- it provides for integration of both public and private clouds such as AWS, Azure, Softlayer, vSphere/vCD, and OpenStack;
- it provides for integration of hybrid cloud frameworks including SaaS, IaaS, and PaaS;
- it works with multiple devices and platforms including Web and mobile;
- it provides a configurable workflow engine;
- it provides roles-based access control; and
- it provides a scalable N-tiered architecture.

Architecture of Jamcracker Cloud Service Brokerage

The architecture of the Jamcracker CSB Platform [3] (https://www.doblerconsulting. com/wp-content/uploads/2017/06/5943a22b1b02a.pdf) is given in Fig. 10.3.

As can be seen from the architecture the Jamcracker CSB Platform consists of four core functional layers:

1. Self-service user portal and service catalog
2. Unified security and policy management
3. Usage reporting and metered/subscription billing
4. Multi-cloud application provisioning and management.

The tool has a provisioning adapter to various cloud service providers such as AWS, Rackspace, Azure, CloudFoundry, and other IaaS, PaaS and SaaS providers. It provides native support for OpenStack cloud management APIs. It provides for integration with various enterprise services such as digital assets, directory/DB, ERP, IT service management (ITSM), and IT operations management (ITOM).

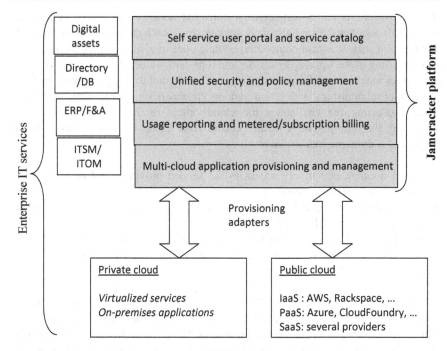

Fig. 10.3   Architecture of Jamcracker CSB Platform

This architecture enables Jamcracker to provide:

   (i)   catalog service;
  (ii)   self-service;
 (iii)   service and user provisioning;
  (iv)   authentication, authorization, and access control;
   (v)   user and service administration;
  (vi)   reporting and auditing;
 (vii)   helpdesk and support; and
(viii)   billing.

10.5.2   IBM Cloud Brokerage

IBM Cloud Brokerage is one of the few purpose-built solutions for hybrid IT. IBM Cloud Brokerage enables enterprises to transform their IT services model from a high-cost, inflexible physical data center model into a next generation, pay-per-use model. IBM Cloud Brokerage provides an automated and self-service view of many cloud providers. It has a distinctive feature that reviews and audits each cloud provider. It assesses the strengths and weaknesses of each cloud service provider. It clarifies cost structures and contractual complexities to give an organization a clear understanding of the upside, downside, and long-term value. IBM Cloud Brokerage even gives enterprises a framework they can use to rapidly integrate their existing contractual relationships with cloud vendors. It was designed to enable hybrid IT while addressing the challenges the cloud brings to the IT value chain. By addressing the multiple steps in the process IBM Cloud Brokerage can with the support of a dynamic marketplace:

- support accurate and timely access to the service providers and delivery environments an enterprise chooses;
- facilitate delivery of a multi-sourced solution using existing service management tools through open APIs; and
- provide a single record system that tracks an order from design through billing and enables centralized governance and cost management by application, virtual data center, and business unit.

The real benefit of IBM Cloud Brokerage is that it helps organizations to move away from cloud complexity toward cloud value. Rather than getting bogged down with vendor RFPs and technology comparisons, IBM Cloud Brokerage offers quick choices based on short-term and long-term objectives. It lets an organization and its users make informed choices in minutes instead of weeks. IBM Cloud Brokerage streamlines that complexity for an organization as per its requirements and objectives.

IBM Cloud Brokerage is a cloud brokerage SaaS offering that facilitates the acquisition of *plan, buy, and manage software* and cloud services from multiple suppliers from a single dashboard in an exceedingly simple manner as illustrated below.

Plan

- Assess workloads to determine which will benefit from the cloud
- Compare IT resources from multiple providers side by side
- Create customizable, reusable solutions or blueprints that include managed services.

Buy

- Explore the service store powered by a dynamic catalog
- Find the best solutions for your business needs.

Manage

- Aggregate bills and navigate payment processes using a centralized billing management solution
- Better manage compliance with enterprise policies.

10.6 Summary

This chapter discussed the modern trend of hybrid IT and its associated complexities. How the challenges in handling hybrid IT can be solved using cloud service brokers was discussed by showcasing typical architectures and exciting tools for brokerage.

10.7 Exercises

1. Why are enterprises adopting hybrid IT?
2. What are the difficulties enterprises face with hybrid IT?
3. How does CSB resolve the difficulties enterprises face with hybrid IT?
4. Write an assignment on the different types of CSB.

References

1. Choudhuri DR, Mohapatra B (2016) Cloud brokerage service, a right buying decision minimizes the risk of hybrid cloud. Int J Eng Innov Technol (IJEIT) 5(11):88–91
2. Giovanoli C, Pulikal P, Gatziu Grivas S (2014) E-marketplace for cloud services. In: The fifth international conference on cloud computing, GRIDs, and virtualization, IARIA, pp 77–83
3. https://www.doblerconsulting.com/wp-content/uploads/2017/06/5943a22b1b02a.pdf

Cloud Orchestration

11

Learning Objectives

The objective of this chapter is to introduce the reader to the basics of cloud orchestration in a multi-cloud environment. By the end of the chapter the reader should have a fair understanding about why we need a multi-cloud environment and hybrid IT, its challenges, and how cloud orchestration helps to resolve some of the challenges. The reader should also gain an insight into the currently available tools used in cloud orchestration.

Motivational Questions

1. What is cloud orchestration?
2. How does cloud orchestration differ from automation?
3. Do orchestration and brokerage mean the same?
4. Why do enterprises need a multi-cloud environment and hybrid IT?
5. How does cloud orchestration help a multi-cloud environment?

Preface

Cloud orchestration is an advanced concept. Having mastered various management-related concepts, such as monitoring, management, and brokerage, in this chapter the reader is introduced to orchestration. The chapter starts by describing the need for hybrid IT, the complexity of hybrid IT, and how orchestration tools play a crucial role in creating and managing workflows that allow more than one activity from multiple providers to be carried out without any conflict and in the best way possible.

© Springer Nature Switzerland AG 2019
S. Chellammal and C. Pethuru Raj, *Essentials of Cloud Computing*,
Texts in Computer Science, https://doi.org/10.1007/978-3-030-13134-0_11

11.1 Emergence of Hybrid Cloud and Multi-cloud Environments

Cloud computing is the most significant technology involved in digital transformation and is currently gaining a lot of momentum as a result of its powerful cloud realization technologies and tools. Business organizations, IT teams, and cloud service providers (CSPs) have been collaborating to put in place a variety of business-specific and generic cloud environments by leveraging well-defined and designed cloud-enabling processes, products, and patterns. The cloud has emerged as the most optimized and organized IT environment in which a growing array of personal, social, and professional applications can reside and run. There are a variety of clouds with different formats: online, on-demand, off-premises, and on-premises. There are public, private, and community clouds in plenty to comfortably cater to different regions and requirements. There are a number of purpose-specific cloud environments catering to different communities. In a nutshell, there are environment-specific, organization-wide, business-centric, private, and localized clouds comprising bare metal servers, virtual machines, and containers. Moreover, there are massive public clouds set up by various providers to meet their clients' computing, networking, and storage needs. The next innovation in cloud computing has already arrived: *hybrid cloud* and multi-cloud. Hybrid cloud and multi-cloud environments have different visions or objectives. In the hybrid cloud environment private and public clouds are integrated toward achieving the *same purpose*. The components of a hybrid cloud typically work together. As a result, data and processes tend to intermingle and intersect in a hybrid environment. However, a hybrid cloud alone is not enough to meet business needs. The main reason is the organizational structure of enterprises. Different divisions and departments in an enterprise focus on their own core areas, such as sales force automation, marketing, customer relationship management, supply chain management, production, and HRA, which results in various lines of business (LOBs). Various LOBs require different types of IT support. LOBs are in constant need of updating to enable or improve automation of their relevant operations to stay competitive in the market. Teams in charge of many LOBs are forced to use their own budgets to take control of updating by turning to various Software as a Service (SaaS) offerings. Furthermore, they approach integration Platform as a Service (iPaaS) providers to link selected *SaaS offerings with their own on-premises data sources*. The key point to be noted in a multi-cloud environment is that enterprises mix services from more than one public cloud provider (because enterprises want unlimited scalability, availability, and rapid resource provisioning) and an on-premises data center (because enterprises want to keep their IT assets safe and secure). This pattern of ad hoc outsourcing has accelerated the trend toward multi-cloud environments. In a multi-cloud environment an organization uses multiple different public cloud services, often from multiple different providers along with on-premises physical, virtual, and private cloud infrastructure.

There are a number of benefits to using the latest combined operating models of hybrid cloud and multi-cloud:

- They provide a foundation for elastic resources to increase resilience, accelerate development and test efforts, access more geographic locations, and select best-of-breed providers for various tasks.
- They bring the agility, flexibility, and innovation needed to drive any business forward.
- They increase customer engagement, share of wallet, satisfaction, and loyalty.
- They create new areas of profitable growth and differentiation.
- They reduce risk and lower operational costs by accelerating and driving efficiency.

11.1.1 Challenges in Managing Hybrid Cloud and Multi-cloud Environments

Establishing hybrid cloud and multi-cloud environments is not without challenges. Such challenges can be broken down into three categories (as shown in Fig. 11.1).

Technical challenges

- *API*: No single model of integration or infrastructure automation can work in isolation as each cloud provider supplies a different API to access different cloud services.
- *Behavior*: There are many differences in how clouds behave under certain circumstances and even for common actions. For example, some clouds automatically provision storage on launch of a server or instance, while others do not.
- *Resource sizes and types*: Each cloud provider offers different sizes and types of compute, storage, and network resources. Hence the IT team must take this into account when looking for the optimum resource size and type needed for their workloads.

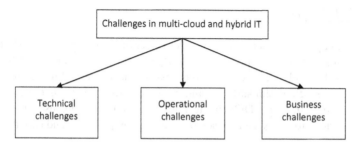

Fig. 11.1 Challenges in multi-cloud and hybrid IT environments

- *Operating system images*: Each cloud provider provides a unique set of operating system (OS) images. This makes it difficult to run workloads using the same image in other clouds.
- *Hypervisors*: Each cloud provider leverages different and sometimes proprietary hypervisor options.
- *Application stacks*: Some cloud providers supply a selection of common and preconfigured application stacks (such as LAMP, Java, or .NET).
- *Add-on services and features*: Each cloud provider offers extra add-on services and proprietary features beyond the common compute, network, and storage resources. These may include load balancing, application servers, analysis tools, or databases.
- *Security capabilities*: Access control capabilities vary across cloud providers. This becomes more complex if different providers demand different password complexities or authentication measures.
- *Network capabilities*: Each cloud provider offers different ways to define subnets, security groups, and network gateways, increasing the difficulty in network planning.

Operational challenges

- *Testing*: Deploying applications to multiple clouds requires platform-specific testing, which involves many separate automated tests targeting multiple cloud platforms.
- *Maintaining security and governance*: Companies need to go through the rules and regulations of each cloud service provider to fully adhere with security compliance.
- *Managing applications and infrastructure configurations across multiple cloud stacks*: This can be difficult since cloud platforms do not share a common API, which highlights the problem of dealing with different service definitions and billing models.
- *Technical support and expertise*: Extra administrative work and research are required to determine the best provider and whether the provider's services are compatible with the needs of the enterprise.

Business challenges

- *Billing and pricing*: Each cloud provider offers different pricing models for services with different quality-of-service (QoS) attributes. Multiple billing and pricing is definitely a challenge for businesses to leverage multiple clouds. There has to be a single dashboard showing all the clouds' service charges.
- *Skill sets and training*: Different technologies and tools are used by different cloud service providers. Hence lack of education, experience, and expertise in the

organization about different clouds can lead to outages of workloads and increase cost/effort.

- *Planning and execution*: It can be difficult to choose services that match a company's business needs, pricing, governance, and expertise.

11.2   Cloud Orchestration

Orchestration is concerned with automating multiple tasks together. Processes typically comprise multiple tasks and systems. The tasks inscribed in a process need to be executed in sequence to be fruitful. That is, a process starts with an appropriate workflow representation and ends with workflow execution. Thus a process from workflow representation to workflow execution is simply termed orchestration. Orchestration deals with the end-to-end process, including management of all related services, taking care of high availability (HA), post-deployment, failure recovery, scaling, and more.

Automating tasks or orchestration of workflows within a single enterprise may be easier as all the services, such as APIs, interfaces, standards, regulations, and policies, are confined within the enterprise. *However, enterprises now find themselves compelled to look at cloud offerings to meet many critical needs such as reduced capital and operational cost, uncertain loads, dynamic and unlimited scalability needs, and high availability. They depend on public clouds because of their inherent capabilities. At the same time enterprises have to depend on on-premises setups to protect legacy and sensitive data.* In spite of the challenges associated with a multi-cloud environment (see previous section), enterprises are compelled to opt for multi-cloud and hybrid IT because of their benefits (again see previous section). Cloud orchestration resolves *some of the challenges associated with operations in* multi-cloud environment. *Before looking at how orchestration can be used to solve challenges the concept of orchestration needs to be distinguished from its related terms automation and brokerage* [1]:

- *Automation versus orchestration*: Automation is the process of automating a single task using some scripts. An example is starting a web server. It is a single task with a limited or confined scope. *However, orchestration is the process of automating a business process that executes many tasks according to specific execution patterns like sequential workflow.* Orchestration manages the execution of several tasks in sequential order to achieve a broad business goal.
- *Brokerage versus orchestration*: Cloud service brokerages are useful *business support services* that provide intermediation between various clouds (private, multi-host, public, and SaaS providers) and provide consistent and centralized purchasing and billing while ensuring *business rules including budget and cost management* are met across multiple cloud environments. However, *orchestration has its focus on operational support services*, which include advanced

workflow engine capabilities and the means for management consolidation to drive standardization and realize efficiency.

Cloud orchestration is carried out across all layers of the cloud architecture.

11.2.1   Types of Orchestration

Orchestration can be categorized into three types:

(i)   resource orchestration;
(ii)   workload orchestration; and
(iii) service orchestration.

Resource orchestration

Each type of service offering in the cloud (i.e., IaaS, PaaS, and SaaS) has different types of resources:

- *IaaS layer* (compute, storage and network): Cloud orchestration is tasked with automatic resource provisioning of the *compute, storage, and network nodes* that are distributed over *geographical* locations while keeping company policies and regulations intact. It should be kept in mind that resources differ and are provided by different providers.
- *PaaS layer*: PaaS layer resources include load balancers, authorization servers, required guest OS, platforms, web servers, application servers, database servers, middleware, development and runtime platforms such as .NET and JDK, and different languages such as Python and Java. The PaaS layer is very important in meeting a cloud user's required levels of various QoS attributes such as availability, performance, security, reliability, software licensing, software upgrade, performance statistics, and SLA compliance.
- *SaaS layer*: The SaaS layer orchestrates operations that manage the life cycle of SaaS-level resources.

How *orchestration operations* related to provisioning of different resources (of different service offerings) differ from one another is shown in Table 11.1.

Workload orchestration

A workload is an application to be deployed in an infrastructure. Workload orchestration is automatic deployment of a workload into an appropriate infrastructure (as shown in Fig. 11.2).

As already mentioned, a workload is an application to be deployed in an infrastructure. The workload to be deployed is described using a declarative workload definition language. Resources required for the workload and required

Table 11.1 Different orchestration functions involved in different resources over different layers

Layer	Resources	Orchestration functions
IaaS	Compute node	Start, stop, restart, select, mount off instance storage, monitor, reconfigure, assign IP, select cloud location, select availability zone, scale-in, scale-out, authorize, and authenticate
	Storage node	Create new buckets, upload file, download file, scale-in, scale-out, monitor, encrypt, decrypt, authorize, and authenticate
	Network node	Allocation of IP addresses, URL, ports, availability zone, VPN to CPU resources, and monitor
PaaS	Load balancers, authorization servers, required guest OS, platforms, web servers, application servers, database servers, middleware, development, and runtime platforms	Start, stop, restart, select, allocate hardware resources, integrate with other appliances, install script, monitor, create, migrate, scale-in, scale-out, login, logout, install software, replicate, synchronize, backup, delete, encrypt data, decrypt data, authorize, and authenticate
SaaS	SaaS applications	Automatic provisioning of SaaS applications into PaaS and IaaS. Life cycle management of SaaS applications

See Rajiv et al. [2]

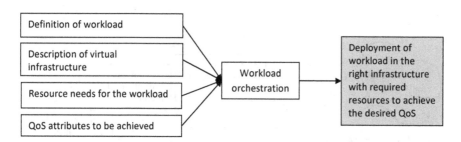

Fig. 11.2 Workload orchestration

levels of QoS attributes, such as reliability, availability, and performance, are given as input to an orchestration engine.

Service orchestration

Service orchestration is the process of integrating more than one service so as to form a business goal. Services are executed according to a given workflow (as shown in Fig. 11.3).

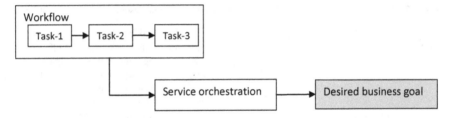

Fig. 11.3 Service orchestration

As Fig. 11.3 shows, service orchestration automatically executes several tasks in different infrastructures provided by different providers with the required QoS while meeting compliance requirements.

11.2.2 Key Functions of Orchestration Engine

By and large an orchestration engine performs the following *key functionalities over different layers of the cloud* (as shown in Fig. 11.4):

- helps automate delivery of infrastructure, application, and custom IT services;
- supports direct integration of service management capabilities;

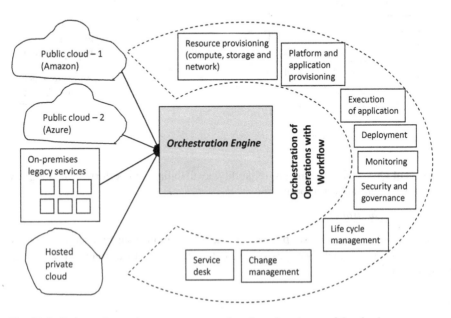

Fig. 11.4 Orchestration engine automates operations in various layers of the cloud

- deploys application workloads across on-premises and off-premises cloud environments;
- provides policy-based governance and logical application modeling to help ensure that multi-vendor and multi-cloud services are delivered at the right size and service level for each task performed;
- includes both build/deployment and delivery/support orchestration and automation services; and
- enables intelligent orchestration and smart automation with cognitive functions.

As mentioned earlier, an orchestration engine automates various *operations* in different layers of the cloud.

An orchestration engine orchestrates:

- automatic resource provisioning of compute, storage, and network nodes provided by different providers dispersed at different geographical locations;
- automatic platform and application provisioning by bringing interoperability among heterogeneous APIs, platforms, interfaces, etc.;
- orchestration of *life cycle management* activities;
- orchestration of *monitoring* among multiple clouds;
- orchestration of *change management* and *service desk* tasks; and
- security and compliance requirements throughout orchestration activities.

11.3 Some Leading Cloud Orchestration Tools

Chef

Chef is a powerful automation platform that transforms complex infrastructures into code bringing servers and services to life. Chef automates the configuration, deployment, and management of applications across the network. Chef uses **cookbooks** to determine how each node should be configured. Cookbooks consist of multiple **recipes**; a recipe is an automation script for a particular service that is written in Ruby. **Chef client** is an agent that runs on a node and performs the actual tasks that configure it. Chef can manage anything that can run Chef client such as physical machines, virtual machines, containers, or cloud-based instances. **Chef server** is the central repository for all configuration data. Chef client and Chef server communicate in a secure manner using a combination of public and private keys, which ensure that Chef server responds only to requests made by Chef client. There is also an option to install a standalone client called **Chef solo**.

Puppet

Puppet requires installation of a master server and client agent in target nodes and includes an option for a standalone client, which is equivalent to Chef solo. Deployment modules can be downloaded and installed using Puppet commands. Like Chef, Puppet comes with a paid Enterprise edition that provides additional features such as reporting and orchestration/push deployment. However, while Chef and Puppet perform the same basic functions they differ in their approach. Chef seems to be significantly more integrated and monolithic, whereas Puppet consists of multiple services. This can make Chef somewhat easier to get up and running and manage. Both have their pros and cons, so we need to evaluate which makes the most sense for our operations teams and infrastructure development workflow.

OpenStack

OpenStack is a free and open-source cloud computing software platform that is primarily used as an Infrastructure as a Service (IaaS) solution. It consists of a series of interrelated projects that control pools of processing, storage, and networking resources throughout a cloud center. Users manage them through a Web-based dashboard, command line tools, or a RESTful API. The key components of the OpenStack platform are shown in Fig. 11.5.

The main components of OpenStack include Nova (compute), Cinder (block storage), Glance (image library), Swift (object storage), Neutron (network), Keystone (identity), and Heat (orchestration tool):

- *OpenStack Compute* (Nova) is a cloud computing fabric controller, which is the main part of an IaaS system. It is designed to manage and automate pools of computer resources and can work with widely available virtualization technologies and top-performance computing configurations.
- *Storage*: The two types of storage in OpenStack are object storage and block storage. Cinder is block storage and Swift is object storage.
- *OpenStack Networking* (Neutron) is a system for managing networks and IP addresses.
- *OpenStack Identity* (Keystone) provides a central directory of users mapped to the OpenStack services they can access. It acts as a common authentication system

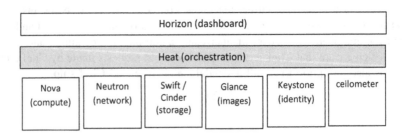

Fig. 11.5 Key components of OpenStack platform

across the cloud operating system and can integrate with existing back-end directory services.

- *OpenStack Image* (Glance) provides discovery, registration, and delivery services for disk and server images.
- *OpenStack Telemetry* (Ceilometer) provides a single point of contact for billing systems.
- *Heat* is a service to orchestrate multiple composite cloud applications using templates through an OpenStack-native REST API and a CloudFormation-compatible Query API. The software integrates other core components of OpenStack into a one-file template system. The templates allow for the creation of most of the OpenStack resource types (such as instances, floating IPs, volumes, security groups, and users) as well as more advanced functionality such as high availability, instance auto-scaling, and nested stacks.

11.4 Summary

This chapter began by discussing the need for enterprises to adopt multi-cloud and hybrid IT technology. How the multi-cloud environment introduces modernization and optimization to businesses was discussed along with its associated challenges. After describing the challenges the chapter explained cloud orchestration and how useful it is in solving some of the challenges associated with a multi-cloud environment. The chapter ended by giving a brief description of the different cloud orchestration tools.

11.5 Exercises

Imagine you are a cloud administrator in a company that is seeking to adopt a multi-cloud environment:

1. Prepare a table of existing orchestration tools with special emphasis on features and capabilities of tools (assume you are working with Amazon IaaS and Azure PaaS).
2. Do you really need orchestration tool support? Justify your answer.
3. If you need tools, which ones would you choose? Why?

References

1. https://www.cmg.org/2017/08/orchestration-cloud-services/
2. Ranjan R, Benatallah B, Dustdar S, Papazoglou MP (2015) The NetherlandsCloud resource orchestration programming overview, issues, and directions. IEEE Internet Comput 2–12

Disaster Recovery

12

Learning Objectives

Like security, disaster recovery is a major concern of IT industries. Enterprises want to maintain business continuity (BC) whatever happens. The objective of this chapter is to present the basics of disaster recovery (DR), how to prepare a DR plan, and how DR can be implemented using cloud infrastructure.

Motivational Questions
1. What is the need for DR?
2. How can cloud provide help for DR?
3. Is cloud DR fit for purpose for business continuity?
4. What approaches are there for DR?

Preface

When a natural or man-made disaster occurs data centers and IT server farms may fully or partially go down. Disaster recovery (DR) mechanisms have been devised that should guarantee business continuity. The affordability, multi-region availability, agility, and adaptability of cloud environments have inspired worldwide enterprises to embrace the cloud idea, which is especially true when it comes to fulfilling the distinct goals of disaster recovery. In this chapter the reader should learn about what, why, and how DR environments can help rescue enterprise-class applications and data.

© Springer Nature Switzerland AG 2019
S. Chellammal and C. Pethuru Raj, *Essentials of Cloud Computing*,
Texts in Computer Science, https://doi.org/10.1007/978-3-030-13134-0_12

12.1   Disaster Recovery and Its Requirements

In general, IT systems and business workloads have and continue to be intrinsically designed, developed, and deployed in a highly available and scalable fashion to ensure business continuity. An important feature that has been incorporated is fault tolerance, which has been designed to tolerate and survive any kind of internal errors and external attacks. Nevertheless, the computing resources of an enterprise could go down during natural or man-made disasters. Disaster recovery is all about having a secondary data center to support the recovery of data and services during disasters. Traditional disaster recovery (DR) approaches typically result in off-site duplication of data, applications, and infrastructures (software and hardware). Hence if something catastrophic happens to the primary data center or cloud center, it is possible to quickly switch to the backup/secondary data center to get critical applications up and running again. Such a secondary data center is termed a *disaster recovery* (DR) center and mandates:

- real estate to house the IT infrastructure;
- human resources to administer, operate, and manage the DR center;
- electricity, cooling facility, and connectivity infrastructure; and
- server machines, storage devices, and network and security solutions.

As enterprises increasingly adopt cloud environments as a one-stop IT solution to all kinds of issues facing business acceleration, augmentation, and automation, embracing one or more cloud environments (public or dedicated) is gaining significant traction these days. Many advantages have been put forward for the adoption of the cloud paradigm for all kinds of IT needs, especially the establishment of a DR facility.

12.2   Benefits of Cloud for Disaster Recovery

Cloud environments bring a number of distinct advantages for institutions, individuals, and innovators. This section throws some light on why the cloud is being lauded as a best-in-class solution when it comes to DR capability:

- *Saves time and money*: Building data centers and manning them in an efficient manner definitely incurs a lot of time, talent, and money. However, leveraging a cloud facility for DR purposes is a cheaper option. It involves entrusting DR requirements to one or more cloud service providers (CSPs). As IT becomes the fourth social utility as a result of widespread cloudification the pay-per-usage model is increasingly being adopted for computing. Moreover, since the cloud idea fulfills the properties of on-demand and online computing, increasingly the DR task is being fulfilled through cloud environments. The cloud paradigm also steadily ensures the goals of autonomous computing through a host of pioneering technologies and tools. Cloud reliability, availability, scalability, security, affordability, agility, etc. are being systematically realized. In short, the cloud phenomenon can best be described as a tectonic shift in IT.

- *Offers multiple options*: The cloud journey thus far can best be described as exciting and enigmatic. Cloud enablement processes, patterns, platforms, procedures, and practices have been unearthed to speed up cloud adoption in a risk-free and rewarding fashion. There are cloud centers across the globe leveraging competent design, development, and operational and management technologies. A wide variety of premium services are being offered by various cloud service providers to retain customers and attract new ones. Ever-persistent competition in the cloud space means businesses are going to gain immense benefits when it comes to securing their data and applications. Not only have cloud centers been built and rented to businesses they are also available to the general public in many locations (i.e., there are more options to back up customer, confidential, and corporate data). Not only data but also all kinds of business-critical applications are being stocked in cloud-based DR centers. The cloud offers many options when it comes to housing your backup, adding to the resilience of applications to avoid regional disasters.
- *Supports simplified design with high reliability*: Disaster recovery (DR) solutions are relatively easy to set up in the cloud. All the right and relevant hardware infrastructures, software infrastructure solutions, platforms, databases, enterprise and mobile applications, etc. have been and continue to be made available in cloud environments. An enterprise simply has to choose the appropriate resources and software packages, etc. in a standard format and submit it to a cloud service provider to get everything ready in a moment. The cloud includes various concepts such as consolidation, sharing, automation, simplicity, accessibility, modifiability, remote management, orchestration, and governance. Cloud storage is relatively cheap and storage cost is still low even for long-duration storage. Furthermore, if something bad happens to the primary data or cloud center, the DR center comes to life immediately so that there is no slowdown and breakdown of service and data delivery. There is no need for transportation and restoration of backup tapes to get applications up and running again. All data can be accessed quickly and easily through the internet when using the cloud for DR. In short, DR is simply easy in the cloud.
- *Scalability*: Cloud resources are innately elastic and hence cloud applications are scalable. When there are more users and hence more data loads, fresh cloud infrastructures, such as virtual machines and containers, can be provisioned immediately to tackle such loads. The cloud environment has simplified such non-functional requirements (NFRs).

Many other noteworthy benefits have come from the cloud idea. All kinds of non-functional requirements (NFRs), such as scalability, availability, modifiability, performance/throughput, affordability, universal accessibility, simplicity, sustainability, and security, are easily and quickly accomplished using a host of automation, optimization, orchestration, and integration tools.

12.3 Primary Components for Disaster Recovery

Data are critical to any enterprise offering premium services to its consumers and clients. Data trustworthiness and timeliness have to be maintained at any cost to extricate actionable insights out of data heaps. The emergence of pioneering technologies and tools that can stream large amounts of data quickly has led to the value, variety, volume, velocity, veracity, and viscosity of data changing fast and acquiring special significance not only for businesses but also for individuals. Hence data security, safety, and privacy are indispensable. This is the reason data recovery is being touted as a success factor and key differentiator for any enterprise to survive and surge ahead. The two primary components for data recovery are:

- *Data backups*: Backing up data involves simply copying data from the primary means of IT storage and storing it in the DR environment. Backups help to recover data at times of data loss or unavailability, or when data are corrupted in the primary center. Typically, data backups have a small to medium recovery time objective (RTO) and a small recovery point objective (RPO) (RTO and RPO are discussed in the next section).
- *Database backups*: Database backups are slightly more complex than data backups because database recovery typically involves recovering at a given point in time. Hence the importance of knowing how to carry out and restore database backups. The challenge here is that the recovered database system has to mirror the production configuration (the same version and mirrored disk configuration). It is also important to know how to back up transaction logs. The first thing that should be done during recovery is to restore database functionality. This should be followed by applying the latest database backup and the recovered transaction logs that were backed up after the last backup. This is quite complicated. It is better to adopt a *high-availability first approach* to minimize the time to recover from a situation that could cause unavailability of the database server. This allows enterprises to achieve smaller RTO and RPO values.

12.4 Designing a Disaster Recovery Plan

It is important to have a comprehensive and well-tested DR plan [1] and make use of the cloud to implement it. Designing a DR plan includes three major steps:

1. Audit the infrastructure and assess possible risks
2. Perform a business impact analysis
3. Design a DR plan according to the RTO and RPO.

Audit the infrastructure and assess possible risks

It is important to note the existing IT assets (servers, storage devices and arrays, networking and storage solutions) and carry out risk analysis. Mapping has then to be done between IT infrastructures and business applications and data. Yearly data growth has to be precisely calculated. Application user size has to be identified to get a firm grip on the DR strategy. It is very important to ascertain risks from all sides. For instance, onsite risks include fire, flood, hurricane, earthquakes, power outages, network collapse, cyber attacks, and natural or man-made disasters. Once you have carried out a deep and decisive analysis of what assets might be at risk and what events might impact business continuity, the resulting DR execution plan can be deemed valid.

Perform a business impact analysis

The next step is to perform a business impact analysis. This will help better understand the thresholds under which a business can operate after a disaster occurs. As is well known DR is a subset of business continuity planning. Any DR plan is determined by *two critical factors*:

1. Recovery time objective (RTO)
2. Recovery point objective (RPO).

- *Recovery time objective (RTO)*: The RTO is the maximum acceptable length of time that an enterprise's application can be offline before seriously impacting its business operations. If the company is a business-to-consumer (B2C) application, any downtime is a big loss. Not a single transaction can be made while the software is down. In this case the RTO might be set at 15 min or less, and hence the enterprise will have to invest heavily in the DR plan to achieve full recovery in that short amount of time. This value is usually defined as part of a larger service level agreement (SLA). For not-so-critical applications the RTO can be set for an hour, a day, or even more. Understanding the value of the RTO is very important because that length of time directly correlates to the amount of resources an enterprise needs to invest in its disaster recovery (DR) plan.
- *Recovery point objective (RPO)*: The RPO is defined as the maximum acceptable length of time during which data might be lost from an application due to a major incident. An RPO informs how often an enterprise should back up its data. In the case of mission-critical applications the RPO might be as little as 5 min because of the data-intensive and high-compliance nature of the business concerned.

Typically, the smaller the RTO and RPO values (i.e., the faster the application must recover from an interruption) the more it will cost to run the application. Because smaller RTO and RPO values often mean greater complexity the associated administrative overhead is also on the high side. A high-availability application might require an enterprise to manage distribution between two physically separated data centers, manage replication, and more.

RTO and RPO values can typically be rolled up into another metric called the service level objective (SLO), a key measurable element of an SLA. An SLA is the entire agreement that specifies what service is to be provided, how it is supported, the frequency at which backups are undertaken, and the locations, costs, performance, penalties, and responsibilities of the parties involved. SLOs are specific and measurable characteristics of an SLA such as availability, throughput, frequency, response time, or quality. An SLA can contain many SLOs. RTOs and RPOs are measurable and hence should be considered SLOs.

Design a data recovery plan according to the RTO and RPO

Based on RTO and RPO thresholds an enterprise designs its DR system to fulfill varying DR goals:

- *Design according to recovery goals*: An enterprise should design its DR plan by incorporating application and data recovery techniques, analyzing RTO and RPO values, and then finding which DR pattern can be adopted to meet those values. For example, in the case of historical compliance-oriented data there is no need for speedy access to the data, hence a large RTO value and cold DR pattern is appropriate. However, if an online service experiences an interruption, then it becomes essential to recover both the data and the customer-facing part of the application as quickly as possible. In that case, a hot pattern would be more appropriate. Moreover, an email notification system, which typically is not business critical, is probably a candidate for a warm pattern.
- *Design for end-to-end recovery*: It is not enough just to have a plan for backing up or archiving data. An enterprise should ensure that its DR plan addresses the full recovery process from backup to restore to cleanup.

12.5 Proven Disaster Recovery Approaches

- *Backup and restore approach*: If an enterprise has a relatively long RTO and RPO threshold the way forward is to create a straightforward *backup and restore* DR plan (i.e., an enterprise can back up its on-premises data in a public cloud storage such as Amazon S3 or Azure Storage). Cloud service providers should ensure the restore mechanism is in place so that if any disaster befalls on-premises data the enterprise can recover its data quickly to avoid prolonged downtime. This helps to bring down the DR cost to that of storage and data transfer.
- *Pilot light approach*: In the pilot light approach a minimal version of an enterprise's IT environment is running in the cloud. Since this is a lighter version it can immediately be spun up in case of emergency. If and when a disaster scenario rears its ugly head the enterprise can quickly build the full version of the IT environment around that core to fully restore its applications. This approach helps an enterprise to recover its systems as quickly as possible. This approach is better

than the backup and restore approach since the enterprise already has its core components in place and creating the full version takes much less time. Prominent elements include replication of data in the cloud environment, a set of preconfigured servers ready to be launched at short notice, and the storage of installation packages or configuration information. Additional database instances are required to achieve data resilience. When the recovery need arises the enterprise can fire up the preconfigured cloud servers quickly, route the traffic to the newly carved-out servers, and scale them up as per the brewing needs.

- *Warm standby*: Warm standby mandates the creation of a scaled-down copy of an enterprise's fully functioning environment in the cloud. This approach drastically speeds up recovery because there is a replica of the company's primary environment. Although this is a contracted one, it is always running in the cloud to support disaster recovery quickly. A company may set up a small number of low-cost and low-capacity virtual machines (VMs) and a few cloud databases where the company can mirror its on-premises data regularly. If the on-premises environment goes down due to an unavoidable cause the company can certainly increase the capacity of VMs at the cloud, use a load balancer to balance the load across VMs, and direct its traffic to them instantaneously. It can also scale its databases to ensure that its DR environment in the cloud can handle the increased load without any issue.
- *Full replication in the cloud*: Full replication in the cloud is the fastest and most expensive approach to DR goals. It is all about having the exact IT infrastructure in the cloud (i.e., both the on-premises environment and the DR environment in the cloud are running actively). In this approach an enterprise would completely replicate its on-premises environment in the cloud and distribute the traffic between the two environments. If an emergency causes the enterprise's on-premises environment to go offline, it can route the full traffic to its cloud environment and scale appropriately. While this approach will help to achieve a short RTO, it can be the costliest option because two different environments are running concurrently. The connectivity cost between two geographically different environments also matters.
- *Multi-cloud approach*: In the multi-cloud approach enterprises employ two or more cloud environments to host and run their applications. One acts as the primary environment and the other cloud setup is for DR purposes. By using two different cloud providers an enterprise's infrastructure can be more resilient since there are no dependencies between the services at all.

12.6 Implementation of Disaster Recovery Using Cloud

Selecting a Suitable Cloud Service Provider
Once the formalities of deciding on a comprehensive approach to achieving DR goals are completed, choosing an appropriate cloud service provider is the next

action to be taken, which should of course be based on all the insights. The following features should be analyzed before deciding on a cloud service provider:

- *Analyze cloud-based DR cost*: Affordability is one of the main reasons for widespread adoption of the cloud. Enterprise data are held in cloud storage devices as a backup. Network cost is another consideration when budgeting for a sustainable cloud-based DR solution. The technologies used for DR play a major role in deciding cloud DR cost. Typically, DR cost centers around the backup and recovery of files, physical/bare metal servers and virtual machines, databases, and 24/7 engineer-level support. Operational costs also contribute to escalating DR costs in a major way.
- *Determine the backup speed*: The size, speed, and scope of data are very important when preparing a functional DR strategy. It all comes down to data transfer speed when selecting the most appropriate DR service provider. A high-speed data transfer rate reassures organizations that applications and data can be backed up and recovered with minimal disruption and discrepancies.
- *Transition from hardware-focused approach*: Legacy backup and recovery systems involve tape backup and hardware that is neither cost efficient nor has the capability to effectively withstand data onslaught prevalent in organizations today. This can be overcome by using a cloud-based approach, which accelerates data recovery and reduces DR costs substantially. Moving from a hardware-based approach to software-defined cloud centers is a strategically sound solution to cloud-centric DR. Other important parameters that merit consideration when looking for a cloud-centric DR solution and choosing a DR solution provider include reliability, speed of recovery, usability, simplicity of setup and recovery, scalability, and security and compliance.

There is a growing array of purpose-agnostic cloud environments offering multi-faceted services, of which DR is one (note that there are exclusive DR service providers).

Setting up Cloud Data Recovery Infrastructure
Once an appropriate cloud service provider is chosen as the DR partner an enterprise can work together with the DR partner to implement the design and set up the DR infrastructure. There are a number of logistical issues to be considered and performed:

- How much of each infrastructural component will the enterprise need?
- How will the enterprise copy its data and take the data to the cloud?
- How should user authentication and access management be implemented?
- How should security and compliance management systems be set up?
- How to minimize the likelihood of disasters?

In short, what is the best way for an enterprise to set up its DR so that it can meet the RTO and RPO values identified and approved? The primary goal is to get applications up and running as soon as possible after a disaster strikes.

Document the Recovery Plan
It is imperative to document any DR plan precisely. Each member of the DR team has to know his or her role in deploying the cloud disaster recovery infrastructure. Deployment descriptors, scripts, and other instruction details should be comprehensively documented.

Test the Plan Regularly
Once a DR plan is created and documented, it has to be continuously tested and refined to proactively find and eliminate any gaps or issues. The plan should be given dummy runs to check whether it is robust and will work in a real-world situation. So many things can go wrong that it is a tough ask to visualize every possible DR situation. DR processes may not be as far-sighted as expected. Nevertheless, many deviations and deficiencies will be found with care and can then be pre-emptively addressed. In short, it is essential to test the DR plan thoroughly and regularly.

The more complex the DR plan, the more important it is to test it often. Full DR tests should be run every quarter and a company should take weekly or daily snapshots of its backup infrastructure to ensure that it is all running properly.

12.7 Disaster Recovery—Best Practices

- *Use cloud storage as part of daily backup routines*: Cloud storage cost is declining due to technological advances. Cloud service and storage providers are obliged to offer cloud storage in an affordable manner to ward off rising competition. When enterprises use cloud storage to store their data backups they need to make sure that the buckets containing their backups have appropriate permissions applied to them.
- *Treat recovered data like production data*: All the security controls (encryption, access permission, audit requirements, etc.) applied to production data should also be applied to recovered data. Any recovery process should be audited to gain the most critical insights into what, how, and why the disaster happened.
- *Making sure the data recovery plan works*: An enterprise should doubly ensure that DR execution is as per plan through one or more dummy runs.
- *Maintain more than one data recovery path*: In the event of a disaster there is a possibility that connectivity will go down as well. Hence it is important to have additional network connectivity to the DR site. It is mandatory to regularly test that the backup path is operational.
- *Automate infrastructure provisioning*: An enterprise can use any cloud and container orchestration platform solutions to automate VM provisioning and container creation. If an enterprise is running its production environment

on-premises it should have a monitoring process and tool that can start the DR process when it detects a failure and can trigger appropriate recovery actions.

- *Monitor and alerting processes*: Monitoring the primary IT environment is crucial to capturing various operational metrics and logs in detail. Should there be a threshold break-in, then the alerting tool springs to life to initiate recovery proceedings. Disaster can occur at any point of time. As a result of their unique DR strategy and means of implementing it, enterprises should be ready to face any situation so that business continuity can be guaranteed through technological solutions. The surging popularity of cloud IT is generally presented as the best DR solution. A well-designed solution in association with cloud service providers works well in fulfilling DR needs. ·

- *Disaster prevention measures*: In addition to DR an enterprise should put in place control measures to proactively predict and prevent disasters. It is paramount to add appropriate controls to prevent disasters from occurring and to detect issues before they occur. For example, an enterprise should ensure suitable monitoring agents are available to send alerts when a data-destructive flow occurs such as a deletion pipeline, unexpected spike, or other unusual activity. Such monitoring could prevent a catastrophic situation.

- *Preparing the software*: A critical part of DR planning is to make sure that the software, which has to be instantaneously recovered in case of any disaster, innately supports the recovery process. Moreover, it has to be verified that the chosen application software can be installed from a source or from a preconfigured image.

- *Design continuous deployment for recovery*: The continuous deployment (CD) toolset being leveraged has to be an integral part of the recovery plan to enable quick deployment of recovered applications in the case of any mishap in the primary IT center.

- *Implementing security and compliance controls*: Security should be given high priority when designing a quality DR implementation plan. The same controls have to be replicated in the DR environment. There should be no compromise when it comes to security. Furthermore, compliance with all regulations should be faithfully applied to the recovered environment too. It is pertinent here to make sure that network controls in the DR environment provide the same separation and blocking as provided in the production environment.

- *Verify DR security*: It is essential to verify that all security controls are in place. A comprehensive test should be performed to see whether there is any gap, hole, or leak. Identity and access management policies should be tested. Access control given to various users should be verified and validated (there are automated tools that can help in this regard).

- *Make sure users can log into the DR environment*: Similarly, it is imperative to check whether users can access the DR environment before any disaster strikes. An enterprise should make sure that it has granted appropriate access rights to various users (developers, operators, data scientists, security administrators, network administrators, etc.). If there is a local identity management system, then it has to be synchronized with the identity management system at the DR site.

Because the DR environment will be the production environment until the primary IT environment springs into life, it is vital to get users who need access to the DR environment to log into proactively test and eliminate any access issues.

Thus there are a few important steps to be considered and incorporated to prevent the occurrence and recurrence of disaster-like situations. Hackers and other evil-doers will easily find security loopholes and vulnerabilities in systems to bring them down. Hence all kinds of attack prevention have to be analyzed along with their risks proactively to put appropriate countermeasures in place.

12.8 Prominent Workloads for Disaster Recovery

Transactional, analytical, and operational applications are typical of those running in enterprise servers in on-site environments. Moreover, due to the growing popularity of the cloud, even enterprise-grade, business-critical, and customer-facing applications are being accordingly modernized and migrated to cloud environments. Similarly, IT platforms, middleware, database systems, etc. are being hosted in cloud servers. Hence cloud infrastructures, such as bare metal (BM) servers, virtual machines (VMs), containers, and functions, host and manage a variety of software infrastructure solutions and business workloads. To achieve disaster recovery capability there should be interconnects between on-premises local/private clouds, traditional IT centers, and off-premises public and dedicated cloud environments. For instance, a private-to-public cloud combination works well to ensure business continuity. Not every application needs to be considered for real-time or near-real-time recovery. Those that do need DR facility are given below:

- *Batch-processing workloads*: Batch-processing workloads tend not to be mission critical, hence an enterprise does not need to incur the cost of designing a high-availability (HA) architecture to maximize uptime; in general, batch-processing workloads can deal with interruptions. This type of workload can take advantage of cost-effective products, like pre-emptible VM instances, which are instances that can be created and run at a much lower price than normal instances. Big data analytics typically uses batch processing to do the data crunching. This happens at scheduled times and hence the HA need for this sort of business application is not insisted on.
- *E-commerce sites*: As a result of widespread usage of the internet, online applications, services, databases, and platforms are acquiring special significance. In particular, e-commerce and business applications are increasingly popular. All kinds of commercial and business activities are being accomplished online at any point in time using any device from any part of the world. These applications are generally transactional and increasingly analytical. Hence the need for a high-end disaster recovery facility is mandated to avoid any kind of application slowdown. In e-commerce sites some parts of the application can have larger RTO values.

For example, the actual purchasing pipeline needs to have high availability, but the email process that sends order notifications to customers can tolerate a few hours' delay. Although customers expect a confirmation email, they know what they have bought and notification is not a crucial part of the process. This is a mix of hot (purchasing) and warm/cold (notification) patterns. The transactional part of the application needs high uptime with a minimal RTO value. Hence an enterprise can use HA, which maximizes the availability of this part of the application. This approach can be considered a hot pattern.

- *Video streaming*: Many components of a video-streaming solution need to be highly available, from the search experience to the actual process of streaming content to the user. In addition, the system requires low latency to create a satisfactory user experience. If any aspect of the solution fails to provide a great experience, then it is just as bad for the supplier as it is for the customer. Moreover, customers today readily turn to a competitive product if they are not happy. In such a scenario an HA architecture is a must-have and small RTO values are needed. This scenario requires a hot pattern throughout the application architecture to guarantee minimal impact in case of disaster.

12.9 Disaster Recovery as a Service

Disaster Recovery as a Service (DRaaS) [2, 3] uses a cloud provider's computers, networking, and storage devices as the target site for replication and recovery of a company's critical data and applications. DRaaS) is a new offering that is turning out to be a key differentiator when it comes to adopting the cloud. The cloud-inspired DR facility has become the default and preferred option these days because of the flexibility, reliability, cost-effectiveness, sustainability, and universality of the cloud. Zerto is a good example of a DRaaS platform.

Zerto—The Only IT Resilience Platform for DRaaS
Zerto Virtual Replication (ZVR) provides enterprise-class disaster recovery and business continuity software for virtualized infrastructure and cloud environments. Zerto is dual-headquartered in Israel and the United States.

Zerto enables cloud service providers to offer a robust, cost-effective system of DRaaS. It is the first IT resilience platform built with the cloud in mind. With Zerto, effective DR is possible within the private cloud, to the public cloud and in the public cloud.

Enterprises are starting to see the value of the cloud, but are hesitant to trust an emerging technology with mission-critical data due to concerns about availability, performance, and security. Providing DRaaS, in which the enterprise replicates its production applications to the cloud, is a win–win situation. The enterprise has the opportunity to safely evaluate what the cloud service provider has to offer and become comfortable with the concept of the cloud.

Zerto's hypervisor-based replication technology is the first disaster recovery system that lets cloud service providers offer cost-effective, auto-mated, enterprise-class DRaaS. With Zerto, cloud providers can deliver a solution that is:

- *Multi-site*: The ability to replicate between more than one sites enabling enterprises to support many customers.
- *Multi-tenant*: Full integration with VMware vCloud Director enables cen-tralized and simplified management of all virtual data centers as well as effectively leveraging resources within the cloud to realize economies of scale.
- *Array agnostic*: This replicates any customer environment to the relevant enterprise's cloud regardless of their storage vendor or architecture.
- *Deployed quickly and remotely*: This installs remotely in hours without requiring any changes to the customer environment.
- *Tested and validated anytime*: This recovers customer applications in the relevant enterprise's cloud with one click of a button.
- *Granular*: This allows customers to pick specific applications to protect regardless of their physical server or storage location.
- *Comprehensive*: This provides robust replication and offsite backup in one simple product.
- *Consistent and reliable*: This provides scalable, block-level replication with RPO of seconds and RTO of mere minutes.

The reason enterprises want to move disaster recovery to the cloud is the huge savings in costs and resources compared with setting up a replication site and other necessary systems. In addition, moving disaster recovery to the cloud replaces upfront investments with ongoing monthly bills, which puts pressure on cloud service providers to ensure high performance and reliability. From the perspective of cloud service providers DRaaS represents a critical offering that inevitably attracts enterprises to the cloud.

12.10   Summary

Enterprise servers, data centers, and IT server farms may fully or partially go down during natural or man-made disasters. To guarantee business continuity even during a disaster, disaster recovery (DR) mechanisms have been and continue to be worked out. This chapter discussed the basics of disaster recovery, how to go about designing a DR plan, and the different approaches taken to mitigate DR. Moreover, the benefits of cloud computing in the context of DR and how cloud computing can facilitate the implementation of DR were explained in detail. The chapter ended by describing how DR is available as a service (DRaaS).

12.11   Exercises

1. Why do we need disaster recovery mechanisms?
2. Can security policies stick together during a disaster? Explain how?
3. What level of support can the cloud provide for disaster recovery and business continuity.
4. Explain briefly how you would go about preparing a DR plan.
5. What is the significance of testing to a DR plan?
6. Which type of DR approach would you suggest for an enterprise providing e-commerce? Justify your answer.

References

1. http://ijarcet.org/wp-content/uploads/IJARCET-VOL-4-ISSUE-5-1796-1801.pdf
2. https://ieeexplore.ieee.org/document/7976645
3. https://leapfrogservices.com/ribbit/wp-content/uploads/2017/07/cloud_based_disaster_recovery.pdf

Index

© Springer Nature Switzerland AG 2019
S. Chellammal and C. Pethuru Raj, *Essentials of Cloud Computing*,
Texts in Computer Science, https://doi.org/10.1007/978-3-030-13134-0

Printed in the United States
By Bookmasters